T0305457

Globalisation Under Threat

Globalisation Under Threat

The Stability of Trade Policy and Multilateral Agreements

Edited by

Zdenek Drabek

Senior Adviser, World Trade Organization, Geneva, Switzerland

Edward Elgar
Cheltenham, UK • Northampton, MA, USA

Published by
Edward Elgar Publishing Limited
Glensanda House
Montpellier Parade
Cheltenham
Glos GL50 1UA
UK

Edward Elgar Publishing, Inc.
136 West Street
Suite 202
Northampton
Massachusetts 01060
USA

A catalogue record for this book
is available from the British Library

Library of Congress Cataloguing in Publication Data

Globalization under threat : the stability of trade policy and multilateral agreements / edited by Zdenek Drabek.
    p. cm.
  Includes bibliographical references and index.
   1. Free trade. 2. International trade. 3. Economic stabilization. 4. Globalization. I. Drabek, Zdenek.

 HF1713 .G564 2001
 382'.3—dc21

                                          2001023647

ISBN 1 84064 658 6

Printed and bound in Great Britain by MPG Books Ltd, Bodmin, Cornwall

Contents

List of Figures vii
List of Tables viii
List of Boxes ix
List of Contributors x
Preface and Acknowledgements xii

Introduction: The Stability of Trade Policy and Multilateral Agreements 1
Zdenek Drabek

PART ONE: TRADE AND MACROECONOMIC POLICY

1. Exchange Rate Overvaluation and Trade Protection: Lessons
   from Experience 43
   Howard J. Shatz and David G. Tarr
2. Macroeconomic Conditions and Import Surcharges in
   Selected Transition Economies 75
   Piritta Sorsa

PART TWO: TRADE AND LABOUR

3. Trade-Labour Link: A Post-Seattle Analysis 101
   Arvind Panagariya
4. Paved with Good Intentions: Social Dumping and Raising
   Labour Standards in Developing Countries 124
   W. Max Corden and Neil Vousden

v

PART THREE: TRADE, ENVIRONMENT AND COMPETITION

5. Reforming Environmental Policy: Harmonisation and
   the Limitation of Diverging Environmental Policies:
   The Role of Trade Policy   147
   Scott Vaughan
6. The Relationship Between International Trade Policy and
   Competition Policy   172
   Edward M. Graham

PART FOUR: MULTILATERAL AGREEMENTS

7. European Lessons for Multilateral Economic
   Integration: A Cautionary Tale   203
   Peter Holmes and Alasdair R. Young

Index   229

Figures

2.1 Evolution of Trade Policy Stance with the Trade Restrictiveness
    Index   82
2.2 Developments in Key Macroeconomic Aggregates: The Czech
    Republic   84
2.3 Developments in Key Macroeconomic Aggregates: Hungary   86
2.4 Developments in Key Macroeconomic Aggregates: Poland   87
2.5 Developments in Key Macroeconomic Aggregates: Slovak Republic 88
2.6 Productivity in the Four Transition Economies   95
2.7 Real Interest Rates in the Four Transition Countries   95
4.1 Distributional Effects in the 'Wage-Differential' Model   127
4.2 Distributional Effects in a Modified 'Wage-Differential' Model   130

Tables

1.1   Comparing Great Depressions: Cameroon, Côte d'Ivoire and the
United States   54
1.2   Real Growth Rates in Africa, 1981-1995 (annual averages)   63
2.1   Regression Results   90
7.1   The EU Framework of Regulation   209

Boxes

1.1 Update of Events: Devaluation and Liberalisation in Kazakhstan   48
2.1 Exchange Rate Arrangements   85

Contributors

W. Max Corden is the Chung Ju Yung Distinguished Professor in International Economics at the Paul H. Niztze School of Advanced International Studies of the Johns Hopkins University in Washington, DC. He was formerly Nuffield Reader in Economics at Oxford University and Fellow of Nuffield College, Oxford and Professor of Economics at the Australian National University.

Zdenek Drabek is a Senior Adviser at the World Trade Organization, in Geneva. He was previously Minister's Plenipotentiary in the Czechoslovak Government and, prior to that, Senior Economist at the World Bank in Washington and Chairman of the Department of Economics, University of Buckingham.

Edward M. Graham is a Senior Fellow in the Institute for International Economics in Washington, DC. He served on the faculties of MIT, North Carolina and Duke Universities as well as in the US Treasury Department. He has been consultant to the WTO, the IMF, the World Bank, the OECD and UNCTAD.

Peter Holmes is Jean Monnet Reader in the Economics of European Integration at the University of Sussex. He has also taught at the University of British Columbia and College of Europe. He has been advising at the World Bank, OECD and the European Commission.

Arvind Panagariya is a Professor of Economics and Co-Director of the Centre for International Economics at the University of Maryland. He also taught at Rajasthan University in India and has been consultant to the World Bank, Asian Development Bank, IMF, WTO, and UNCTAD.

Howard J. Shatz is a post-doctoral fellow at the Center for International Development at Harvard University. Prior to his current appointment he was a research associate in the Trade Group of the World Bank Research Department in Washington, DC.

Piritta Sorsa is Deputy Director in the Policy Review Department in the International Monetary Fund in Washington, DC. Previously she was Senior Economist in the IMF Resident Office to the international organisations in Geneva and Senior Economist in the World Bank in Washington, DC.

David G. Tarr is Lead Economist with the Development Research Group of the World Bank in Washington, DC. On behalf of the World Bank he has provided trade policy advice in more than 15 countries, mostly in the former Soviet Union, Central Europe and the Middle East.

Scott Vaughan is a Director of the Trade and Environment Division with the North American Commission for Environmental Cooperation. Previously he was Counsellor in the World Trade Organization in Geneva.

Neil Vousden is a Professor of Economics at the National Centre for Development Studies, the Australian National University, and author of a recent book on the theory of protection.

Alasdair R. Young is currently a Jean Monnet Fellow at the Robert Schuman Centre for Advanced Studies at the European Institute in Florence. He has written extensively about transnational regulatory politics, particularly in the European Union, and about the interaction between trade and regulatory policies.

Preface and Acknowledgements

One of the major achievements of the multilateral trading system has been the commitments of countries to maintain their markets relatively open and subject to transparent and mutually agreed measures and rules to facilitate international trade. This has created conditions to ensure that trade policy remains stable and the risks of policy slippages and reversals to protectionism are minimised. Unfortunately, these achievements cannot be taken for granted. The WTO system, which has been the guardian against these reversals, has been recently under severe attacks from different corners of the world, from different intellectual movements and groups of civil society. This book addresses four of such dangers and attacks – specific labour interests, local environmental groups and people concerned about anti-competitive practices. Another serious danger that potentially may undermine the stability of the international trading system is the poor conduct of macroeconomics policies – an issue that is well known to economists but one that is continually underestimated or even ignored by policy makers in many countries. This book discusses these threats from a unique perspective – it looks at the existing role of international agreements and evaluates their future evolution. It consists of seven chapters written by eminent international scholars and experts in their respective fields.

I am grateful to a number of persons who stimulated my interest in this subject. The book is partly dedicated to all my colleagues at the WTO who have been concerned about the future of their organisation. Their fear has nothing to do with a worry about their jobs but it reflects a genuine concern about the credibility of the multilateral trading system and its future role. The book has also been stimulated by the growing interest in the academic literature and among policy makers with regard to the role of domestic regulation – a subject that has until recently escaped the mainstream of economics. I had very useful and thought provoking discussions about the linkages of labour, environment, competition and macroeconomic conditions to trade with Andre Sapir, Bijit Bora, Ake Linden, Rolf van der Hoeven, Richard Anker, Marion Jensen and, of course, with each of my contributors. I am grateful to Trudie Sarks for her excellent editorial assistance, and to my wife Sylvie for putting up with my moods. But, most of all, to my children

Bianca and Alexandre, who will hopefully do a better job of defending good causes than I might have done in this book.

Zdenek Drabek,
Geneva.

Introduction: The Stability of Trade Policy and Multilateral Agreements

Zdenek Drabek*

STABILITY OF TRADE POLICY AND MULTILATERAL AGREEMENTS: AN INTRODUCTION

Globalisation has become a household word all over the world. We are increasingly aware of events, activities and people in other parts of the world. Companies are becoming greater 'global players' as they serve not only domestic, but also foreign markets, and as they draw on input from the cheapest sources. Governments are responding by taking regional and multilateral initiatives to facilitate or manage the process. Our cultures are intertwining, people are travelling more frequently around the globe than ever before. The international community is setting up new institutions and reviewing the activities of established ones to address the changes in global economic, social and political environments.

One reason for the enormous interest in globalisation is the fact that the process has become synonymous with liberalisation of economic policies. We have seen a dramatic change of government attitudes and policies, even in countries which traditionally have been relatively closed and interventionist as their governments have embarked on the road of privatisation, elimination of government subsidies, lower taxation, restrained government spending, lower trade barriers and better access for foreign investors and to capital markets.[1] The agenda of liberal economic policies has

* The views expressed in this chapter are personal and should not be attributed to the WTO Secretariat or to the WTO Members. I am grateful to my hard-working research associate Fabrizio Zarcone for his assistance in collecting and sorting out the background information and literature. My thanks, without implicating, are also to Andre Sapir and Ake Linden for their valuable comments on an earlier draft of this chapter.
1. For a review of international trade policies, see Drabek and Laird (1998).

been pushed to the forefront of international financial institutions such as the World Bank, the International Monetary Fund (IMF) as well as that of arguably the most up-and-coming multilateral institution of today – the World Trade Organization (WTO).

However, these gains in economic policy reform are not necessarily permanent. The world has experienced two periods of free trade – from the 1840s to the 1870s, and from the mid-1940s to the mid-1970s. In both instances, the periods of free trade were followed by two relapses into moderate protectionism – from the 1880s to 1913, and in the 1980s following the oil shocks of the preceding decade.[2] Most importantly, the experience of the 1930s, when most countries went on a rampage of massive protectionism and autarchy, is undoubtedly the best reminder of the fragility of liberal trade policies.

As the work of researchers as well as the events at the WTO meetings, including those in Seattle, demonstrate, the recent trade policy reforms around the world have been subject to considerable pressures. While attacks against liberal economic policies and against globalisation are not new, they have tended to be sporadic and much more isolated in the past. What makes the Seattle events of December 1999 rather different is not only the scope and intensity of the criticism, but also the fact that the demonstrations represent groups of highly diversified interests. In this respect, it was perhaps the first major public attack against globalisation. Seattle brought together critics of human rights violations with respect to child labour or the oppression of Falun Gong, and the opponents of free trade and of cheap imports from developing countries. The opposition also included those concerned about environmental degradation, the power of multinational corporations and the plight of developing countries – to name just the main themes.

Globalisation clearly means different things to different people, and the criticism comes from different directions. Recognising the dangers of generalisations, globalisation is seen as (1) a threat to national *cultures*; (2) a process implying trade-offs and hard choices since it produces winners and losers – globalisation is not a *'win-win'* situation;[3] (3) a threat to national *sovereignty* while (4) a process in which multinational corporations dominate

---

2. For more details, see Boltho (1996).
3. For example, Professor Joe Stiglitz, the former chief economist of the World Bank, proposed at the 2000 Development Conference in Paris that 'countries should reject funding programmes that damage social cohesion even if they promote growth. *Financial Times*, 30 June 2000, p. 8.

and disregard the proper environmental and labour *standard;* and (5) a factor leading to increased *instability* of financial markets.[4]

The Seattle attacks are especially significant because of the target of the demonstrations. While in the past the criticism of liberal policies has mainly been targeted at the World Bank and the IMF, the target of the Seattle demonstrations was another multilateral institution – the WTO and its Ministerial Conference held in Seattle at the time. For the WTO Member countries, as well as the WTO management and the Secretariat, the demonstrations were a major surprise and setback. From an institution widely respected and admired only a few months prior to the Seattle events, the WTO arguably became the most controversial and, in some circles, even feared international institution.

However, the multilateral trading system is not only challenged by its foes, but also by its friends. In his speech to the World Bank conference on development in Paris on 26 June 2000, the French prime minister Lionel Jospin said: 'Trade rules should take account of human rights, of social rights, of the defence of the environment and of the necessity to preserve cultural diversity'. Clearly, this was a call for multilateral negotiations to treat issues that are not currently a subject of the existing trade agreements, but are presented as proposals of new issues for the New Round of trade negotiations.

There is no doubt that globalisation is under attack. Seattle was not a unique event. A few months later, similar demonstrations took place in Washington, DC on the occasion of the Interim and Development Committee Meetings at the IMF and the World Bank. Subsequent demonstrations in Europe occurred in late June 2000 at the Social Summit held in Geneva which had globalisation and its impact on poverty as the main theme, and at the regular annual conference on development of the World Bank in Paris with globalisation and its treatment by the World Bank as its subject. There are now perhaps no topics more frequently researched, discussed and the subject of international and national conferences or public meetings than the topic of globalisation. The opponents of multilateral institutions and globalisation have taken the initiative, and clearly are very much encouraged by their 'success' in Seattle. Whilst the supporters of globalisation have since awakened and re-grouped, they are facing a strong and an increasingly vocal group of critics.

---

4. The recent financial crises in Asia, Russia and Latin America are explained by some economists by the pre-mature liberalisation of financial markets in these regions. Moreover, financial capital is extremely mobile and can be a source of inflationary capital surges and paralysing capital flights.

INSTABILITY OF TRADE POLICY

The most serious danger emanating from the criticism of the multilateral trading system is its potential impact on the conduct of trade policy. There are real reasons to believe that the criticisms could lead to reversals in trade policy, especially to movements away from 'open-market' policies to derogations of international trade policy commitments and, in general, to trade policy 'backsliding'. Such an effect would be unfortunate if not tragic, given the positive contribution of world trade and foreign investment to the growth of world output that we have grown accustomed to over the last fifty years, and given the high costs of protection and the dangers of retaliation.

How real is the danger of policy slippages or policy reversals? Are policy reversals 'costless' or do they carry a heavy 'price-tag' for those who are responsible? Is the danger of policy slippages large enough for us to be concerned about, or are we unnecessarily anxious about this issue? The answers to all these questions are, I believe, quite straightforward. Protectionism puts countries on a collision course with those countries that favour open trade regimes. Trade policy slippages may lead to disrespect of existing international commitments. Relatively minor policy slippages and backsliding can occur unnoticed by policy makers, academics and the general public at large. However, if the instability of trade policy were to become more widespread and of a general pattern, or if the policy reversal of a single but large country had serious global implications, this would have serious consequences for the credibility of national policies, international agreements, lending practices of international financial institutions and, last but not least, for the merits of liberal trade policies *per se*. It is clear that the costs of trade policy reversal would be very high for individual countries and the international community. Moreover, as is the case in such situations, the distribution of costs among countries would be uneven. The rich and/or large countries would do relatively better than the poor and/or small countries.

The policy backsliding has not been prevented by countries' Membership in the WTO and other multilateral financial institutions.[5] Under the provisions of Articles XII and XVIIIB of the General Agreement on Tariffs and Trade (GATT), countries are permitted to derogate from their international commitments and to introduce protective measures if they face genuine balance-of-payments (BOP) difficulties. In such cases, the countries submit their requests to the BOP Committee of the WTO and, once their case is heard, in the presence of the IMF representative, examined and approved,

---

5. Even though the IMF has been by and large a champion of free trade, it has also been known to support government policies raising extra fiscal revenues through higher tariffs.

they may be allowed to introduce a temporary protection. Such extra restrictive measures are usually required to be removed within about a year of their introduction.[6]

How will the BOP experience in the WTO affect the credibility of these countries? If the request for protective measures, and consequently the derogations, are exceptional, it is most likely that the adverse effects will be negligible. They will be treated by countries and markets as a result of 'acceptable mistakes' or temporary difficulties and, as such, will be tolerated. Even markets and the most liberal governments can be forgiving!!! However, if a country concerned approaches the BOP Committee on repeated occasions, or if it succeeds in maintaining the extra protection for a prolonged period of time, it is likely that its credibility will be adversely affected.

Arguably, the worst case scenario is when the country concerned is not a member of the WTO and it has no or few bilateral/regional commitments. In such a case, policy backsliding most probably will be seen by markets as a dangerous precedent and a hostile intervention to the smooth operations of markets. It is for this reason that countries typically do make international commitments since the latter provide the additional element of credibility to complement domestic legislation and policy measures.

We already have a considerable amount of empirical evidence to suggest that policy slippages are a matter of concern. Starting with the experience of the BOP Committee of the WTO, the number of countries requesting derogations from their commitments by invoking the BOP provisions has increased considerably in recent years. During the period of 1994 to 1999, the BOP Committee of the WTO examined the cases of 18 Members. Some of these countries invoked the BOP provisions twice, and more. An extremely interesting feature of all these cases is that the requests have only come from developing countries and from countries in transition, not a single case so far involving a developed country. Many of these countries, such as Slovakia or Brazil, were before the BOP Committee at least twice during that period. For the guardians of the purity of the WTO agreements this raises the questions as to why the pattern of derogations has been so skewed, and whether there is not indeed something 'specific' about these two groups of countries. In particular, do not these examples provide striking evidence that the speed of liberalisation may have been too fast in the light of these countries' weak banking systems, incomplete legislative reforms, poor legal enforcement or, for some other reasons?

---

6. Nevertheless, there has been at least one WTO Member who has claimed extra protective measures on BOP grounds for decades. See McCusker (2000).

Countries sometimes also introduce specific protective measures that are not in violation with GATT Articles but are nonetheless trade restrictive. There are several legal venues for them to do so under the WTO provisions. Countries may increase applied tariff rates up to their respective bound rates. Since it is the latter and not the former that constitutes the violation of GATT commitments, such practices are tolerated, albeit grudgingly. Countries may apply anti-dumping and safeguard provisions of GATT to protect their markets if they believe that the relevant anti-dumping and safeguards conditions are violated. These provisions are regulated by Articles VI and XIX respectively, and have been used extensively in recent years. For example, between 1987 and 1997 the total number of anti-dumping investigations that were initiated in GATT/WTO almost doubled – the actual numbers increased from 120 to 233 per year during this period. Moreover, while new users of anti-dumping provisions accounted for only 20 percent in 1987, the corresponding figure increased to 49 percent by 1997.[7] Most of the latter increase is attributed to countries such as Mexico, Argentina, Brazil, South Africa, India, Korea and Poland. It is clear that anti-dumping measures have been more frequently used by countries to protect themselves against unfair competition and that the corresponding provisions are increasingly being used by new Members and/or Members from the groups of developing and transition countries.

Further empirical evidence of trade policy reversals and backsliding can be found in the chapter by Sorsa in this book, and in a paper co-authored by the present author and Professor Brada.[8] Both of these writings examine the experience of certain transition countries and find that in the last decade these transition countries have introduced a variety of trade restrictive measures, being mostly on a temporary basis but long enough to be a matter of concern. Even though many of these measures have been subsequently reversed, the frequency of and the extent to which the measures have been applied has raised a great deal of questions about these countries' commitments to free trade.

Regionalism may be considered as another potential threat to liberal trade regimes. We have recently seen a proliferation of regional trading arrangements sought by countries as a complement and sometimes as a substitute for their membership in the multilateral trading system. The establishment of regional groupings such as NAFTA, MERCOSUR, or ASEAN was motivated by the idea of complementing the countries' Memberships in the WTO with the creation of regional blocs. On the other

---

7. These figures come from Miranda *et al.* (1998), pp. 6-7.
8. See Drabek and Brada (1998).

hand, the customs union between Russia, Kazakhstan, Kyrgyzstan and Belarus was established as an instrument of a regional initiative in which the four countries were to be free from external pressures of other countries to reduce their external tariffs. In other words, Russia's tariff remains relatively high – one that is unlikely to be acceptable to the WTO Members once Russia negotiates its tariff schedule in its accession negotiations in the WTO. Moreover, regional groupings themselves may not be stable. The BOP difficulties experienced by Brazil in 1999 forced the Brazilian government to devalue, which in turn led to the retaliation by Argentina to protect certain industries. As a result, Brazil decided to suspend its negotiations with Argentina on the auto, sugar and footwear sectors.[9]

'Complementary' regional blocs may also be seen as trade 'restrictive'. A relatively recent World Bank study of MERCOSUR argued, on the basis of empirical evidence, that MERCOSUR tends to lead to 'trade diversion'.[10] The study generated a great deal of interest, controversy and strong criticism. Nevertheless, the controversy itself reminded us that the treatment of regional trading arrangements is difficult; their treatment as *bona fide* 'trade creating' institutions is subject to complex legal and economic investigations to ensure that they are fully consistent with the relevant provisions of Article XXIV of GATT. Therefore, it is not surprising that out of some one hundred regional agreements notified to the WTO, so far only the customs union of the Czech Republic and Slovakia has been recognised and accepted as being fully compatible with the provisions of Article XXIV. The latter case was quite simple for the WTO Members to assess since both countries were a part of the same country prior to the break up in 1993!

For many observers, these and other pressures have reflected a movement away from free trade. Boltho, for example, writes:

> a movement away from free trade was clearly taking place (after 1973). One significant landmark was the 1994 adoption of the Multi-Fibre Agreement initially designed to regulate and subsequently used to restrict, textile imports from developing countries. And all of the major industrialised participants in world trade made increasing use of various forms of non-tariff barriers. Export restraint arrangements, virtually unknown in the early 1970s, may have covered not less than ten percent of world trade, and about 12 percent of world non-fuel trade by mid-1980s, with hard-core non-tariff barriers applying, perhaps, to as much as 18 percent of the Organisation for Economic Cooperation and Development (OECD) imports in 1986. To this end must be added the inhibiting effects of the more frequent use of countervailing duties

---

9. Dow Jones, 28 July 1999.
10. See Yates (1997).

and anti-dumping cases, as well as trade distorting impact of a proliferation of subsidies.[11]

In addition, there are also the recent calls for protection against imports produced by *'cheap' labour* in developing countries and against imports from countries with no or different *environmental standards*. We already had to deal with the sensitive cases of genetically modified foods that are leading to serious ripples in the transatlantic relationship between the European Union (EU) and the United States (US), to discussions concerning the New Agenda for the New Round of trade negotiations and to pressures for domestic protection. The first well publicised cases have recently involved imports of genetically modified maize and soya and hormone beef.[12] Furthermore, there are also growing pressures in many countries to address the question of *competition* in their markets as they increasingly worry about market power of transnational corporations. The importance of competition policies is rising particularly in view of the dramatic reduction of trade barriers, the slippages noted above notwithstanding.

At the same time, the concept of 'unstable trade policies' is gaining a new meaning. The 'classical' case of unstable trade policies is when countries actually increase trade barriers. If they are restrained from doing so by their international commitments, protectionism can 'creep in' through other forms, as described by Boltho above. Moreover, with the expansion of the 'trade agenda', protectionism can potentially take other shapes and forms. Among the less orthodox forms is, in particular, the threat of sanctions. The use of trade sanctions has been proposed already as an instrument to enforce certain environmental and labour standards. Thus, a country need not increase import restrictive measures to 'force' other countries to restrain their exports of environmentally 'unfriendly' products. The threat of sanctions may be enough. In such a case, the effect will be the same as that of increased tariffs, namely, the exporting country is penalised as a result of lower exports even in the absence of higher tariffs or other more trade restrictive measures.

Another 'new' element of modern protectionism is the threat of higher protection if the multilateral system does not continue to liberalise. In discussing the role of regionalism in East Asia, Bergsten writes: '[The East Asians] want better access to foreign markets. Moreover, they realize that

---

11. See Boltho (1996), p. 252. Other well known observers have taken a similar line including, for example, J. Bhagwati, the late J. Tumlir, F. Bergsten and many others.

12. The case concerning genetically modified maize and soya was brought to the WTO under the heading of eco-labelling. It was requested by the EU to inform its consumers about the origins of the products. The latter has been an issue in the WTO under the Sanitary and Phytosanitary agreement.

there is a constant risk of a relapse towards protectionism if the system does not continue to liberalise. They know that the system is particularly acute in the United States, their largest market'.[13] In a way, this threat constitutes a pressure for countries to negotiate new measures to open their markets. If they do not, the 'threatening' countries have enough instruments at their disposal to restrict imports from the rest of the world.

In the present context, it may be useful to distinguish between two strands of 'new' protectionism, both of which have the potential to affect the conduct of trade policy. The distinction is based on whether the threat stems from 'inside' or 'outside' the system of the existing WTO agreements. The 'outside' threats to globalisation include those issues that are neither part of the existing trade agreements nor constitute an agenda of existing WTO committees or working groups. Such threats are 'brought' into the debate concerning the role of the WTO by those who see the WTO as a convenient and powerful instrument of achieving their goal, and are drawn from other arenas such as the International Labour Organization (ILO) ('core' labour standards), UNESCO (culture), the United Nations (human rights) and the World Bank (development strategies).

The 'inside' threats to globalisation include, in particular, macroeconomic instability. Macroeconomic discipline is critical for the conduct of trade policies and is already the subject of the WTO's disciplines, as discussed below. Another important 'inside' issue is trade and environment which constitutes the subject of the WTO Working Group on Trade and Environment. Anti-competitive practices can also be treated as an 'inside' issue since the existing agreements address various aspects that are normally the subject of competition laws and policies (for example, anti-dumping). With the exception of macroeconomic instability, all of the preceding 'inside' threats constitute topics proposed by a number of countries for the New Agenda of the next Round of the WTO negotiations where sanctions will play an important role. Therefore, it is appropriate to look at these threats as the origins of potential trade frictions.

The topics which are the focus of this book are, macroeconomic policies, labour, environment and competition policies. Such focus is not to suggest that these topics constitute the greatest threats to the stability of the international trading system. It may be, in fact, that there are other issues that currently endanger the system even more. For example, the ongoing transatlantic conflicts between the EU and the US with respect to the US law on foreign sales corporation, genetically modified foods and the banana

---

13. See Fred Bergsten: 'Towards a Tripartite World', *The Economist*, 3 August 2000, pp. 19-21.

import regime of the EU are issues that are all testing the WTO system to the limits. Moreover, the labour and environment threats are qualitatively differently to those originating in macroeconomic instability or in the lack of competition. Our choice for the focus of this book was dictated by two simple considerations. First, the labour and environment issues arguably constitute the most dangerous threat to the WTO's stability, even though such threat is not immediate. Second, both macroeconomic instability and distorted competition are 'dormant' threats that can be ignited into 'active' threats if not handled with care.

We shall be asking two simple questions: What is the role of international agreements in providing the right environment for stable trade policies? Is the present system of multilateral trade-related agreements conducive to maintain stable trade policies? In order to answer these questions, we shall focus on the above four subjects by looking at the linkages between trade policies on the one hand, and macroeconomic, labour, environmental and competition policies on the other. With regard to economic policies, we shall start by examining the evidence that good macroeconomic policies are critical for the pursuit of stable trade policies. In order to better understand the reasons for policy slippages, we shall further discuss the interplay between trade and macroeconomic policies. There are three global institutions that oversee the conduct of macroeconomic policies – the IMF, the World Bank and the WTO. This naturally leads to the question – is the countries' membership in these institutions a guarantee of stable trade policy?

With regard to labour, environment and competition issues, our approach will be somewhat different. Both labour and environment are already subject to a large number of international agreements and conventions. This is not the case of competition, but many countries are now calling for inclusion of competition in multilateral trade negotiations. However, the proposals to pursue the negotiations of these three issues in the framework of the WTO have been met with a great deal of reluctance and opposition from a large number of countries. The resistance has been particularly strong in the case of labour and environment. We shall, therefore, examine in the book the reasons why labour and environment constitute the greatest threats to the international trading system and why there has been so much reluctance to negotiate a global competition agreement. On a more specific level, several contributors to this book will identify and evaluate the most controversial issues surrounding the global discussions on labour, environment and competition. We shall discuss the major difficulties of negotiating multilateral agreements on labour, environment and competition, and address questions concerning the distribution of benefits of multilaterally agreed universal standards. We shall analyse the reasons why these issues have been 'pushed' to the WTO forum and whether it would not actually be easier to negotiate these issues outside the WTO framework. The fact that all of these issues have been brought to the WTO demonstrates the perception (and perhaps the reality) of the fact that international agreements may not always be effective in meeting their objectives.

One of the problems encountered in the negotiations of new trade agreements is the disagreement among governments and experts as to whether or not labour, environment and competition standards should be universal. The topic has already received some attention in the professional literature which has tended to take a theoretical and academic approach.[14] Our approach in this book is more practical – virtually all contributors review the recent experiences with domestic and international legislations and discuss their policy implications.

TRADE AND MACROECONOMIC POLICIES

The greatest underestimated danger to the stability of trade policy stems from poor economic policies. Governments, in the face of large and prolonged current account deficits, are often tempted to increase import protection in the belief that higher restrictions on imports will reduce imports and thus lower or eliminate the current account imbalance. Whilst this policy response may reflect the power of domestic lobbies, equally importantly is that it represents an instinct of governments as old as the policy discretion given to governments following the abolition of gold standard and its automatic BOP adjustment mechanism.

But as any trained economist knows, there is a close link between current account of BOP and domestic economic variables, and hence there are important linkages between trade and other domestic policies. Current account imbalance has a mirror image in the imbalance between domestic savings and investments. A current account deficit implies a corresponding excess of investments over savings, and vice versa in the case of current account surplus. This means that current account deficits cannot be eliminated by import restrictions alone unless they also affect the imbalance between savings and investment. As an economic issue this is a well known problem, and, as noted further below, the only unresolved question for policy makers, is which domestic policy measures should be used to restore the external balance – macroeconomic policy measures or appropriate structural

---

14. The most prominent among such studies are the two collected volumes edited by Professors Bhagwati and Hudec (1996).

policy measures? It is remarkable how frequently this simple policy question is misunderstood or ignored by policy makers, media and the general public at large.

Consider the following examples. When the US was running large current account deficits in the 1980s, there were strong pressures by the US Congress to increase import restrictions. Similarly, the US has been placing pressure on Japan to open up its market in order to reduce Japan's current account surpluses. Would policies to restrict US imports in the first case and to increase Japan's imports in the second case, succeed? The answer depends on what would happen to the balance of savings and investments as a result of these changes. As Corden puts it when addressing the former example, 'the essential issue is whether the combination of increased protection and appreciation of the dollar would reduce the budget deficit, increase private savings, or reduce private investment'.[15] Whilst this was written in the 1980s, we are today still addressing similar issues and trying to correct the same mistakes.

Similar concerns about the conduct of macroeconomic policies and its impact on trade policy have recently been raised by critics of euro. Martin Feldstein, former chief economist in the Reagan administration and Harvard Professor, has been for some time very critical about the prospects of the euro. In his most recent paper, in which he assesses the experience of the first year of the euro, he concludes that a 'one size fits all' monetary policy is not suitable for Europe because cyclical and inflation conditions vary among countries. He concludes that this, together with distortionary labour market policies, may lead to trade protectionism.[16]

The experience and evidence from the BOP Committee of the WTO provides, in my view, another serious warning that good conduct of macroeconomic policy cannot be taken for granted and that macroeconomic conditions may lead to, or be used as a justification for, the introduction of new trade policy barriers.[17] It is true that other factors of a structural nature may, in fact, play a role and be primarily responsible for external imbalances. Nevertheless, macroeconomic policies are typically also at fault because, at the very least, they accommodate the distortions generated by poor structural policies.

As I have noted above, the only unresolved issue for policy makers is the choice of domestic policies to restore external imbalance. For many economists, the appropriate tool is macroeconomic policy. Structural policy

---

15. See Corden (1994) p. 258.
16. See Feldstein (2000).
17. See the relevant discussion in the previous section.

tends to be limited to exchange rate policy with the aim of changing the relative resource allocation through changes in relative prices of tradeables in terms of non-tradeables. Other structural policies such as reform of financial sector, changes in the pattern of public expenditures, funding of pension or health schemes etc. have tended to be seen as long-term issues and therefore outside the framework of adjustment programmes which require immediate and consequently, relatively short-term solutions. The constraint of structural policy is reflected in the usual package of adjustment policies recommended by the IMF to countries with BOP difficulties. Such a package places a great deal of emphasis on fiscal and monetary restraint which is intended to increase the level of domestic savings and reduce spending. Critics underline the presence of policy and market failures. The latter should be addressed by the use of primarily structural policies as instruments of external adjustment.

While economic theory is relatively clear about the remedies for external imbalances, the links between trade and other domestic policies are not yet well understood by policy makers. The first chapter of this book is an attempt to bridge this gap. In this regard, rather than adopting the theoretical approach common in economic literature, the approach here is instead to examine the experiences of different countries. The focus is on macroeconomic policy failures even though it is recognised that structural policies failures may be equally or sometimes even more important.[18] In this way, such a focus on macroeconomic conditions and policies does not go all the way in explaining the variability of trade policy. Nevertheless, it does go at least a part of the way.

The specific questions which need to be addressed are: What policy measures should be applied in the face of serious current account imbalances? Are countries with unstable macroeconomic conditions more likely to resort to import restrictions? Given the fundamental identity between savings-investment and current account balances, what role should be played by macroeconomic policies in the process of current account adjustment? Since the efficiency of economic instruments may vary, what is the role for the exchange rate policy, and what are the costs and other consequences of poorly conducted exchange rate and other macroeconomic policies ?

---

18. Using a multivariate model and a sample of 26 transition countries, a recent IMF paper has argued that structural reforms are pre-eminent over both initial conditions and macroeconomic variables in explaining cross-country differences in performance and the timing of economic recovery. See Berg *et al.* (1999). A similar conclusion is reached in Caballero (2000) using three case studies of Latin American countries.

This book contains two empirical chapters to address the above questions. In the first chapter *Exchange Rate Overvaluation and Trade Protection: Lesson from Experience,* Howard Shatz of Harvard University and David Tarr of the World Bank discuss the importance of exchange rate policies. Beginning with an examination of the level of exchange rate policies in a large number of countries, they find that exchange rate overvaluation is a serious problem. About a quarter of the countries in their large sample had overvalued exchange rates, with 'black market' premiums ranging from ten percent to more than 100 percent. The origins of overvaluation may vary from country to country starting from the inappropriate use of fixed exchange rates to different speeds of adjustment in domestic wages and prices. These authors review and discuss the evidence of consequences of overvaluation and of governments trying to defend an overvalued exchange rate. One of the 'classic' outcomes of these policies is an attempt to defend an overvalued exchange rate by protectionist trade policies. In other words, poor exchange rate policies may lead to pressures to increase trade restrictions with adverse consequences for economic growth. Competitive exchange rates are, therefore, a key to avoiding pressures for increased trade protection.

The extent to which exchange rate policies can actually be the key variable explaining the trade policy reversals is addressed in the second chapter *Macroeconomic Conditions and Import Surcharges in Selected Transition Economies*. The author, Piritta Sorsa of the IMF, questions whether the frequent use of trade restrictive measures is a reflection of the fact that the first best policies are not available to governments. The latter should include an appropriate mix of macroeconomic policies as well as exchange rate policies. It may be, for example, that governments are temporarily unwilling to adjust a nominal anchor such as exchange rate. The effectiveness of monetary policy may also be reduced in the presence of fixed exchange rates and free movement of capital. Fiscal adjustment may take too long or may be undesirable in a particular state of economic cycle. Taking a sample of the Czech Republic, Hungary, Poland and Slovakia – four countries that have introduced import surcharges to deal with BOP disequilibria – the author provides econometric evidence that appreciation of the real exchange rate was the main explanation for trade policy reversals, while output growth, or the fiscal-monetary policy mix in terms of interest rates, had no significant impact on demand for protection.

It is implicit in the analysis of Shatz and Tarr, as well as that of Sorsa, that pegged exchange rates tend to lead to overvaluation and hence to greater pressures for trade restrictions. The question that could also be asked is whether flexible exchange rates are even more conducive to greater variability in inflation and output rates and hence to greater pressures for more trade protection. This is, in fact, precisely what has been argued recently in a paper by Bleaney and Fielding (1999) who found that inflationary expectations are lowered when exchange rates are pegged to some other currencies. This issue of optimal exchange rate regimes in the context of stable trade policy (addressed neither by Shatz and Tarr nor by Sorsa) is one that cannot be ignored.

In sum, it is clear that macroeconomic policies play a critical role, especially monetary and fiscal policies, in view of their most direct impact on savings and investments. At the same time, the right structural policies, such as those affecting the financial sector, are also important. The financial sector provides for intermediation and allocation of savings to the most efficient uses and, in the absence of an efficient financial sector, macroeconomic policies will not work. For example, Aghion *et al.* (1999) show that countries with an intermediate level of financial development are more unstable than very developed economies. The depth and liquidity of the former countries' capital markets are relatively limited and the balance sheets of commercial banks are exposed to higher risks than in sophisticated and mature markets of developed countries. It follows that such countries are also more likely to be more exposed to protectionist's pressures.[19] Similarly, savings-investment imbalances are known be to be sensitive to other factors, in addition to macroeconomic policy, such as capital movements, rigid labour markets, policy distortions or political instability,[20] but none of these factors are the subject of discussion in this book. Whilst macroeconomic policies are probably dominant in the short-run, the importance of the structural policies tends to increase in the long-run.

TRADE AND LABOUR STANDARDS

The second danger for the stability of trade policy under consideration in this book stems from *labour policies*. Labour policies have been most forcefully brought to the table by trade negotiators a few years after the conclusion of the Uruguay Round and as part of preparations for the New Round of multilateral trade negotiations.[21] The push primarily came from several

---

19. Interestingly enough, the countries are also more unstable than the very undeveloped countries, presumably because the latter are unlikely to have open capital accounts. For more details see Aghion *et al.* (1999).
20. See, for example, Bussiere and Mulder (1999).
21. The labour issue has, however, a longer history in WTO. It was already raised and discussed during the Kennedy Round negotiations, and consequently a closer cooperation between GATT and the ILO was sought. I am grateful to A. Linden for this interesting point.

developed countries – such as France and the US – but it has not necessarily been shared by all of them. This initiative has been vigorously opposed by developing countries. There have been fewer issues in the WTO that have divided the developed world from developing countries more than that of labour standards.

How are labour issues linked to the stability of trade policy? Simply, the discussion of labour issues is a discussion about the extent to which some countries should modify their labour policies or, in the absence of any changes, whether countries with 'high' labour standards should be allowed to protect their markets against imports from countries with 'low' labour standards or enforce them through sanctions or other trade restrictive measures. It is not, therefore, surprising that developing countries see this new labour initiative as an attempt of developed countries to protect their markets through the 'back-door' of the negotiating process. Perhaps the only difference between these 'attempts' for protection and those that arise from *ad hoc* protectionist pressures is that the latter are spontaneous while the former may lead to formal and negotiated commitments.

The sharp divisions among countries concerning the approach to labour issues is related to the question of labour standards. Developed countries argue that one reason for the phenomenon of 'cheap imports' is the fact that developing countries do not respect labour standards that are common in developed countries. The ILO has, over the years, negotiated 182 conventions on labour standards and related issues, but the acceptance of these standards has been stalled by the slow and ineffective ratification process. Most countries recognise that a successful, world-wide ratification of the existing labour conventions, or reaching a full agreement on a complete set of labour standards, is unrealistic. As a result, the discussion is currently focused on 'core' labour standards such as child labour, employment of women, prison labour and the right of workers to associate themselves in labour unions.

Many critics refer to the present trade system based on labour standards as 'social dumping'. This reflects two different concerns. On the one hand, there are those critics concerned about the impact of 'cheap' imports on their industries – they represent 'protectionist' sentiments. But there are also those critics who are concerned about the 'cheapness' of imports in the context of shop floor practices and their impact on human rights. They argue that the current labour practices allow firms to apply inhuman labour standards and treat workers under poor working conditions.[22] These critics represent 'humanitarian' sentiments.

---

22. This criticism constitutes a twist to the general argument. The critics argue that liberal trade and investment regimes allow transnational corporations to misuse weak legislative rules and

For many an uninformed observer, the introduction of labour issues on the agenda of trade negotiations is surprising and difficult to understand. After all, trade is supposed to be about exchange of goods and services and, as such, any link to labour can be seen as exceeding the boundaries of trade *per se*. In order to better understand the reasons why labour has been proposed as a new subject for trade negotiations, one needs to go beyond the concept of *products (or services)* that are subject to international trade and consider the question of *process*, i.e., the way these products (services) are produced. If we accept that the process matters in determining the equity of international exchange – and there are good reasons to argue that this is indeed the case as we shall see further below – it is only natural that labour is brought into the discussion about fairness of international trade. The real issue concerns the conditions under which inputs used in the production of internationally traded goods (or services delivered) are priced. If prices of inputs somehow reflect the 'genuine', 'normal' and 'true' economic conditions, the prices of commodities produced with the help of these inputs are considered in the market to be 'fair'. On the other hand, if the relevant input prices are seen as 'distorted', the corresponding output prices are seen by the market as 'unfair' and the producers of these commodities are considered to have gained an unfair competitive advantage.

The distinction between product and process is not an artificial one. The issue has been recognised by international negotiators in the previous rounds of multilateral trade negotiations. Thus, according to Article VI/3 of GATT, countries can levy countervailing duties up to the amount 'of subsidy determined to have been granted, directly or indirectly, on the manufacture, *production* or export of such product in the country of origin or exportation, including any special subsidy to the transportation of a particular product'. (Emphasis mine). The issue has also been brought to light in the two recent famous cases in the WTO dispute settlement mechanism – the 'tuna/dolphin' case and the 'shrimps/turtles' case. The subjects of the disputes were, respectively, the treatment of externalities in the fishing of tuna and in the fishing of shrimps or, to put it differently, the process or production techniques used in the fishing industry. In both cases the panel essentially ruled in favour of the producing countries, against the challenge of importing countries to unilaterally adopt trade restricting measures against countries on the grounds of 'wrong' production processes.[23] The verdict has been recently

---

procedures in developing countries in order to 'exploit' cheap labour, thus violating one of the fundamental human rights.

23. The specific issues at stake were whether or not the challenge of importing countries was GATT-consistent, and whether countries could take unilateral trade measures on the grounds of protecting the global environment. These issues will be discussed in greater detail in this

attacked by a number of legal scholars, such as by Howse and Regan (2000) on the grounds of the product-process distinction.

Central to a discussion of labour standards is the controversial issue of whether or not labour standards should be universal. Would not the adoption of universal labour standards threaten the functioning of markets? In particular, what would be the impact of universal labour standards on international trade and on the distribution of gains from trade between the rich and poor countries and within the poor countries? Can the reluctance of developing countries to accept universal ('higher') labour standards be explained by their impact on these countries' comparative advantages? What are the intellectual arguments in favour of the trade-labour linkage and how valid are these arguments? Would universal labour standards be 'protectionist' while being 'humanitarian' since they would improve working conditions of those who are employed? How should the issue of labour standards be addressed in international negotiations?

The link between labour and trade has also been dismissed in the literature on other grounds explored in detail in this book by Panagariya in his chapter *Trade-Labour Link: a Post-Seattle Analysis.* In brief, his criticism is based on the following arguments. First, optimal labour standards are not uniform either over time in the context of welfare of one country, or across countries in the context of world welfare. Second, the WTO is not the appropriate place to address poor labour standards of countries since they are neither endemic to trade as an exclusive determinant of labour practices, nor will the inclusion in the WTO improve individual countries' welfare or world welfare. Third, the trade-labour link is also extremely difficult to justify on moral grounds – given the diversity of moral values among countries and the question of who pays for the costs of adjustment. Fourth, as noted above, the link has been often made on the grounds of fairness and equity – i.e., that 'cheap' imports are 'unfair' to labour intensive industries in rich countries. However, to the extent that 'cheap' imports represent trade based on comparative advantage, this is clearly a question of different efficiencies rather than unfair trade practices.

The question of social dumping is addressed by Corden and Vousden in their chapter *Paved with Good Intentions: Social Dumping and Raising Labour Standards in Developing Countries.* Their starting question is, what would be the effects if developing countries' governments, or multinationals operating in developing countries, gave way to the protectionist and humanitarian concerns and raised labour cost in developing countries' export

---

book in the following section of this chapter and, in particular, in a separate chapter written by Vaughan.

industries. With the help of a theoretical model, they find, not surprisingly, that employment in export industries would fall, and labour would transfer into the residual sector where wages and average income would fall. Hence, inequality among wage earners would increase. The average wage for the economy would not necessarily increase – it would rise or fall depending on relative elasticities. The impact on exports is potentially also negative as employment may fall or profits are reduced which would induce multinationals to invest elsewhere. Corden and Vousden identify some interesting situations in which humanitarians are satisfied as wages and working conditions are raised in developing export industries, but the situations do not satisfy the objectives of protectionists who seek higher LDC prices and lower LDC exports. 'What may be good for the humanitarians may not be good for the protectionists', they conclude.[24]

The Seattle events have exposed the political sensitivity of the trade-labour link. As Panagariya argues in his chapter, it will be very difficult to make a strong case for the inclusion of labour issues on the New Agenda of the WTO negotiations. He finds no convincing intellectual ground for linking labour issues to trade – whether it be on grounds of efficiency, or morals, appropriateness or fairness or, even on practical grounds, as already noted. His arguments about the inefficiency of using trade measures to address labour issues and about their negative impact on world and on an individual country's welfare, are particularly persuasive. He strongly favours leaving the labour issues outside the WTO system and reserving them for the ILO.

The chapter by Panagariya and that by Corden and Vousden point to the inherent instability of the trade-labour link and, consequently, to the strong possibility of unstable trade policies. The introduction of universal labour standards would have the same effects as increased protection in countries with poor labour endowment. The introduction of labour issues would most likely destabilise the whole WTO negotiating process since the market access of labour-abundant countries will be adversely affected. The linkage could be a heavy price to pay for pushing the frontiers of multilateral negotiations.

TRADE AND ENVIRONMENTAL STANDARDS

The third danger for the stability of trade policies is the link between trade and environment or, to put it more precisely, the attempts to link trade

---

24. For a more general elaboration of the labour standards in international trade see Brown *et al.* (1996). Not surprisingly, the authors reach the same conclusion when they address the question of trade between high and low income countries.

policies with environmental policies and standards. As in the case of labour standards, these attempts are relatively new and intensified in recent months, especially after Seattle. The critics blame international trade for environmental hazards, even though the problem is often a matter of domestic policies or related to other activities such as investment. The criticism is focused on the WTO trade rules – specifically, the rules are criticised for their implications on domestic environmental policies and for provisions that have extra-territorial effects on domestic environmental standards. These issues have received a great deal of attention in the literature.[25]

In brief, the critics have targeted different aspects of the trade-environment linkage.[26] They argue that environmental regulations hurt and undermine the competitiveness of countries. Since regulatory compliance always leads to higher costs for producers, environmental regulations are also not costless. Moreover, countries with higher environmental standards are thought to be at a competitive disadvantage to those countries with lower environmental standards. The question which then arises is whether a country's competitive position in world markets is threatened by universal standards and, if so, by how much. In addition, who is hurt more and who is hurt less by the regulations? The critics also claim that multinational firms relocate from developed to developing countries to take advantages of lax environmental standards. This is an issue that is more relevant to the discussion of location of foreign direct investment, and often has been raised in the context of NAFTA and the US investment in Mexico. Some critics have also suggested that any multilateral agreement involving environmental standards would be highly ineffective since it would lead to the adoption of the lowest quality of standards as the only acceptable common denominator. This is, of course, the well known 'race to the bottom' argument. Developing countries are anxious that environmental standards could be used as a form of a non-tariff barrier to deny them access to developed countries' markets. These, and related topics, have already received considerable attention in the literature, most notably in a recent WTO report.[27]

The chapter *Reforming Environmental Policy: Harmonisation and the Limitation of Diverging Environmental Policies: The Role of Trade Policy*, written for this book by Vaughan, addresses a different, but complementary set of questions. The chapter is focused on the direction of domestic environmental policies and international environmental agreements, their

---

25. See, for example, Howse and Regan (2000) and their bibliography.
26. The debate is reviewed, for example, by Esty (1994).
27. See WTO (1999).

treatment of environmental standards and policies and their harmonisation. The main question asked by the author is the role of trade policy in the process of harmonising environmental standards and policies. In responding to some of the criticism, Vaughan reviews the trends in domestic environmental legislation as well as those pertaining to the major international agreements. He makes the strong point that 'regulatory reforms … in the environmental arena are not primarily influenced by the pursuit of environmental quality, but rather by the principles of trade liberalisation and related open-market principles'. While the harmonisation of environmental standards 'is supported by all governments in principle, (it is) increasingly complex to enact in practice'. Whilst Multilateral Environmental Agreements (MEAs) typically set environmental objectives, their implementation is left to individual countries. Consequently, in his view, the design of environmental policies is becoming more, rather than less, diverse. The WTO and NAFTA, agreements with trade and environmental contents, appear to play two important roles – they influence the agenda for negotiating the new MEAs and they only give *preference* to relevant universal standards. As he rightly points out, two recent WTO panels 'leave open the contentious question of how to allocate the burden of proof in proving that international standards are not applicable in meeting domestic policy objectives'.[28] Such divergences in environmental policies and standards can be observed even in the EU where the harmonisation of environmental standards is most advanced.

It is clear that – as in the case of labour standards – the question of harmonisation of policies and standards, namely, whether the policies and standards should be universal or not and how they should be linked to trade policy measures, is a matter that is critical for the conduct and the stability of trade policy. Since countries may perceive differences in environmental standards as affecting their comparative advantages, this could lead to pressures for increased protection in various forms. For example, if a country must increase its 'low environmental standards', the costs of compliance may reduce the scope of the country's exports. As a result, the existing exporters may seek additional support from their government to maintain their competitiveness. The government may also be under pressure, for macroeconomic reasons, as the country's BOP will deteriorate. Furthermore, the government may have to seek alternative ways of raising fiscal revenues due to slower growth of output and of maintaining external equilibrium due to slower growth of exports.

---

28. The cases involved the tuna/dolphin and the shrimp/turtle disputes and, in particular, the dispute between the US and the EU concerning the beef hormones case.

The design and implementation of environmental policies raises the inherently difficult issue of the quality of environmental policies. Poor environmental policies may also be a destabilising factor for the international trading system. Given the recent trend in the design and implementation of domestic environmental policies towards greater reliance on non-uniform or heterogeneous approaches, as argued by Vaughan, it is possible that we shall see in the future growing frictions in the domestic and international community over the treatment of trade and environment issues. The friction could be between those who point to the successes of the international trading system to harmonise international trade rules and for the preference that is placed in the WTO on the adoption of relevant international standards, and those who believe that environmental policies can rarely be applied in a uniform manner because of the different approaches to the design and implementation of domestic environmental policies as noted above.

Moreover, and similarly with respect to labour standards, the pursuit of universal environmental standards through international environmental agreements has been, so far, rather limited. This 'failure' might also lead to pressures for the critics to turn their attention to the 'wrong' agreements and 'wrong' targets. Such misconceptions could also endanger the stability of the international trading system. It is more appropriate for environmental issues to be addressed in domestic legislations or in international environmental agreements. Unfortunately, this has not necessarily been the practice. Instead, the critics have often turned to the WTO as if it were the institution that sets international environmental standards or that determines the environmental policies of Member countries. On both accounts, the critics have targeted the 'wrong' institution.

TRADE AND COMPETITION POLICIES

When the German car manufacturer Volkswagen acquired the right to purchase the Czech car manufacturer Skoda in the early 1990s, it negotiated a clause that required the Czech government to increase tariffs on imports of cars. The clause, accepted by the Czech government, gave Volkswagen extra protection despite a massive devaluation that had proceeded the deal. Moreover, since Skoda was virtually the only car manufacturer in the country, the clause gave the Germans the monopoly position in the market. As this example demonstrates, competition policies, or rather the absence of proper competition policies, can have adverse implications for the conduct of trade policy and its stability.

The example of Volkswagen is by no means unique. Similar pressures from foreign investors have recently occurred in the Ukraine, Romania, Slovakia and other countries. All these examples refer to the car manufacturing sector, but the experience is probably wider. There are, of course, many examples of foreign direct investment which have not led to changes in the level of protection of their industries. These are most likely more typical cases than the preceding examples. Nevertheless, the examples are used to illustrate a linkage between trade and competition policies.

Now suppose that Volkswagen were to be denied the benefits of the extra tariff protection by the Czech government. If the German company decided to proceed irrespective of the extra tariff protection, it would remain the sole Czech car manufacturer with a dominant market position. Should the government competition authorities under such circumstances have treated Volkswagen as a monopolist and take, therefore, an appropriate stand? Should they take the necessary measures to protect consumers and maintain an acceptable level of competition in the Czech market? If so, how would it ensure that Volkswagen's dominant position does not lead to an abuse of that position through, for example, price fixing? Should it be guided by principles applied, for example, by the Spanish authorities which also face a similar problem with a dominant car manufacturer (which happens to be the same Volkswagen) but in a much larger market. How are the competition authorities in such situations deciding? Are the goals of trade and competition policies different or the same? Do the authorities look for *universal* competition standards and policies? Would universal competition policies be conducive to world trade? Are trade and competition policies complementary and, if so, why and how? Are there any limitations on competition policies in creating conditions conducive to trade? If so, what kind? Could international agreements help?

These are the main questions that are addressed in the last of the 'new issues' raised in this book. They are discussed in Graham's chapter, *The Relationship Between International Trade Policy and Competition Policy.* Graham commences with an examination of the goals of trade and competition polices and makes a convincing case that they are, in fact, the same goal – the enhancement of consumer welfare through increased production efficiency. However, while the goal may be the same, the procedures through which trade and competition policies are implemented tend to be different. This raises the obvious question whether or not the absence of universal competition standards creates problems for the conduct of the WTO business. His answer is – an unequivocal 'yes'. Many competition issues have an international dimension with 'cross-border' implications. Anti-competitive practices such as mergers, price discrimination, cartels, exclusive dealerships or supplier arrangements are often perceived as measures not only affecting profits, prices and competition in a given market, but also market access. As a result, it is only natural that such anti-competitive practices may be brought to the WTO *viz.*, for example, the Kodak/Fuji dispute. However, the treatment of these disputes is problematic – they may be subject both to competition and trade policy standards and are, therefore, controversial and highly problematic to resolve.

There is a great similarity between the linkage of trade and competition policies on the one hand, and that of environment and trade policies on the other. Graham finds that virtually the same broad answers apply with regard to the link between competition and trade policies as Vaughan has found for the link between trade and environment policies. On the one hand, the objectives/goals of each respective set of policies are more or less the same, but the implementation of these policies is different. The implementation depends on the selection of standards and neither in the case of environment nor in the case of competition policies is it realistic to believe that countries will adopt universal standards any time soon. In fact, the present trend seems to point in the opposite direction. Graham chooses the EU and the US to demonstrate the differences between their competition laws. His explanation of the legal differences lies in the different structure of political pressures that lobby for protection of their particular interests, and in historical and cultural differences.

The implications of the difficulties to globally manage competition for the stability of trade policy at the national and multilateral level, are again serious. They are also strikingly similar to those discussed already in the context of trade and labour issues and trade and environment policies. In fact, one could more or less re-write the last paragraph of the previous section to argue that the failure to agree on international competition standards has already posed serious threats for the WTO, and has allowed the critics of the multilateral trading system to target the 'wrong' agreement and 'wrong' institution. It is also clear that multilateral agreements have not performed all the functions that their supporters hoped to achieve. Multilateral agreements must play a better role than they have done so far – an issue to which we shall now turn.

MULTILATERAL AGREEMENTS AND INSTITUTIONS

Global issues require global solutions – it is difficult to imagine a world in which markets, the power of nature or social processes are regulated solely by individual citizens and governments without some form of international cooperation. By the same token, it is difficult to imagine a world without multilateral agreements.[29] Yet, in spite of the proliferation of multilateral initiatives, we have not so far succeeded in making the globalisation process smooth and fully acceptable to all, and one in which multilateral agreements can be seen as an effective tool for controls of social and economic processes. Judging from the experience of Seattle, as well as from the emergence of powerful social, environmental and competition lobbies, we are still a long way away from the situation in which multilateral agreements perform their intended functions and meet their expectations. The evidence and material compiled in this book provides a powerful reminder of our failures.

Nowhere are the shortcomings of multilateral cooperation more visible than in the area of international trade. On the one hand, we have the Uruguay Round Agreements which have so far proved to be quite successful, at least judging from the continuous expansion of Membership as well as from the functioning of the WTO Dispute Settlement Mechanism. On the other hand, there are other areas and agreements with implications for international trade where the cooperation of countries has been far less successful. This book looks at what arguably constitutes the three most important areas – labour, environment and competition. In looking at the developments in these three areas, one cannot be overly pleased with their current status in international fora, nor with the progress that has been achieved so far.

A Failure of Policies or Failure of Markets?

While environmental degradation, the abuse of labour rights as well as economic instability are all matters of serious concern, it is necessary to first address the question of whether these problems, or 'externalities' as we economists like to call them, represent market failures or policy failures. Restrictive business practices of private economic agents may lead to failure of markets, while poor government policies may lead to policy failures. The distinction is important because market failures will require different responses to those for policy failures.

As we shall see in the rest of this section, there are clear indications of failures of governments to pursue effective international cooperation. However, governments are not entirely to be blamed for environmental

---

29. In theory, this outcome may not necessarily be the case. The theoretical literature has identified cases when self-enforcing international environmental agreements may not be able to substantially improve the countries' welfare over the non-cooperative outcome. Starting with the work of Demsetz (1967) who first justified 'free-riding' as the superior solution as compared to the cooperative outcome, the literature has recently expanded. For an extension of the argument see, for example, Barrett (1994).

degradation or other social and economic problems. Another origin of these problems could be behaviour of economic agents in general, and business practices of firms in particular. Notwithstanding this comment, the discussion in this book is almost exclusively focused on failure of policies rather than on failure of markets. Clearly, this constitutes our own bias which should be pursued in a separate study. The bias should be kept in mind particularly when reading the last section on policy implications.

Failure of Domestic Policies and Guarantees of Multilateral Agreements

It must be borne in mind that multilateral agreements do not necessarily provide a guarantee of stable trade policies. The current situation concerning remedies for BOP disequilibrium is a good example. As I have argued above, the Membership in the WTO alone is not a guarantee that countries will not take recourse to trade policy measures to correct imbalances on current account. The existing WTO agreements allow the necessary 'loophole' for countries to use trade restrictive measures, albeit temporarily and subject to other disciplines. The problem of BOP pressures typically originates in poor domestic policies, and no multilateral agreement can offset the effects of such policies.

Local Competition Laws

Business practices in world markets are currently not subject to a world-wide competition law. In fact, many countries are still without any competition law although the numbers of such countries are declining. To the extent that business practices are subject to regulations, the latter tend to be of local, i.e., national character. The two contributions to this book that specifically address competition issues – chapters by Graham and by Holmes and Young[30] – start from the position of *given* pressures that call for an establishment of multilateral rules on competition, and then proceed to explain the reasons why countries are reluctant to do so.

Since national competition policies are closely linked to trade policy, it may be useful to remind the reader of the reasons why many countries are actually pushing for a multilateral agreement on competition. The reasons are clearly summarised in the 1995 EC Expert Group Report on 'Competition Policy in the New Trade Order: Strengthening International Cooperation Rules' as follows:[31] (1) the lack of national competition laws (currently in

---

30. The contribution of Holmes and Young is reviewed further below in this section.
31. The list is adapted from Petersmann (1996).

only approximately 100 countries), or their effective enforcement, gives rise to market access barriers, concerns over reciprocity, trade conflicts and retaliatory trade measures; (2) international trade is subject to the problems of business practices with cross-border implications (for example, international cartels); (3) the differences and risks of conflict among domestic competition rules generates uncertainty and higher transaction costs; (4) unilateral extra-territorial enforcement of domestic anti-trust laws, *vis-à-vis* foreign businesses, generates international conflicts; and (5) developing countries, in particular, are subject to greater risks and costs of anti-competitive behaviour of firms.

Uncertain Status and Impact of Multilateral Agreements on Environment and Labour

In the area of labour and environment, we have seen an enormous proliferation of multilateral agreements. With regard to environment, there exists already 185 MEAs and some 900 regional and bilateral environmental agreements.[32] With regard to labour, countries have signed, under the umbrella of the ILO, virtually the same number of conventions – 182 by the end of 1999. The number of conventions concerning the 'core' labour standards – an issue of particular importance to the WTO – is seven. These standards include freedom of association, forced labour, elimination of child labour and elimination of discrimination in respect of employment and occupation.[33] In brief, there is no lack of international agreements on environment and labour.

Despite the number of these 'agreements', they certainly have not been as effective as their supporters may have wished. For one thing, the ILO 'agreements' are (a) 'only' conventions meaning they are not legally binding. Their enforcement relies on 'peer' pressure rather than on legal instruments. This lack of a powerful and effective enforcement system is similarly a

---

32. See Vaughan in this book.
33. The relevant seven conventions include: Forced Labour Convention 1930, (No. 29 =151), Freedom of Association and Protection of the Right to Organize Convention, 1948 (No. 87=127), Right to Organize and Collective Bargaining Convention, 1949 (No. 98=145), Equal Remuneration Convention, 1951 (No. 100=143), Abolition of Forced Labour Convention, 1957 (No. 105=145), Discrimination (Employment and Occupation) Convention, 1958 (No. 111=141), and Minimum Age Convention, 1973 (No. 138=59). The numbers in brackets identify the relevant ILO Convention Number and the total number of countries that have ratified the relevant convention as of 31 December 1999, respectively. In 1999, a new convention called the Convention on the Worst Forms of Child Labour (No. 182) was signed. The ILO now lists this convention along with the other seven as well and, presumably, includes it among the 'core' standards.

problem for MEAs. (b) There are a limited number of conventions that have actually been ratified by parliaments. For example, the Convention on Minimum Age has only been ratified by 83 countries as of 31 December 1999!! Furthermore, (c) some of these conventions have not even been ratified by several large developed countries. This does not bear well for the rest of the international community that sometimes needs to be convinced about the merits of these agreements. For example, the Convention on Employment and Occupation has not yet been ratified by the US and the United Kingdom. (d) Last, but not least, the conventions have not been signed by all countries, a fate also suffered by MEAs.

In brief, the labour and environmental conventions/agreements are subject to two basic problems. The incomplete coverage of countries permits 'free-riding' by countries.[34] This means that non-signatories can benefit from externalities, the costs of which are borne by signatories. The other problem arises from the absence of an effective enforcement mechanism. This would lead to an unstable equilibrium, even under the conditions that all countries sign on a given agreement. The reason for this is that countries may not follow up on their declared intentions to bear the costs of abatement since they face no legal consequences for their failure to meet their 'commitments'.

In addition, there is the problem of the existing environmental agreements. As already noted, the agreements only set targets and objectives, and governments have a discretion as to the manner in which the agreements are implemented. As discussed extensively by Vaughan in this book, the discretion is freely used by countries which sometimes leads to divergent domestic policies as well as to different environmental effects. Similar concerns have been raised by Graham in this book in his review of competition policies in various countries and of regional agreements.

Independent Course of Multilateral Agreements on Environment and Labour

International agreements appear to have a 'life' of their own. They are 'born' as a result of different forces, motivations, pressures. Their 'life' is built on different support systems and is subject to different political interests. For example, the evolution of international agreements on environment and labour, as well as that of various cooperation agreements among different

---

34. Recently, there has been a growing interest in studying the impact of international trade on incentives to free-ride on global agreements. In one of the first papers in this area, Barrett (1997) argues that the threat to impose sanctions is vital to maintain equilibrium – i.e., to eliminate incentives for free-riding.

competition authorities, have so far been quite different to the evolution of the WTO agreements. The one big difference is that while the WTO agreements have succeeded in the adoption of the same, universal standards, the other agreements have not!! Trade negotiators have been able to negotiate universal standards for trade policy, while competition, labour and environment authorities have been far less successful in this respect. This is not only serious, as we note below, but also disappointing. It is disappointing because labour, environment, and competition international agreements share the same ultimate goals as the WTO agreements. Therefore, one would think that this should provide the fundamental condition for reaching a full set of international agreements. Unfortunately, we have a long way to go to reach this conclusion.

Since the implementation of MEAs can be vastly different, it is critical that these MEAs are consistent with the WTO agreements. Are they formulated in such a way that they reflect and/or are dependent on other relevant agreements? Do they depend on the evolution of domestic legislations of particular countries? In particular, are they complementary to the WTO agreements?

The evidence collected by the Committee on Trade and Environment in the WTO has identified areas in which the WTO agreements and MEAs are *complementary,* but also those where conflicts can arise. While the work of the Committee has not yet been completed, some interesting observations have already been made. The Committee has identified 23 MEAs that contain trade provisions. The Committee has also identified at least two potentially serious problems for the conduct of trade policy. First, the list of signatories of MEAs is not identical with that of the WTO Members. Hence, the WTO Members may theoretically bring cases against those countries that violate MEAs even though the latter countries are not signatories of the 23 MEAs.[35] Second, signatory countries of MEAs are permitted under the terms of these agreements to apply trade sanctions against violators of agreed environmental standards. This poses a problem under the WTO agreements. For example, if the sanctions are to be applied on a discriminatory basis, they would violate the MFN provisions of GATT. Moreover, there are specific provisions under the WTO agreements that call for a due process under which trade policy measures can be applied. Hence, there is also room for a potential conflict between MEAs and WTO provisions.

The evidence collected and discussed by Vaughan in this book suggests that MEAs are developing independently from domestic legislation. He goes

---

35. The possibility of WTO measures is, in theory, open even though no case has to date been brought to the WTO.

even further when he suggests that the agenda of multilateral and national environmental legislations has been driven by the agenda of liberal trade policies. This, he concludes, may be good for trade policies, but possibly bad for environmental policies.

The Critical Problem: Universal Standards or Not?

The critical issue for countries in general and for international negotiators in particular, is whether it is desirable to aim at a system with universal standards applicable to all countries across the board. As noted above, international trade negotiators have succeeded in negotiating universal trade standards while the negotiations of labour, environmental and competition standards have been marred by serious difficulties. This is undoubtedly one reason why some people wish to move the discussion and negotiation of labour, environment and competition issues to the WTO in the hope that these issues will be handled with success equal to that of the handling of the issues of 'technical barriers to trade' or 'sanitary and phytosanitary measures'. But the point of substance remains – should we all subscribe, for example, to the same standards on labour?

The answer is not simple. The introduction of universal standards could have serious *economic* consequences as we have seen above. The chapter by Corden and Vousden make this point very clear in their examination of the potential impact of universal labour standards on developing countries. Another problem is the *complexity* of issues that pertain to the labour, environment and competition agreements. And, as we know from the literature, the similarity of rules does not in itself guarantee that decentralised decision-making will be conflict free.[36] Any agreements on universal standards in the environmental, labour and competition area are also elusive because regulators typically face two or multiple overlapping objectives. For example, competition authorities often have to consider the trade-off between efficiency considerations on the one hand and market stability on the other.

There is also the problem of potential *conflicts between different multilateral agreements*. While it is true that some multilateral agreements are complementary with the WTO agreements, it is not always the case. With regard to environmental agreements, we already have a mechanism for determining the degree of complementarity between MEAs and the WTO

---

36. For a good discussion of this issue see Bhagwati (1996), Bliss (1996) and Brown*et al.* (1996). Further evidence is reviewed in the study by Cadot *et al.* (2000).

agreement – the Working Group on Trade and Environment in the WTO.[37] No such mechanism exists with regard to labour and competition. In the absence of complementarity, the problems of jurisdiction and policy implications are serious. For example, competition policies are typically conducted on a national level or, at best, on a regional level. However, decisions of competition authorities often have a 'cross-border' dimension. Take the example of a cross-border merger between two companies. Which country should adjudicate in conflict situations? Should it be the competition authorities of country A or those of country B? Or should the dispute be settled by the authority of the dispute settlement mechanism of the WTO? In practice, in fact, both routes, that of the competition and the WTO authorities, have been tried, as in the infamous case of the Kodak-Fuji dispute.

Another policy implication arising from the absence of universal standards and non-complementary multilateral agreements is the need to address new uncertainties. On the one hand, the WTO agreements already include provisions for protection of the environment, as can be seen from the following. Article XX on Rule of Exceptions allows exceptions for measures 'necessary to protect human, animal or plant life or health' and 'relating to the conservation of exhaustible natural resources'. The Agreements on Technical Barriers to Trade and on Sanitary and Phytosanitary Measures specifically target environmental protection and recognise the legitimacy of government policies to address their objectives. The Agreement on Subsidies and on Countervailing Measures also has special provisions for environmental subsidies and similarly the Agreement on Agriculture. The TRIPS Agreement (Article 27) and GATS Article XIV define conditions under which the relevant policies are exempt from normal WTO disciplines. On the other hand, the presence of specific environmental provisions can lead to uncertainties about the agreement under which disputes can be resolved. Such uncertainties are also costly and may even lead to cancellations of projects.

In brief, if standards are not universal, the costs of compliance with national or regional standards would increase. International disputes will be

---

37. The agenda of the Committee on Trade and Environment includes the relationship between WTO and environmental agreements, between trade liberalisation and sustainable development, developing guidelines for eco-labelling and packaging requirements, the study of the relationship between the WTO provisions and environmental taxes and charges, the study of exports of domestically prohibited goods, building up transparency in WTO negotiations and environmental policies, the consideration of relevant provisions on TRIPS and Services, the impact of environmental standards on competitiveness, the definition of appropriate limits for unilateral trade actions in support of environmental policies and the handling of environmental disputes within the WTO and other frameworks.

subject to different jurisdictions which may mean that for each dispute we shall have a different dispute settlement authority. Moreover, as countries become more and more mutually intertwined, more international disputes can be expected in the future with more agencies being involved in the process. To put it differently, independence is not a free good – there is a price to pay.

Poor Transplantability of Standards

Whilst universal standards on labour, environment and competition are at best far away and a remote possibility, there is still the theoretical and perhaps academic question whether one could not, after all, transplant standards from one legislation to another. There are already historical examples of such transplantations. The most recent example is the adoption of the *Aquis Communautaire* – the EU legislation – by the new acceding countries of Central and Eastern Europe.[38]

This book provides a rather different picture and conclusion to that offered in the chapter by Holmes and Young, *European Lessons for Multilateral Economic Integration: A Cautionary Tale*. Their topic is the question of regulatory convergence which they address by looking at the experience of the EU in four areas – technical barriers to trade, services, investment and competition policy. The EU was chosen as an example partly on the ground that the EU constitutes a fairly homogenous group of developed countries – at least by the standards of multilateral institutions such as the WTO. Hence it should be relatively easier to reach agreements in areas where value judgements about norms and standards are required than in countries which have substantially different economic needs, political structures and loyalties, cultures and histories. The review by Holmes and Young of practices over time leads them to the conclusion that, at best, 'any simple transposition of EU frameworks would be very tricky'. In competition policy area, for example, they conclude that it is only now that 'the EU has moved towards the beginnings of a single competition policy for a single market'. This view is confirmed by the chapters by Panagariya and Graham in this book.

Political Sensitivity

Given the controversies and complexities surrounding the question of universal standards and policies, it goes almost without saying that

---

38. There are, of course, other examples including the case of GATT/WTO agreements when the WTO Members agreed to adopt in full the WTO legal provisions. This point is particularly relevant for newly acceding countries.

international agreements and their negotiations are always politically sensitive. This holds particularly for standards of labour, environment and competition. The adoption of these standards is likely to be a very difficult task. As we are reminded by Graham in this book, the adoption of universal standards in business practices was already attempted at the time when countries were proposing the establishment of the International Trade Organization (ITO) – an intellectual idea of the predecessor to GATT. The proposal failed, *inter alia,* because the original draft of the Treaty of Havana, calling for the establishment of the ITO, made explicit provisions on restrictive business practices. It was only when these provisions were dropped that GATT was established.

There are two highly sensitive political issues involved in negotiating labour, environment and competition issues. The first is sovereignty – a matter of concern for governments in all situations involving international negotiations. The second is each of the special topics covered by this report – labour, environment and business practices – each bringing specific political issues of its own. Moreover, one of the major problems for governments is the conflict between open markets and goals of public policy. The strife of the WTO is for open markets, without much explicit concern for public policy issues. However, the latter is an important prerogative of governments, a prerogative that is strong in some countries and weak in others. All chapters in this book point to the sensitivity of all of the topics under discussion. The sensitivity has undoubtedly increased over time, as the events of Seattle clearly demonstrate.

A WAY FORWARD?

We have started this discussion from the situation in which the so-called New Trade Agenda has been expanded by the proposal to negotiate under the auspices of the WTO the linkages between trade and environment, trade and labour and trade and competition. To this we added the discussion of the relationship between trade and macroeconomic policy. With the exception of the latter, the linkages respectively between environment, labour and competition on the one side and trade on the other, are not immediately evident. Yet, as the discussion in this book demonstrates, the linkages are quite strong. By way of summary, the most important *linkages* are:

- There is a direct link between trade and macroeconomic policies given by the fundamental economic (and accounting) identity.

- There are direct linkages between multilateral trade and environmental policies. The WTO agreements include various environmental provisions, while several MEAs contain trade provisions.
- The WTO agreements contain direct provisions on competitive practices.
- Both labour and environment are linked to foreign trade through production processes since they are inputs in the production of trade goods.

Thus, the linkages exist and the real question is what are the implications for policy-making, especially on the multilateral level. The discussion in this chapter and throughout the book suggests that international cooperation and multilateral agreements with trade implications appear to be a weak point of globalisation. There is no multilateral agreement on competition, the existing multilateral agreements on environment and labour are weak (with respect to country coverage, absence of an implementation and enforcement mechanisms), our ability to strengthen them through 'transplants' of standards is probably limited and they have become very politically sensitive – all of which makes harmonisation of standards and domestic policies difficult.

All of the shortcomings could be quite serious since the choice of policy instruments to address trade, environment, labour, or any other issue is very important. At present, as we are reminded by the contributions in this book; trade, environment, and labour issues are treated by a variety of instruments. By way of a reminder, environmental issues are already a part of MEAs, unilateral environmental policies and trade-related agreements such as the Uruguay Round agreements. In the absence of effective international agreements, there is always a danger that trade policy will be used as an instrument to target the wrong issues and institutions. If this were to happen, as there are signs of it happening, this will greatly complicate the negotiations about 'pure' trade issues, and there are good reasons to believe that such a situation would be highly unstable and could lead to more, not less protection.[39]

This is not a report to address the question of the impact of trade policies on environment or labour standards. Our objective is the reverse – to study the impact of poor environmental and labour policies on the stability of trade policy. The purpose of the book is to point out certain anomalies in the

---

39. The literature on optimal policy intervention, together with the literature on trade and environment, clearly demonstrate that trade policy is a poor instrument to target environmental degradation or the abuse of labour practices. For more details, see, for example, WTO (1999).

international institutional architecture which affect world trade. Nevertheless, some policy conclusions, mentioned below, also emerge from our book.

1. Globalisation of Policies?

Since there is no multilateral competition agreement at present, it is logical to ask the question whether some form of a global competition policy is desirable. A related question is whether we should seek the expansion of the multilateral framework of agreements on environment, labour and other issues. Has the multilateral system gone too far or has it not gone far enough? On this issue, the authors are not unanimous.

For Holmes and Young, there is enough evidence to suggest that the current system has probably gone too far. They feel that the system is trying to address cross-border issues as well as applying a binding dispute settlement mechanism, and that is too big a task to accomplish. This is consistent with the view of those who argue against global competition policy. For example, several Asian countries have argued for some time that the question of consistency between trade and competition policies is not an issue of bad business (non-competitive) practices, but that of trade policies. This would imply that what needs fixing is trade rather than competition policy.

On the other hand, there are the arguments of those who call for a greater complementarity of international agreements. This would require even greater cooperation of governments than in the past. In addition, the pressures for unilateral standards are very strong in all three areas – competition, labour and environment. The question is whether these pressures can, or should, be accommodated. In the area of competition, the most sensible route is a greater cooperation of competition authorities in the form of cooperation agreements between competition authorities. However, this could raise a problem; in some countries the competition authorities may not be a full-fledged government authority, hence jealousy and poor support from governments can arise and block these efforts.

2. Legitimacy

The multilateral system must be seen as legitimate by the 'participants' in order to succeed. How does one achieve legitimacy? One way to do so would be through democratic processes, but such a 'democratic legitimacy' is highly unrealistic at present. It is hard to imagine that, for example, the institutional set-up of multilateral institutions would be obtained through countries' votes. Alternatively, the system must be based on transparency and performance and, add Holmes and Young, on 'sufficient sensitivity to regulatory preferences'.

3.   Ensure Complementarity of Multilateral Agreements

The lack of complementarity constitutes a serious danger for the multilateral system. Conflicting multilateral agreements are a sure recipe for discrediting the agreements. At present, we are facing a more fundamental problem – insufficient information about consistency and complementarity of relevant multilateral agreements. Hence, there is a need to identify the degree of the complementarity. The work has already started in the case of environment and should continue.

4.   Harmonisation of 'Core' Standards?

Despite the pressures for universal standards on environment, labour and competition, countries have so far resisted these pressures. They have been more successful in their resistance on some issues than on others. This may suggest that for some standards the task of harmonisation may be easier than for other standards. An example of the former, given by Graham in the competition area, is harmonisation of policies and standards on the treatment of cartels in the OECD.

Somewhat different tasks can be identified in the area of environment. There appears to be a more fundamental problem for those concerned – the need to identify areas ripe for harmonisation. In NAFTA, for example, domestic environmental standards have been subject to considerable public discussion as well as to concerns about the ability to maintain the independence of domestic environmental standards.

On a multilateral level, one approach could again be to focus on 'core' standards. This implies that in the set of a large number of standards, some standards can actually be acceptable to the world community at large even though the entire package will not. This appears to be the current approach taken in the ILO where the emphasis has been on the 'core' labour standards rather than on any other of the remaining 180 or so conventions. Another route could be to consider *different speeds* with which countries adopt universal standards. Clearly, each one of these proposals would have to be assessed in the light of costs and benefits that are still not fully evident.

5.   Role of the WTO

There is also no reason why at least some of these policies could not be handled by the WTO. This is especially the case of competition policy. Aspects of competition policy are already treated in the existing WTO agreements.[40] For example, GATS recognises, through Article IX, that business practices can become barriers to trade – 'they may restrain competition and thereby restrict trade in services'. As Graham also points out, GATS also calls for the WTO Council for Trade in Services to develop disciplines regarding regulation of service suppliers (qualification requirements, technical standards and licensing requirements). Moreover, Members are not allowed in the *interim period* to apply measures that would 'nullify or impair' their specific commitments. In this respect Graham makes some further concrete proposals. Needless to note, Graham's proposals do not call for the WTO to become a world-wide competition agency, at least at this time.[41] What the proposals suggest is a world of closer cooperation of relevant authorities on matters of competition. This is, to me, quite a sensible suggestion.

Similar arguments can be made about environmental and labour issues. These issues are already at least partially covered by the existing agreements on environment and labour, and trade policy is not the optimal policy instrument as we have already noted earlier. In theory, therefore, the case cannot be made for a more comprehensive coverage of environmental issues in the WTO. Moreover, the practical problem with the proposals to correspondingly expand the WTO agenda is that the WTO system would be over-burdened. This would call, therefore, for alternative arrangements such as parallel, complementary MEAs and Multilateral Agreements on Labour. Most observers would indeed take the line that the latter is far more preferable. Otherwise, the WTO negotiating process is likely to be destabilised which is a heavy price to pay for pushing the frontiers of multilateral trade negotiations. In sum, and on balance, while trade, labour and environment issues are closely linked, the links as well as the environmental and labour issues are best served in their appropriate institutions – outside the WTO.

---

40. For a detailed description of relevant provisions that allow countries to invoke exceptions see Petersmann (1996).
41. Arguments in favour and against an International Competition Policy Agreement (ICPA) can be reviewed in Bilal and Olarreaga (1997). They make an economic argument in favour of a cautious approach towards the pursuit of ICPA. For a contrasting view, see Petersmann (1996).

REFERENCES

Aghion, Philippe, Philippe Bacchetta and A.V. Banerjee (1999), *Capital Markets and Instability of Open Economies*, Discussion Paper Series No. 2083, London, UK: Centre for Economic Policy Research.

Barrett, Scott (1994), 'Self-Enforcing International Agreements', *Oxford Economic Papers*, **46**, 878-94.

Barrett, Scott (1997), 'The Strategy of Trade Sanctions in International Environmental Agreements', *Resource and Energy Economics*, **19**, 345-61.

Berg, Andrew, Eduardo Borensztein, Ratna Sahay and Jeromin Zettelmeyer (1999), *The Evolution of Output in Transition Economies: Explaining the Differences*, Working Paper, WP/99/73, Washington, DC, US: International Monetary Fund.

Bhagwati, Jagdish N. (1996), 'The Demands to Reduce Domestic Diversity Among Trading Nations' in Jagdish N. Bhagwati and Robert E. Hudec (eds) (1996), pp. 9-40.

Bhagwati, Jagdish N. and Robert E. Hudec (eds) (1996), *Fair Trade and Harmonization: Prerequisites for Free Trade?*, Cambridge, MA, US: MIT Press.

Bilal, Sanoussi and Marcelo Olarreaga (1997), 'Competition Policy and the WTO: Is There a Need for a Multilateral Agreement?', mimeo, Geneva, Switzerland: World Trade Organization, Economic Research and Analysis Division.

Bleaney, Michael and David Fielding (1999), *Exchange Rate Regimes, Inflation and Output Volatility in Developing Countries*, CREDIT Research Paper, No. 1999/4, Nottingham, UK: University of Nottingham.

Bliss, Christopher (1996), 'Trade and Competition Control' in Jagdish N. Bhagwati and Robert E. Hudec (eds) (1996), pp. 313-28.

Boltho, Andrea (1996), 'The Return of Free Trade?', *International Affairs*, **72**(2), 247-59.

Brown, Drusilla K., Alan V. Deardorf and Robert M. Stern (1996), 'International Labour Standards and Trade: A Theoretical Analysis' in Jagdish N. Bhagwati and Robert E. Hudec (eds) (1996), pp. 227-80.

Bussiere, Matthieu and Christian Mulder (1999), *Political Instability and Economic Vulnerability*, Working Paper, WP/99/46, Washington, DC, US: International Monetary Fund, Policy and Review Department.

Caballero, Ricardo J. (2000), *Macroeconomic Volatility in Latin America: A View and Three Case Studies*, Research Paper No. 00-10, June, Cambridge, MA, US: National Bureau of Economic Research.

Cadot, Olivier, Jean-Marie Grether and Jaime de Melo (2000), 'Trade and Competition Policy – Where Do We Stand?', *Journal of World Trade*, **34**(3), 1-20.

Corden, W. Max (1994), 'Macroeconomic Policy and Protection', *Economic Policy, Exchange Rate and the International System*, Oxford, UK: Oxford University Press.

Demsetz, Harold (1967), 'Towards a Theory of Property Rights', *American Economic Review*, **57**, 347-59.

Drabek, Zdenek and Joe C. Brada (1998), 'Exchange Rate Regimes and the Stability of Trade Policy in Transition Economies', *Journal of Comparative Economics*, **26**, 642-68.

Drabek, Zdenek and Samuel Laird (1998), 'The New Liberalism: Trade Policy Developments in Emerging Markets', *Journal of World Trade*, **32**(5), 244-69.

Esty, Daniel C. (1994), *Greening the GATT: Trade, Environment and the Future*, Washington, DC, US: Institute for International Economics.

Feldstein, Martin S. (2000), *The European Central Bank and the Euro: The First Year*, Working Paper No. W7517, Boston, US: National Bureau of Economic Research.

Howse, Robert and Donald Regan (2000), 'The Product/Process Distinction – An Illusory Basis for Disciplining Unilateralism in Trade Policy', mimeo, Anne Arbor, Michigan, US: University of Michigan.

McCusker, Karen (2000), 'Are Trade Restrictions to Protect Balance-of-Payments Becoming Obsolete?', mimeo, Geneva: World Trade Organization, Division of International Organizations.

Miranda, Jorge, Raul A. Torres and Mario Ruiz (1998), 'The International Use of Anti-Dumping', *Journal of World Trade,* **32**(5), 5-71.

Petersmann, Ernst-Ulrich (1996), *The Need for Integrating Trade and Competition Rules in the WTO World Trade and Legal System*, PSIO Occasional Paper, World Trade Organization Series Number 3, Geneva, Switzerland: Hautes Etudes Internationales.

World Trade Organization (1999), *Trade and Environment*, Special Study, No. 4., Geneva, Switzerland: World Trade Organization.

Yates, Alexander (1997), *Does MERCOSUR's Trade Performance Justify Concerns about Effects of Regional Trade Agreements?*, PPR No.3, Washington, DC, US: The World Bank.

PART ONE

TRADE AND MACROECONOMIC POLICY

1. Exchange Rate Overvaluation and Trade Protection: Lessons from Experience[*]

Howard J. Shatz and David G. Tarr

SUMMARY: EXCHANGE RATE OVERVALUATION AND TRADE PROTECTION: LESSONS FROM EXPERIENCE

Despite a general trend towards more flexible exchange rate regimes, over half the countries in the world maintain fixed or managed exchange rates. There are clearly advantages and disadvantages of both fixed and flexible exchange rate systems and their variants, and we do not discuss their relative merits in this chapter. Rather, we note that, as a practical matter, exchange rate management in many countries has resulted in overvaluation of the real exchange rate. Estimates suggest that about 25 percent of the countries for which we have data have overvalued exchange rates, with 'black market' premiums from ten percent to more than 100 percent.

Since governments are frequently confronted with the problems of external shocks and external trade deficits in the context of a fixed exchange rate regime, we found that a concise *survey of the literature*, in terms understandable to policy-makers, was needed. This chapter presents world-wide experience regarding what has worked and what has not worked in response to these crises, and why. It also assesses the consequences of

[*] We would like to thank: Julian Berengaut, Dominique Desruelle and Paul Ross of the International Monetary Fund; Arup Banerji, Fred King, Kiyoshi Kodera, Lawrence Hinkle, Albert Martinez, Will Martin, Francis Ng and Maurice Schiff of the World Bank; numerous officials of the Government of Kazakhstan and seminar participants at the World Bank for helpful comments on earlier drafts. The views expressed are those of the authors and do not necessarily reflect those of the World Bank, its Executive Directors, any of its member governments, the International Monetary Fund, the Government of Kazakhstan or those acknowledged.

overvaluation – the frequent result or even the cause of these crises – the consequences of trying to defend an overvalued exchange rate, and the most appropriate policies for addressing an overvaluation.

Although, as a group, developing countries have progressively liberalised their trade regimes during the 1980s and 1990s, some governments take actions to defend an exchange rate that are counter to their long run trade liberalisation. That is, one classic pattern is to attempt to defend an overvalued exchange rate by protectionist trade policies. Experience shows that protection to defend an overvalued exchange rate will significantly retard the growth of the country and delay integration into the world trading community. In fact, an overvalued exchange rate is often the root cause of protection, and the country will be unable to return to the more liberal trade policies that allow growth and integration into the world trading community without exchange rate adjustment.

We briefly explain the benefits of an open trade regime, where we maintain that protectionist policies seriously retard growth and integration into the world trading community. We then provide a brief theoretical discussion of the many channels through which an overvalued exchange rate hurts the economy and growth. We argue that the vast majority of developing countries have downward price and wage rigidities and that with an external trade deficit they require some form of nominal exchange rate adjustment to restore external equilibrium. Next we present the cross-country econometric evidence; this shows that overvalued exchange rates lower economic growth. Subsequently we provide several specific country historical experiences (Chile, Argentina, Uruguay, Turkey, Malaysia) where overvalued exchange rates led to severe problems. In the case of Chile, the reversal of policies, from overvalued exchange rates and protection to competitive exchange rates and low protection, has paved the way for impressive growth. We also discuss the role of a competitive exchange rate policy in the impressive Korean growth experience. Given the significant role overvalued exchange rates have played in Sub-Saharan Africa, we discuss this experience separately and in some detail. We distinguish the Communauté Financière Africaine (CFA) zone from the other countries and provide a case study of Ghana.

World-wide experience has shown that defending the exchange rate has no medium-run benefits, since falling reserves will force devaluation eventually. It is better that the devaluation be accomplished without further debilitating losses in reserves and lost productivity due to import controls. Rather, the world-wide experience with devaluations shows that, post-devaluation, the exchange rate will reach a new equilibrium and that the equilibrium is strongly influenced by the policies of the central bank and the government.

Given that the new trade protection, in response to balance of payments crises, often leads to very diverse tariffs by sector and country, we discuss the adverse world experience with industrial policy that provides very diverse incentives to industries.

1. INTRODUCTION

Despite a general trend in the world towards more flexible exchange rate regimes, over half the countries in the world maintain fixed or managed exchange rates.[1] Moreover, based on a fundamental measure of overvaluation, the 'black market' premium,[2] about 25 percent of the countries in the world have exchange rates that are overvalued by at least 10 percent, and 19 countries have premiums of more than 25 percent. In 10 countries, the 'black market' premium exceeds 100 percent, which implies that the exchange rate fails to serve its role in allocating foreign exchange.[3]

There are many reasons why countries maintain fixed exchange rate regimes: their currencies may be linked to the currency of a partner or partners, for example, the currencies of the CFA zone in Africa. The exchange rate may be used as a nominal anchor, as in the Southern Cone of Latin America in the early 1980s. Or, the exchange rate regime may be employed as a means of regulating foreign trade, as in many of the former communist countries.

There are clearly advantages and disadvantages of both fixed and flexible exchange rate systems and their variants, and we do not discuss their relative merits in this chapter. Rather, we note that, as a practical matter, exchange rate management in many countries in the world has resulted in overvaluation of the real exchange rate. Overvaluation can arise from several factors –

---

1. As of the beginning of 1999 (the latest available data), the International Monetary Fund (1999, Appendix I) reported arrangements for 185 countries. The exchange rate regimes can be divided into pegged (84 countries), floating (75 countries) and limited flexibility (26 countries). Of the 84 with pegged exchange rates, 37 have no separate legal tender, eight use a currency board arrangement, 24 peg to another currency, and 15 to a composite of currencies. Of those floating, 27 maintain a managed float and 48 an independent float.
2. The 'black market' exchange rate is likely to be overly depreciated relative to an equilibrium long run real exchange rate since an actual real depreciation would increase the supply and reduce the demand for foreign exchange. See Ghei and Kamin (1999) for a detailed explanation and econometric evidence.
3. See Global Currency Report (1999). Thirty-eight out of 160 countries had 'black market' premiums of more than ten percent at the end of 1998. Of these: 19 had premiums of more than 25 percent; 13 had premiums of more than 50 percent; and ten countries had premiums of more than 100 percent. These latter ten included Afghanistan, Algeria, Angola, Iraq, North Korea, Liberia, Libya, Myanmar, Sao Tome and Principe, and Somalia.

among them, it is the nature of cycles of international economic activity that from time to time countries are hit hard by external shocks. For developing countries, terms of trade shocks are often quite important, deriving typically from significant swings in energy or commodity prices. Financial crises are another important source of adverse external shocks, as financial crises adversely affect not only the countries involved, but also their trading partners. These external shocks may lead to overvaluation, as in Kazakhstan in 1999. Overvaluation may be the result of a systemic shift in the competitiveness of a linked currency, as in the case of the CFA zone in the late 1980s and early 1990s. In some cases inflation has eroded the competitiveness of the real exchange rate, while the nominal exchange rate served as a nominal anchor (as in the Southern Cone of Latin America in 1979-1982). Or, a multiple exchange rate regime may be used as a means of exercising control over the foreign trade and exchange regime (for example, Poland in the late 1980s).[4]

Although, as a group, developing countries have progressively liberalised their trade regimes during the 1980s and 1990s, some governments take actions to defend an exchange rate that are counter to their long-run trade liberalisation. That is, one classic pattern is to attempt to defend an overvalued exchange rate by protectionist trade policies.[5] In the chapter we present world-wide experience – what are the consequences of defending an overvalued exchange rate regime? Experience shows that protection to defend an overvalued exchange rate will significantly retard the medium- to long-run growth prospects of the country and delay integration into the world trading community. In fact, an overvalued exchange rate is often the root cause of protection, and the country will be unable to return to the more liberal trade policies that allow growth and integration into the world trading community without exchange rate adjustment. Moreover, a devaluation of the nominal exchange rate appears a necessary condition for achieving a large depreciation of the real exchange rate, as virtually all real devaluations (above 25-35 percent) have been accompanied by nominal devaluations (Ghei and Hinkle, 1999).

This chapter is organised as follows. In the remainder of this section, we set the stage by discussing the recent experience of Kazakhstan and defining the key concepts of internal and external balance. In section 2, we briefly

---

4. See Tarr (1990a, 1990b, 1994).
5. Ghei and Pritchett (1999) call this the 'import compression syndrome'. Since devaluations (which reduce imports) are often accompanied by reductions of trade barriers (which increase imports), econometric evidence on the import reducing impact of devaluation has been weak. Ghei and Pritchett estimate that devaluations will reduce imports if import compression is properly accounted for.

explain the benefits of an open trade regime, where we maintain that protectionist policies seriously retard growth and integration into the world trading community. In section 3 we extensively treat the problems caused by an overvalued exchange rate. We begin with a theoretical discussion of many channels through which an overvalued exchange rate hurts the economy and growth. We then argue that the vast majority of developing countries have downward price and wage rigidities that require some form of nominal exchange rate adjustment to restore external equilibrium. Next we present the cross-country econometric evidence; this shows that overvalued exchange rates lower economic growth. Subsequently we provide several specific country historical experiences (Chile, Argentina, Uruguay, Turkey, Malaysia) where overvalued exchange rates led to severe problems. In the case of Chile, the reversal of policies, from overvalued exchange rates and protection to competitive exchange rates and low protection, has paved the way for impressive growth. We also discuss the role of a competitive exchange rate policy in the impressive Korean growth experience. Given the significant role overvalued exchange rates have played in Sub-Saharan Africa, we discuss this experience separately and in some detail in section 4. Finally, in section 5, given that the new trade protection in response to balance of payments crises often leads to very diverse tariffs by sector and country, we discuss the adverse world experience with industrial policy that provides very diverse incentives to industries.

1.1 The Kazakhstan Experience

The first draft of this chapter was written in March 1999 due to the practical need to provide policy advice to Kazakhstan, which was in the middle of a crisis induced by external shocks. The authors found that a concise survey of the literature in terms understandable to policy-makers was needed. This chapter should be useful as a basis of discussion in other countries when similar crises arise.

It is useful to discuss some of the specifics of the crisis in Kazakhstan in early 1999 as a motivation for the broader discussion to follow. Kazakhstan suffered several adverse external shocks in late 1998: it was hit by a fall in the international price of oil (its principal export product), the East Asian crisis and, most importantly, the Russian crisis and the Russian rouble devaluation. Given the lack of sufficient adjustment in the nominal exchange rate, the Kazakhstan tenge became significantly overvalued during early

Box 1.1 Update of Events: Devaluation and Liberalisation in Kazakhstan

On 4 April, the Kazakh Government and the National Bank announced a free float of the tenge's exchange rate. They also announced an end to the highly protective trade measures introduced against Russia, Uzbekistan and Kyrgyzstan. The tenge first slumped to around 150 to the dollar, but later, by mid-April fluctuated between 110-120 to the dollar, and by August 1999 was holding around 132 tenge to the dollar, compared to the pre-devaluation 88 tenge to the dollar rate. The float was intended to boost Kazakh exports and to allow the National Bank to cease its costly efforts to support the tenge. These efforts had depleted hard currency and gold reserves to US$1.7 billion, down from US$1.9 billion in January.

Commenting on the government's actions, prime minister Nurlan Balgimbayev noted that, due to devaluations among neighbour countries, Kazakhstan-produced goods had became uncompetitive. As a result, Kazakhstan industry suffered, enterprises stopped operating and unemployment increased. He indicated that foreign trade turnover of Kazakhstan was reduced by almost nine percent, or US$1.3 billion with exports reduced by US$1.25 billion. Kazakhstan had to undertake urgent measures caused by purely external factors and economic policies of neighbour countries. The trade protection was a response to those pressures.

He emphasised that henceforth the US dollar exchange rate will depend on demand and supply at the foreign exchange market. The National Bank of Kazakhstan (NBK) will not substantially intervene in this process. He said that until the announcement, the NBK was spending its gold and foreign currency reserves in order to support the exchange rate at a certain level, but that will not happen any longer. 'We have no doubts regarding economic stability and our ability to manage the economic situation … BK has significant gold and foreign currency reserves, but what is the reason to give the currency away and support an excessively expensive tenge?' Balgimbayev asked.

Regarding the highly protective trade measures against Russia, Kyrgyzstan and Uzbekistan, he noted that Kazakhstan has borders open for thousands of kilometres with those countries. Cheap goods from those countries easily compete with local producers and take foreign currency out of the country. It is practically impossible to close the borders, and it is also wrong both from economic and political points of view. 'Russia and Central Asian neighbours are our friends, and there is no reason to develop trade wars. From this point of view, the only solution is to introduce a floating exchange rate regime'.

Source: Oxford Analytica, 12 April 1999 and 17 August 1999; Robert Lyle, Radio Free
        Europe, April 1999.
Source: Based on news reports.

1999.[6] Kazakhstan defended the tenge with bans on imports from Russia of many categories of foodstuffs, prohibitively high tariffs on imports of several categories of products from Kyrgyzstan and Uzbekistan, and threatened 'antidumping' actions.[7] These actions were potentially disastrous for Kazakh economic growth.

Some Kazakh authorities feared that devaluation would lead to an unstable downward spiral of the exchange rate and possibly a Russia-style financial crisis. But the banking crisis in Russia was precipitated more by the government default on rouble denominated debt, which dramatically reduced the assets of many Russian banks overnight; these conditions were not present in Kazakhstan. Moreover, the world-wide experience, as well as recent experience in transition countries (for example, Ukraine, Moldova and Russia) has shown that defending the exchange rate has no medium-run benefits, since falling reserves will force devaluation eventually. It is better that the devaluation be accomplished without further debilitating losses in reserves and lost productivity due to import controls. Rather, the world-wide experience with devaluations shows that, post-devaluation, the exchange rate will reach a new equilibrium and that the equilibrium is strongly influenced by the policies of the central bank and the government. In April 1999, Kazakh authorities allowed a float of the exchange rate and reversed the protectionist measures.

---

6. While the tenge depreciated in real terms against the US dollar (by about 15 percent from July 1998 to January 1999) and many other Western currencies, it significantly appreciated in real terms against the Russian rouble (by about 68 percent from July 1998 to January 1999). Since Russia is the most important trading partner of Kazakhstan, the data show that a significant real appreciation of the tenge occurred. Taking all trading partners into account the real exchange rate appreciated. The overvaluation resulted in loss of competitiveness relative to partners in the region, especially Russia, and difficulty in defending the exchange rate. The precise quantitative extent of the overvaluation is beyond the scope of this note, but the data, combined with the difficulties in defending the exchange rate, clearly indicate that the tenge was overvalued.
7. Most countries in the world apply at least some level of tariffs for protective purposes. Compared with tariffs in the customs code or 'safeguard' actions, however, antidumping is an especially inappropriate manner of conducting international trade policy. The reason is that when import protection is applied, the costs and benefits to the nation should be evaluated. Evaluation of the relative costs and benefits is possible in a safeguard action or when the customs code is being changed. Antidumping, however, applies a tariff based on the practice of a foreign company or country and never asks the relevant question of whether application of the tariff is in the interest of the country. Moreover, exporters typically avoid antidumping duties by agreeing to raise the price of their exports, which hurts the importing country by having to pay higher prices for imports. See Finger (1991, 1996) for details and guidelines on how protection should be applied.

1.2   The Need to Restore Internal Balance

When a country experiences a deficit in its trade balance, it is not in 'external' balance. It follows from a national income accounting identity, however, that a trade deficit means that the country is spending more than its income. That is, the trade deficit allows the country to consume or spend beyond its income (otherwise the value of what it is producing). When a country's expenditure does not equal its income, it is not in 'internal' balance. These imbalances can severely impede country economic performance, and it is these imbalances that countries suffering from external shocks often face.

Although a nominal devaluation is designed to correct the problem of external balance, it will also be important to assure internal balance, otherwise the trade deficit may not be corrected by the nominal devaluation. For many developing countries the trade deficit reflects the government's fiscal deficit which is often financed by monetary expansion. The monetary expansion in turn leads to inflation. The impact on the real exchange rate of a nominal devaluation in this environment is likely to be eroded by inflation, since high inflation tends to appreciate the real exchange rate, making elimination of the trade deficit problematic.

In general, monetary or fiscal policies will have to be combined with exchange rate policies to achieve both internal and external balance simultaneously. This is a special case of a more general principle of economics that multiple policy targets typically require multiple policy instruments. In this chapter, however, we focus on the experience of countries that have limited the use of exchange rate adjustment as an economic policy instrument.

2.   THE BENEFITS OF AN OPEN TRADE REGIME

As we elaborate in the next section, a serious problem with exchange rate overvaluation is that it often leads to the imposition of high tariff and non-tariff barriers to international trade. World-wide experience in the last 50 years, however, demonstrates the benefits of open trade regimes. The Organisation for Economic Cooperation and Development (OECD) countries brought trade barriers down through successive General Agreement on Tariffs and Trade (GATT)/World Trade Organization (WTO) negotiations and experienced sustained growth in trade and incomes. Many developing country governments initially felt differently and attempted to promote industrialisation behind high protective barriers. But in the last ten years or so, the balance of opinion has shifted in these countries as well. Evidence accumulated shows that high rates of protection significantly depress economic development, and that open trade regimes are more conducive to growth.[8] Moreover, virtually all recent development success stories have been based on strong industrial export growth and relatively low barriers to imports – Chile, Hong Kong, Malaysia, Mauritius, and Singapore – or continually falling barriers – the Republic of Korea and Taiwan (China). Industrial sectors in these economies not only have higher export growth but generate more employment as well; and trade reforms have usually been accompanied by increased flows of foreign investment.

An effective trade policy is central to the integration of developing countries into the international economic system and to the growth that that will generate. It provides links with international markets, and, together with the exchange rate, forms the transmission mechanism through which international trade affects domestic resource allocation, the efficient and competitive restructuring of industry and agriculture, access to new and diverse technologies, improved incentives to exporters and reduction of smuggling, rent-seeking[9] and corruption in customs.

Tariff policy is the centrepiece of trade policy in a market system. Tariffs are, with very few exceptions, the only acceptable policy tool for protection under the GATT/WTO. They are superior to alternative instruments of protection, such as non-tariff barriers (NTBs) like quotas, licences and technical barriers to trade (TBTs), because they are less likely to lead to rent-seeking and corrupt practices, and because tariffs limit the exercise of domestic monopoly power where it exists, whereas NTBs do not.

3. THE PROBLEMS OF AN OVERVALUED EXCHANGE RATE

Experience has shown that countries that attempt to maintain overvalued exchange rates significantly impede their growth in the medium to long term.

---

8. Sachs and Warner in a recent article (1995) have estimated that open economies have grown about one percent per year faster than closed economies, and that the difference is greater among developing countries. For a review of the extensive literature on the link between open trade regimes and economic growth see Edwards (1993). See also Dollar (1992).
9. Rent-seeking refers to the expenditure of resources to achieve a favourable regulatory intervention by government. In this context, it refers to lobbying of government officials (including bribes) to achieve protection from international competition. It is generally rather inefficient since resources that could be used on productive activities are diverted to influence government decisions regarding protection.

Theory, cross-country statistical studies, and case histories all reinforce the basic findings that exchange rate overvaluation can reduce economic efficiency, misallocate resources, increase capital flight, and most perniciously, lead to exchange and trade controls.

3.1   Problems Caused by an Overvalued Exchange Rate - Theory

Theory suggests that there are many channels through which an overvalued exchange rate hurts the economy and growth: (1) it discriminates against exports. Since a significant portion of the costs of production is paid in domestic currency, the overvalued exchange rate results in a reduction of incentives and ability of exporters to compete in foreign markets. This chokes foreign exchange receipts and damages a country's ability to purchase the imports needed for economic activity; (2) an overvalued exchange rate means that import-competing industries are faced with increased pressure from foreign companies, resulting in increased calls for protection against imports from industrial and agricultural lobbies. The political pressures for protection eventually prove to be overwhelming and governments yield to lobbying and offer increased tariffs on imports. This closes the economy to international competition, reduces access to needed imported inputs and technology, and growth falls as a result. Devaluation serves the dual purpose of uniformly protecting import competing industries and increasing the incentives to exporters; (3) another way that overvalued exchange rates impede growth is that productivity advances are less rapid. This is because the export sectors and the import competing sectors are disadvantaged by an overvalued exchange rate, and it is in these sectors that productivity advances are often most rapid (Cottani *et al.* 1990); (4) overvaluation induces capital flight among domestic citizens anticipating a devaluation. As a result, less foreign exchange is available for needed imports; (5) foreign exchange may become rationed and allocated inefficiently by the government; and finally, (6) efforts to defend an overvalued exchange rate through very tight monetary policy can plunge the country into severe recession. This last concern was very relevant in Kazakhstan before the move to the free float, since monetary and fiscal policies were under too much pressure to defend the exchange rate, risking adverse impacts on investment and output.

3.2   The Problems with 'Automatic' Adjustment Mechanisms to an Overvalued Exchange Rate

Unless the central bank takes offsetting action, a trade deficit will result in a decline in the domestic money supply. Thus, one response to an overvalued exchange rate is to hold the nominal exchange rate fixed and assume that domestic prices and wages will fall to help bring tradeable goods prices back to internationally competitive levels. This is the mechanism known as the 'specie flow mechanism' described by David Hume in the 18th century. The problem with this strategy is that prices and wages tend to be sufficiently inflexible downward in most modern economies, that sustained and substantial periods of unemployment must be endured if the strategy is to have a chance of being successful. Most countries are unwilling to endure these high costs.[10] Some prominent examples are provided here. Further insight is provided in the section below on 'case studies of the effects of overvaluation'.

England 1924
In October 1924, England embarked on a policy of increasing the value of sterling relative to gold to its pre-World War I level. This amounted to a real appreciation of ten percent and required export industries to reduce their prices if they wanted to stay internationally competitive. Furthermore, in order to avoid trade and payments imbalances, the Bank of England increased interest rates and restricted lending abroad. John Maynard Keynes (1925)[11] described the difficulties of this strategy:

> Our export industries are suffering because they are the *first* to be asked to accept the 10 per cent reduction . . . Our problem is to reduce money wages and, through them, the cost of living, with the idea that, when the circle is complete, real wages will be as high, or nearly as high, as before. By what *modus operandi* does credit restriction attain this result? *In no other way than by the deliberate intensification of unemployment* (italics original).

CFA zone
In more recent times, the CFA zone countries in Africa attempted such internal adjustment during the period of their real overvaluation, from 1986 to 1994 (Clément *et al.*, 1996, and Nashashibi and Bazzoni, 1994). This resulted in disastrous consequences for the CFA countries as the economic contractions in some of them were comparable to the Great Depression of the United States. (See Table 1.1 below for data on the two largest CFA countries.) Large increases in poverty and other economic problems ensued (see Devarajan and Hinkle, 1994, and further discussion in section 4).[12]

---

10. See Sachs and Larrain (1999) for a further discussion.
11. pp. 247 and 256-7.
12. For example, the incidence of poverty doubled in Côte d'Ivoire from 30 percent to 60 percent between 1985 and 1992.

Table 1.1 Comparing Great Depressions: Cameroon, Côte d'Ivoire and the United States

All numbers are the percentage decline in per capita GDP.

Measure of Output Decline /Country	Cameroon	Côte d'Ivoire	United States
Purchasing Power Parity[a]	31.4	29.1	N.A.[c]
Purchasing Power Parity with Terms of Trade Adjustments[a]	38.5	34.5	N.A.
Market Prices[b]	41.5	18.8	30.9

Notes
a   Authors' calculations for 1986-1992 from the Penn World Table Mark 5.6, described in Summers and Heston (1991) and available on the website: http://pwt.econ.upenn.edu. Post-1992 data are unavailable.
b   Authors' calculations from the peak to the trough of the depression. This is 1986-1994 for Cameroon and Côte d'Ivoire, and 1929-1933 for the United States. Data are from the World Bank (1999) and U.S. Bureau of the Census (1975).
c   Not Available.

Governments tried especially hard to rein in wage costs, but without success. In fact, wages actually rose relative to GDP. In addition, the high real exchange rate hurt the export and formal manufacturing sectors, undermining the domestic tax base and widening budget deficits. Furthermore, the economic slowdown, called for by internal adjustment, caused a change in the composition of imports to lower-value items, and increased the level of informal imports so that tariff revenues also fell. This meant that at a time when internal adjustment called for the CFA zone governments to decrease their fiscal deficits, these deficits actually increased since the governments could not reduce their spending by as much as their revenue fall. As noted below, the CFA franc devaluation of 1994 – external adjustment – was followed by a return of economic growth and increased trade.

The CFA zone experience also casts doubt on the claim that countries should avoid devaluations in order to retain international investors. The zone certainly had stable prices and exchange rates, but its failure to solve the problems brought on by the overvalued real exchange rate decreased substantially its attractiveness to foreign investors. Capital flight increased in anticipation of an eventual devaluation (Clément *et al.*, 1996).

Chile 1999

Faced with weak demand from Asia and falling prices for its principal commodity export, copper, Chile saw its current account deficit widen and its currency come under attack. At first the central bank raised interest rates, but the high interest rates cut domestic demand on top of the decline in demand for exports, and plunged the country into its worst recession in 16 years and its highest unemployment rate in ten years. On 2 September, the Central Bank allowed the currency to float, suspending its formal commitment to intervene in the foreign exchange markets to keep the peso within a band. The currency immediately fell by a small step, from 519.35 to the dollar to 523.25 to the dollar (Torres, 1999).

3.3   Real Exchange Rate Overvaluation and Cross-Country Economic Performance

Cottani *et al.* (1990) investigated the effects of real exchange rate misalignment and variability on the economic performance of 24 developing countries from 1960-1983. They found that exchange rate misalignment was strongly related to low growth of per capita GDP. Furthermore, misalignment was also related to low productivity. Capital did not go to the companies or sectors that could make the best use of it. Finally, misalignment was also related to slow export growth and slow agricultural growth.

A study of growth in 12 countries from 1965-1985 (Edwards, 1988 and 1989), reinforced these findings.[13] The greater the misalignment, the lower the growth during the period. Furthermore, exchange controls and trade impediments, proxied by the 'black market' exchange rate premium, were negatively related to growth.[14]

In a study of economic growth in 18 Latin American countries between 1950 and 1980, Cardoso and Fishlow (1989) showed that growth was very

---

13. The 12 are Brazil, Colombia, El Salvador, Greece, India, Israel, Malaysia, Philippines, South Africa, Sri Lanka, Thailand, and Yugoslavia.

14. Faini and de Melo (1990) took a somewhat dimmer view of the impact of the real exchange rate on economic performance. They found a positive, but usually not significant, relationship between devaluations and the improvement of the trade balance for 49 developing countries between 1965 and 1985. However, they also found for a smaller sample, different because of data availability, that a depreciated real exchange rate promoted investment. Furthermore, they found that for adjusting countries during the 1980s, the higher prices of imported intermediates brought about by devaluations were not important determinants of depressed investment.

uneven among the countries of the region. They found that the most important determinant of Latin American country growth rates in these years was export performance and access to imports. While they did not discuss the real exchange rate, their findings are valuable for showing the importance of the trade channels through which the exchange rate affects country economic performance. Exports were important not only because competing in international markets induced efficiency, but also because export earnings could avert recurrent stabilisation crises. Imports contributed to growth because the region's industrialisation strategy demanded imported inputs. Countries forced to limit their imports performed less well.

3.4 Case Studies of the Effects of Overvaluation

The economic histories of developing countries that followed a classic import-substituting industrialisation strategy after World War II provide good illustrations of the negative effects of an overvalued exchange rate combined with trade controls. Latin America, more than any other region, followed this strategy but was not alone. We select illustrative episodes from Argentina, Chile, Uruguay, and Turkey.

Argentina, Chile, and Uruguay
Argentina, Chile, and Uruguay all followed import-substituting industrialisation policies that led to a bias against exports, extremely uneven rates of trade protection across sectors, and controlled financial systems. They also experienced recurrent balance-of-payments crises and slow growth (Corbo *et al.* 1986). By the early 1970s, all three had accelerating inflation, bottlenecks in production, slow export growth, and balance of payments difficulties (Corbo and de Melo, 1987).

In response, they went through two phases of stabilisation and reform, one in the mid-1970s and the other from 1979-1982. The second phase is most applicable to judging the effects of an overvalued exchange rate and import controls on economic performance.

In the second phase, all three countries used a nominal exchange rate anchor to halt inflation. The exchange rate appreciated, and when it became apparent that the nominal rate could not be sustained, capital flight resulted. In Uruguay and Argentina, where there were no capital controls, major capital outflows occurred. In Chile, where there were capital controls, people engaged in capital flight by buying imported consumer durables. This capital flight occurred in all three countries well before the onset of the debt crisis in 1982.

Other problems resulted. Profitability fell in the tradeable goods sectors. In Argentina, which remained quite restrictive to imports throughout, the gross margins of exporting businesses were hurt much more than those of import-competing businesses. In Uruguay, the rate of growth of nontraditional exports fell sharply from 1979-1981. And in Chile, the leading growth sectors during the period became construction, internal trade, and financial services – all non-tradeables, even though reforms during the 1975-1979 period had reduced the bias against exports significantly by June 1979.

Chile: the aftermath
Chile is now well known for its economic success. Its average annual rate of growth of real GDP has been more than seven percent since 1984. Its policies following a crisis of 1982-1983 are instructive.

It is true that Chile experienced high rates of growth in the late 1970s. This followed a deep contraction in 1974-1975, and came as a result of a number of deregulation and reform measures, including instituting a uniform ten percent tariff on all goods except automobiles. However, as alluded to above, inflation persisted, hurting the reforms, and Chile fought back with a fixed rate as a nominal anchor in 1979. Combined with other policies, this at first led to large external borrowings, most of which were at variable interest rates. In the early 1980s, the external financing dried up as confidence in the sustainability of the exchange rate ebbed. Making matters worse, Chile experienced a deterioration in the terms of trade, and then foreign interest rates rose, further hurting the Chilean financial and business sectors. In 1982-1983 Chile experienced its worst depression since the 1930s, with real GDP falling 15 percent.

During and immediately after the recession, Chile tried a number of policies, including an increase in tariff rates, to switch domestic spending to domestic products. In June 1982, the government abandoned the fixed rate, and eliminated compulsory wage indexation and initiated a series of nominal devaluations. For a short time, Chile allowed the exchange rate to float (Corbo and Fischer, 1994). However, Chile then followed an erratic policy, implementing five different exchange rate regimes (Labán and Larraín, 1995).

In 1985 the government embarked on the strategy it maintains to this day, specifically, an export-oriented structural adjustment. This included steady devaluations and a staged lowering of uniform tariffs from 35 percent in 1984 to 11 percent by 1991. Importantly, the new nominal exchange rate system featured a crawling band, and policy makers intended to use it to maintain the international competitiveness of Chilean exports (Dornbusch and Edwards, 1994). In fact, though they used the nominal rate as the policy variable, they focused on the real exchange rate, adjusting the nominal rate for the differential between domestic and foreign inflation. Using an index of 100 as the value of the real rate in 1977, the real exchange rate appreciated to 84.5 in 1981, then fell to 118.2 in 1984, and then following the introduction of the new policy, depreciated to 145.2 in 1985. It continued depreciating to 180.1 in 1990 (Corbo and Fischer, 1994). In 1998 the Chilean legislature approved further lowering of the uniform tariff to six percent in stages, and in late 1999 Chile abandoned the exchange-rate band system for a float.

The improved incentives to exporters, from the reduction in the import tariff and the devaluation, led to an expansion of nontraditional exports (10.5 percent per year from 1985-1989) and efficient import substitution. Macroeconomic stabilisation, tax reform, and cuts in government spending combined to promote savings and investment. And privatization of state-owned firms, rehabilitation of the financial sector through re-capitalisation, and the strengthening of bank regulation combined to spur private business activity.

Turkey

Three episodes from the post-World War II history of Turkey, recounted in Krueger (1995), also illustrate the problems created by an overvalued exchange rate combined with import restrictions.

Like the Latin American countries, Turkey followed an import-substituting industrialisation growth strategy. Starting in 1953, export growth ceased for a number of reasons and inflation accelerated. Inflation combined with a fixed nominal exchange rate meant a strengthening of real exchange rate and a bias against exports. Foreign exchange became scarce, so the country started import licensing in 1954. By 1957, export earnings were falling and imports were severely restricted, damaging domestic economic activity. By 1958, Turkey could not finance imports and it appeared that the country would not even be able to obtain gasoline for trucks to move that year's harvest to ports. In response, Turkey adopted an International Monetary Fund stabilisation plan featuring devaluation, import liberalisation, and fiscal and monetary restraint. Real GDP had been declining, but started growing immediately in response to the availability of imports. Inflation fell and export earnings started to rise again. Turkey was among the most rapidly growing developing countries of the 1960s.

In the late 1960s, however, Turkey's exchange rate again became overvalued due to moderate inflation throughout the decade (five to ten percent annually), combined with a fixed nominal exchange rate. The high demand for imports, combined with the bias against exports, caused foreign exchange to become scarce. The resulting problems getting imports caused a slowdown in both production and real investment. The country responded in 1970 with a nominal devaluation, and the result was extremely rapid export growth. Turkey then experienced rapid economic growth through 1975.

The third Turkish episode occurred in the late 1970s. Large fiscal deficits, a failure to change the internal price of oil following the 1973 oil shock, and an overvalued exchange rate, made worse by extremely high inflation, spurred this third crisis. Once again, the country ended up with severely constrained imports, with falling real output and falling income.

3.5   Exchange Rates and Economic Performance in East Asia

Despite the recent Asian crisis, the record of economic development in Asia remains enviable. A large reason for rapid Asian growth was exchange rate management (Roemer, 1994). Successful Asian countries kept their nominal rates close to market-clearing levels, exhibiting low or no parallel-market premiums. Importantly, this flexibility allowed their real exchange rates to remain constant or depreciate gradually, maintaining real returns to exporters over long periods. In some cases, policy makers carried out nominal exchange rate devaluations with the real exchange rate in mind. Oil-exporter Indonesia devalued substantially in 1978 even though export earnings were rising, because policy makers were concerned that a real exchange rate appreciation during the previous six years was hurting non-oil sectors. When oil prices fell in 1983, export earnings were not as badly hurt as in other oil-exporting countries, and further devaluations from 1983 to 1986 encouraged a non-oil export boom (Lewis and McPherson, 1994). We present two more detailed cases, Korea and Malaysia.

Korea
Korea is often viewed as an example of a country that grew despite (or because of) interventionist government policies. While the actual effect of government policies is hotly debated, one fact is clear – Korea avoided overvaluation of its exchange rate to encourage its exporters. Thus, many regard Korea's exchange rate management policy as a key to its successful long-term economic performance.[15] Before 1960, the government kept the nominal exchange rate fixed with only small adjustments, resulting in overvaluation and balance-of-payments problems. These problems forced the government to use multiple exchange rates, import licensing, and high and

---

15. See Nam (1995).

diverse tariffs. In this way, Korea was a typical inward-looking developing
country.

Starting in the early 1960s, however, Korea shifted its strategy to export
orientation. It unified its exchange rate in 1961 and devalued from 130 won
to the dollar to 255 won to the dollar in May 1964. With Korean inflation
much higher than the levels of Korean trading partners, Korea avoided
overvaluation by gradually devaluing the nominal rate, reaching 893 to the
dollar at the end of 1985.[16] Only during the second half of the 1970s, in an
effort to dampen domestic inflation, did policy makers fix the nominal rate at
484 won to the dollar. The fixed-rate policy, along with a number of other
factors, resulted in overvaluation and a stagnation in growth and export
performance. These economic problems led policy makers to devalue the
won in 1980 to 580 to the dollar, the first devaluation since 1974. Afterwards,
they allowed the won to depreciate gradually through the end of 1985.

The most telling result of Korea's policy of exchange rate flexibility is that
from 1953 to 1960, per capita GDP measured in constant purchasing power
parity dollars grew at an average annual rate of 1.8 percent. From 1960 to
1991, it grew at an average annual rate of 6.9 percent, from $904 to $7,251.
Analysing data for 126 countries for the period 1960 to 1992, Pritchett (1997)
showed that Korea had the highest growth rate of real per capita GDP
measured in purchasing power parity dollars.[17] Nam reported that in addition,
exports rose even more rapidly than GNP. The ratio of exports to GNP was
2.4 percent in 1962, and 25.6 percent in 1991. Manufactured goods, as a
share of exports, rose from 27 percent in 1962 to 95.4 percent in 1991.

Malaysia
In some ways, the problems faced by Malaysia in the early 1980s were
similar to those of Africa, to be described in section 4. Malaysia faced
decreases in world commodity prices, a current account deficit, and an
overvalued real exchange rate. The country had a much more successful
adjustment, however, and embarked on a decade of rapid growth.

---

16. The nominal rate appreciated once again between 1986 and 1989, and then depreciated
    through 1991, the end of the period under study in Nam.
17. Using real GNP data from the Bank of Korea, Nam reported an aggregate growth rate of 3.6
    percent annually in the 1950s, and 10.6 percent annually from 1962 to 1991. World Bank
    (1999) showed an average annual growth rate of real aggregate GDP of 8.6 percent from
    1962 to 1991, but did not have data for the 1950s. The per capita GDP figures cited in the
    text and by Pritchett (1997) are from the Penn World Tables Mark 5.6 (Summers and
    Heston, 1991). We downloaded the data from the University of Toronto,
    http://datacentre.chass.utoronto.ca/pwt/index.html

As recounted in Demery and Demery (1992), Malaysia had high levels of economic growth and rapid rates of growth of manufacturing exports between 1968 and 1984, but was a major natural resources exporter as well. Key commodity exports included tin, rubber, petroleum, natural gas, and palm oil. Commodity and oil prices boomed in 1979 and 1980, and the government expanded spending. These prices started declining significantly in 1981. The terms of trade reversals cost the country real income amounting to seven percent of GDP in 1981 and three percent in 1982. However, expecting the reversals to be temporary, the government maintained its fiscal expansion, relying on foreign borrowing to finance growing government deficits. The large inflows of debt finance, combined with government spending tilted towards the non-tradeables sectors, resulted in an appreciation of the real exchange rate.

Starting in 1984, the Malaysian government embarked on an adjustment programme. It cut government spending to reduce the deficit.[18] To restore external competitiveness and profitability in tradeables, it depreciated the nominal exchange rate and reduced external borrowing. Combined with lower domestic inflation, these policies led to a real depreciation between 1985 and 1987 of just under 30 percent.

The change in the real exchange rate, along with the other adjustment policies, had several beneficial effects. The current account returned to surplus in 1986 and 1987 and resources started to move back to the tradeables sectors.[19] The adjustment also restored growth. According to World Bank data (World Bank, 1999), aggregate real GDP growth averaged 8.3 percent annually from 1987 to 1991, well above the rates before the adjustment.[20] And for the whole decade 1987 to 1996 aggregate real growth averaged 8.5 percent.

---

18. Lower tax revenues resulted in the deficit rising again in 1986 and 1987, though the government financed this mostly with domestic borrowing. Foreign borrowing was actually negative in 1987. Another result of the government's expenditure reduction policies was that private consumption and investment fell from 1984 to 1987. This kept demand for imports flat while the level of exports rose, helping bring the current account back into balance.
19. Between 1979 and 1984, these sectors (agriculture, mining, and manufacturing) fell from 56 percent of GDP to 52 percent, but recovered to 54 percent in 1987.
20. Although GDP grew by 6.8 percent annually between 1980 and 1984, Demery and Demery (1992) attribute this largely to government spending, which was unsustainable, given the current account deficit, the growth of government debt, and terms of trade reversals. During 1985, real GDP fell by 1.1 percent, and then rose by 1.2 percent the next year.

4.   EXCHANGE RATES AND ECONOMIC PERFORMANCE IN SUB-SAHARAN AFRICA

4.1   Introduction

While the countries of post-colonial Africa represent a remarkable diversity of people and geography, their economic policies leading up to the 1980s bore a striking similarity (Foroutan, 1997). They established tight control over economic activity using import and export quotas and prohibitions, price controls, foreign exchange controls, interest rate ceilings, state-owned enterprises, and marketing monopolies. This produced a layering of policies with a strong bias against trade (Nash, 1997). By the early 1980s, many countries faced balance of payments crises and economic decline.

Terms of trade shocks played a large role in triggering these problems (Bouton *et al.* 1994). Commodity booms in the second half of the 1970s led to higher government revenues and the rapid expansion of government spending. In the early and mid-1980s, commodity prices fell, but governments did not adjust. Continuing to spend, they financed their mounting deficits with external debt and inflation. For example, Madagascar's budget deficit grew from four percent of GDP in 1978 to 17 percent in 1982, inducing inflation. Kenya's foreign debt, very low at the beginning of the 1970s, reached 50 percent of GDP a decade later. The foreign borrowing appreciated the equilibrium real exchange rate. Inflation and a lack of adjustment of nominal exchange rates led to significantly overvalued real exchange rates throughout Africa.

In response to the real appreciation, countries imposed exchange controls and import restrictions rather than devalue, and this triggered a downward spiral. The overvalued rate reduced incentives for exporters and the trade balance worsened, forcing officials to impose even tighter restrictions. Many countries ended up with negative growth. Ghana's real per capita income, for example, declined 30 percent between 1970 and 1983, and real export earnings declined 52 percent. Throughout Africa, real per capita income fell by 15 percent between 1977 and 1985 and export performance collapsed from about ten percent annual growth in the early 1970s to declines in the early 1980s (Jones and Kiguel, 1994). These problems resulted in a period of painful adjustment programmes.

The valuation of the real exchange rate proved a key to successful reforms. Comparing three areas of policy – exchange rate, fiscal, and monetary – Bouton *et al.* (1994) conclude that exchange rate reforms had the biggest effect on growth.

4.2 The Exchange Rate: Cross-Country Studies

Any analysis of the continent's experience must differentiate between the CFA franc countries, which peg their currency to the French franc, and the countries of the rest of Sub-Saharan Africa, which independently determine their exchange rate policies.[21] The growth records of these two groups are very different, as shown in the following table. The resumption of aggregate growth for each group coincided with real exchange rate adjustments.

Table 1.2 Real Growth Rates in Africa, 1981-1995 (annual averages)

Country Group	1981-1985	1986-1993	1994-1995
Non-CFA Zone Countries			
GDP Growth	0.4	4.4	3.0
Per-Capita GDP Growth	-2.5	2.1	-0.2
CFA Zone Countries			
GDP Growth	4.3	-0.4	2.8
Per-Capita GDP Growth	0.6	-3.2	-0.8

Source: Klau (1998)

Outside the CFA zone, most Sub-Saharan African currencies experienced large real appreciations in the 1970s and early 1980s, estimated at about 44 percent on average. The CFA-zone overvaluations started a bit later, in the mid-1980s.

There is strong evidence that the overvaluation of real exchange rates contributed a great deal towards Africa's poor economic performance. Ghura and Grennes (1993) analysed the relationship between the real exchange rate and macroeconomic performance in 33 Sub-Saharan African countries between 1972 and 1987. They found that misalignment, or overvaluation, was associated with lower levels of growth of real GDP per capita, lower

---

21. The West and Central African Monetary Unions, which together with Comoros form the CFA zone, have convertible currencies pegged at a fixed rate against the French franc. Their monetary arrangements help guard against large losses of reserves and shortages of foreign exchange. Membership in the zone has changed somewhat over time, but in general has included Benin, Burkina Faso, Cameroon, Central African Republic, Chad, Congo, Comoros, Côte d'Ivoire, Equatorial Guinea, Gabon, Mali, Niger, Senegal and Togo.

levels of exports, lower levels of imports, lower levels of investment, and lower levels of savings, even when correcting for other causes.

Klau (1998) showed that the CFA franc overvaluation of the late 1980s and early 1990s was one of the principal causes of output decline in those countries. In both CFA zone and non-CFA zone countries, he showed that real devaluations are associated with short-run and long-run improvements in economic activity, as suggested in Table 1.2.

Real devaluations are also associated with improvements in African export performance. Sekkat and Varoudakis (1998) analysed the real exchange rate and manufactured exports in three sectors in 11 African countries from 1970 to 1992. They found that an overvaluation was negatively associated with exports in all three sectors, textile products, chemical products, and metal products, for the non-CFA zone countries.

The next section presents case studies of Ghana, one of the non-CFA reformers, and the CFA countries as a group.

4.3   Case Studies of Reform and Adjustment

Ghana
Ghana's reform record has been one of the better in Africa, as detailed in Nowak *et al.* (1996). Part of this record included the transformation of the currency, the cedi, from one of the most overvalued in the world to a convertible currency by 1992. Ghana also moved its budget towards balance and liberalised its trade policies, and began to see significantly improved growth.

Reforms, known as the Economic Recovery Programme (ERP), took place in two phases – from 1983 to 1986 and then from 1987 to 1991. In the period leading up to the programme, 1978 to 1983, real GDP fell at an average annual rate of 1.6 percent, and gross investment, merchandise exports, and merchandise imports were all about five percent of GDP. One sign of the problems of the economy was the currency's 'black market' premium – the exchange rate in informal markets compared to the official rate. It finished the period at 223 percent in 1983, after exceeding 500 percent earlier in the 1980s (see Sekkat and Varoudakis, 1998).

The first phase of reforms aimed at stabilisation, along with major changes to the trade and exchange rate rules. Ghana lowered the level and dispersion of average tariff rates, eliminated quantitative restrictions, and corrected the exchange rate. Inflation fell from almost 123 percent in the years before the programme, to 24.6 percent during the first period of the programme. Real GDP started growing again at an average annual rate of 3.6 percent, and gross investment rose to 7.5 percent of GDP. Exports and imports both rose above eight percent of GDP, though exports remained concentrated in cocoa.

The second period of reforms attempted further structural and institutional changes. The unification of foreign exchange markets in 1990 brought an end to the 'black market' premium, which measured 0.4 percent in 1991. GDP grew even faster in the second period at an average annual rate of 4.8 percent. Gross investment rose to 14.7 percent of GDP, while merchandise exports and imports rose to 15.5 percent and 19.1 percent respectively. Exports rose despite a decline in the terms of trade. Nowak *et al.* (1996) find econometric evidence that the elimination of the exchange rate overvaluation helped improve both investment and growth.

Poverty fell between 1987 and 1988, and 1991 and 1992, especially in rural areas, partly due to increased trade (World Bank, 1995). Overall, the incidence of poverty decreased from 36.9 percent to 31.5 percent. Rural areas account for two-thirds of Ghana's population, and rural poverty fell from 41.9 percent to 33.9 percent. Poverty increased in Accra, the capital, from 8.5 percent to 23.0 percent, but fell in other urban areas, so that urban poverty actually fell from 27.4 percent to 26.5 percent. Decreases in poverty were especially sharp for female-headed households and for non-farm rural households, but were present in nearly all population groups.

Economic growth caused most of the reduction in poverty, with the bulk of income growth in non-farm self-employment, especially wholesale and retail trade. Part of the increased activity in domestic trade came from a rebound from depressed levels before the start of the ERP. However, the other factor was the surge in both imports and exports, a direct result of the ERP and its exchange rate and other reforms.

While Ghana was a successful reformer on many dimensions, its experience also illustrates the difficulties of reform in a highly distorted economy with a history of government intervention. Not all reforms remained in place. In 1992, with a new constitution in April and elections in November and December, the government gave large increases in wages and benefits, throwing the budget far out of balance and increasing the rate of inflation. Private saving and investment subsequently declined as well.[22]

Despite those problems, Ghana has benefited from its reforms. GDP growth has remained strong, averaging more than four percent each year from 1995 to 1997, and the 'black market' premium has stayed almost non-existent.

---

22. See Nowak *et al.* (1996).

The CFA zone countries – background and devaluation

Until the second half of the 1980s, the countries of the CFA zone experienced stable and positive economic performance (Elbadawi and Majd, 1996). For example, their average annual real GDP growth rate from 1973 to 1981 was 5.7 percent, compared to an average of 2.8 percent for 18 non-CFA Sub-Saharan African countries. In addition, their annual average export growth rate was 7 percent, compared to 1.2 percent, while their investment and savings rates were about equal with those of the rest of Africa. This better economic performance was partly due to the exchange rate link, at 50 CFA francs to one French franc, at a time when the French franc was depreciating against the US dollar and the terms of trade were relatively favourable on average.

However, the economic performance of the CFA zone countries began to deteriorate in the mid-1980s for two reasons: the appreciation of the French franc, and a series of primary-commodity price shocks (Azam and Devarajan, 1997). Devarajan (1997) shows that for most of the CFA countries, these changes brought about real exchange rate overvaluations. Studying 12 countries,[23] he found an average overvaluation of 31 percent in 1993 on the eve of the devaluation, with Cameroon's real exchange rate the most overvalued (78 percent) and Chad's real rate the only undervalued one. Eight of the 12 countries had overvaluations of 20 percent or more. Making matters worse, other African countries were devaluing during the 1980s, contributing to the overvaluation of the real rates of the CFA zone countries compared to those of their export competitors.

Because of the overvaluations and mounting structural problems, such as rigidly high wages, economic performance started to deteriorate. The zone saw no economic growth between 1986 and 1994 when other Sub-Saharan African countries were growing at 2.5 percent annually (Clément, 1994). In fact, as mentioned above, for some of the countries there was an output contraction comparable to the Great Depression in the US.

There were a large number of other ill effects from the period of overvaluation in the CFA zone. A number of countries suffered large increases in poverty (Devarajan and Hinkle, 1994). For example, the incidence of poverty doubled in Côte d'Ivoire from 30 percent to 60 percent between 1985 and 1992. Devarajan and Hinkle (1994) also note that banking systems in a number of countries became insolvent or illiquid as a result of the private sector's inability to repay debts, government and public enterprise arrears, and capital flight. Export earnings collapsed in response to the

---

23. Countries analysed included Benin, Burkina Faso, Cameroon, Central African Republic, Chad, Congo, Côte d'Ivoire, Gabon, Mali, Niger, Senegal, and Togo.

adverse terms of trade shocks and the overvaluation of the real exchange rate. The contractionary macroeconomic policies adopted by most of the CFA countries reduced import levels and inflation remained low; but budget and external deficits rose. The fixed nominal rate and various policy-induced rigidities in domestic prices – particularly in wages and non-tradeable goods prices – meant adjustment had to come through reduced employment, output, and growth.[24]

Analysing data through the end of the 1980s, Elbadawi and Majd (1996) showed the effects on CFA economic performance by comparing average annual changes in various economic aggregates for the CFA countries with other sub-Saharan African countries. The CFA countries had real GDP growth of 2.9 percent between 1982 and 1985, but 0.4 percent from 1986 to 1989. The other African countries had –0.2 percent growth in the first period, when they were starting to adjust, and 2.8 percent growth in the second period. Export growth fell from 3.4 percent to –4.4 percent for the CFA countries, but rose from 0.6 percent to 4.4 percent for the other African countries. Investment fell in both groups, while savings rose only in the non-CFA group. Elbadawi and Majd (1996) showed statistically that CFA membership, and by implication the high real exchange rate level, was partly to blame for the poor economic performance of the late 1980s.

Constrained by their fixed exchange rates, at least two of the CFA zone countries tried to undergo so-called mock devaluations, with subsidies to exports and increases in import tariff rates. In Côte d'Ivoire, the scheme collapsed after a short trial because of administrative difficulties, inability to give the export subsidy plan a sufficient budget, and lack of support by the government. In Senegal, administration proved difficult, and the scheme encouraged over-invoicing by exporters and smuggling and under-invoicing by importers. The plan also proved costly to the budget, as tariffs were already high and the increases could not generate much more revenue.

Finally, the countries held a 'maxi-devaluation' on 12 January 1994, changing their rates to the French franc from 50 CFA francs to one French franc, to 100 CFA francs to one French franc.[25]

---

24. For example, both Senegal and Côte d'Ivoire had rigid labour laws that kept wages high throughout the pre-devaluation period (Foroutan, 1997). Clément (1994) noted that throughout the CFA zone, rising wage costs contributed to substantial drops in public enterprise profitability, expanding the public sector financing requirement. Extensive controls over both producer prices and retail prices, particularly non-tradeable goods prices, also added to the price rigidities in many countries.

25. The Western and Central African Monetary Unions (comprising Benin, Burkina Faso, Cameroon, CAR, Chad, Congo, Côte d'Ivoire, Equatorial Guinea, Gabon, Mali, Niger, Senegal, and Togo) changed their rates from 50 CFA francs to one French franc to 100 CFA

The CFA zone countries – results

The CFA devaluation has had excellent intermediate-term effects on growth. For the 12 CFA countries in Devarajan's (1997) sample, real GDP growth from 1990 to 1993 averaged almost –0.3 percent annually weighted by GDP, according to World Bank data (World Bank, 1999). However, from 1994 to 1997, growth in these same countries averaged 5.1 percent annually, according to the same data source.[26] Cameroon, the largest country in the CFA zone, grew at an annual rate of –3.4 percent in the first period, but 4.5 percent in the second period (World Bank, 1999). Devarajan (1997) found that a year after the devaluation, the average undervaluation was 2 percent for the group, but with significant variance.

4.4   Lessons from Africa

The countries of Sub-Saharan Africa have made significant strides in correctly valuing their exchange rates. In 1980, 45 African countries had pegged exchange rates, four had managed floats, and none had independent floats. By 1996, 25 had pegged exchange rates, six had managed floats, and 19 had fully independent floats, according to Sekkat and Varoudakis (1998). In both years, 14 were pegged to the French franc. This move towards a flexible exchange rate allowed most non-CFA zone countries, beginning in 1984-1985, to experience a real depreciation. The CFA zone countries had their own depreciation in 1994.

By the late 1990s, much of Africa had returned to growth. Hernández-Catá (1999) reported that real GDP grew 4.25 percent annually from 1995 to 1998, up from less than 1.5 percent from 1990 to 1994, with per capita output up one percent in the later period, against a decline of 2.25 percent in the earlier period. Inflation peaked at 47 percent in 1994, and dropped to 10 percent in 1998. He credited the improved performance to better policy, rather than to adverse external developments in 1998.

A great deal of policy reform remains for Africa. Though policy makers have taken large steps, there has been backsliding and failure to implement some important measures. Aggregate growth has returned, but per capita growth is only slightly positive and investment and savings both remain lower than in other developing regions. However, the continent has seen significant successes, and a realistically valued exchange rate has proved essential to these successes.

---

francs to one French franc. Comoros changed its rate from 50 Comoros francs to one French franc to 75 Comoros francs to one French franc at the same time.
26. The unweighted averages are 0.1 percent for 1990 to 1993, and 4.7 percent for 1994 to 1995.

5. DIVERSE VERSUS UNIFORM TARIFFS AND INCENTIVES

In defence of the exchange rate, countries often apply trade protection that is very high or prohibitive on selected products or countries. The experience in Kazakhstan in early 1999 is a case in point. We question the efficacy of these policies. Even with a limited objective of reducing the demand for foreign exchange, depending on how porous the borders are, we will observe an increase in imports through informal channels. And with diverse protection, while some sectors will be protected, the burden of the costs of adjustment to the overvalued exchange rate will be borne by the unprotected sectors, those sectors that are more susceptible to informal or illegal imports, and the export sectors.

Although protection is unlikely, the appropriate response to a balance of payments crisis, if any protection is offered for this purpose, it should be uniform, not a diverse protection structure.[27] A uniform tariff is sometimes applied for balance of payments reasons; this achieves the same impact on reducing imports as exchange rate depreciation, but it fails to achieve the beneficial effects on the export side. The optimal tariff structure, given that it is a surrogate for a devaluation (without export incentives), must uniformly induce resources to flow into import competing industries in general, rather than any particular import competing industry.

At the practical level, the arguments for a diverse tariff structure rest on the ability of governments to: (1) 'pick the winners', i.e., to identify the candidates that are most likely to meet the conditions justifying intervention, and choose and maintain the appropriate level for the policy variable (for example, tariff, subsidy). In general, the market is a more reliable indicator of the industries that have comparative advantage than any economic model. Over time this is particularly true, as comparative advantage changes with technological development; (2) be immune to the pressures from vested groups that inevitably arise once the willingness to grant special status is established; and (3) prevent any protection granted from becoming permanent.

The empirical evidence in both developed and developing countries during the past three decades casts doubt on most governments' ability to meet the preceding conditions. Endorsement of a more general approach – with little differentiation in the level of assistance – thus emanates from a wider scepticism about the practical merits of *targeting* of any kind.[28]

---

27. See Tarr (1999) for an elaboration of the arguments for and against a uniform tariff.
28. See Westphal (1990) and Krugman (1989, 1992) for details.

Moreover, the economy must provide its most talented members with the incentive to engage in entrepreneurial activities such as starting or expanding firms, developing new products and lowering costs. If the economy provides tariffs that differ greatly by sector, or extensive subsidies or tax exemptions to industries or firms, or presents a difficult regulatory framework within which to do business, talented people will find it more profitable to engage in the socially wasteful activity of lobbying the government for tariffs, subsidies, protection, tax or regulatory relief (Murphy *et al.*, 1991). This socially wasteful lobbying is especially harmful because it attracts one of the scarcest resources in developing countries – entrepreneurial talent that would otherwise be helping the economy grow. Thus, World Bank experience indicates (see Lieberman, 1990; Atiyas *et al.*, 1992) that the best industrial policy is for the government to provide a stable macroeconomic and regulatory environment conducive to business development, with neutral incentives to all firms and industries.

REFERENCES

Atiyas, Izak, Mark Dutz and Claudio Frischtak, with Bita Hadjimichael (1992), *Fundamental Issues and Policy Approaches in Industrial Restructuring*, Industry Series Paper No. 56, The World Bank, April.

Azam, Jean-Paul and Shantayanan Devarajan (1997), 'The CFA Franc Zone in Africa: A Symposium', *Journal of African Economies*, **6**(1), 1-2.

Bosworth, Barry P., Rudiger Dornbusch and Raúl Labán (eds) (1994), *The Chilean Economy: Policy Lessons and Challenges*, Washington, DC, US: The Brookings Institution.

Bouton, Lawrence, Christine Jones and Miguel Kiguel (1994), 'Macroeconomic Reform and Growth in Africa, *Adjustment in Africa* Revisited', Policy Research Working Paper 1394, The World Bank, December.

Cardoso, Eliana and Albert Fishlow (1989), 'Latin American Economic Development: 1950-1980', NBER Working Paper No. 3161, Cambridge, MA, US: National Bureau of Economic Research, November.

Clément, Jean A.P. (1994), 'Striving for Stability: CFA Franc Realignment', *Finance and Development*, **31**(2), 10-13.

Clément, Jean A.P. with Johannes Mueller, Stéphane Cossé and Jean Le Dem (1996), *Aftermath of the CFA France Devaluation*, Occasional Paper 138, Washington, DC, US: International Monetary Fund.

Corbo, Vittorio, Jaime de Melo and James Tybout (1986), 'What Went Wrong with the Recent Reforms in the Southern Cone', *Economic Development and Cultural Change*, **34**(3), 607-40.

Corbo, Vittorio and Jaime de Melo (1987), 'Lessons From the Southern Cone Policy Reforms', *The World Bank Research Observer*, **2**(2), 111-42.

Corbo, Vittorio and Stanley Fischer (1994), 'Lessons from the Chilean Stabilization and Recovery', in Barry P. Bosworth, Rudiger Dornbusch and Raúl Labán (eds) (1994), pp. 29-68.

Cottani, Joaquin A., Domingo F. Cavallo and M. Shahbaz Khan (1990), 'Real Exchange Rate Behavior and Economic Performance in LDCs', *Economic Development and Cultural Change*, **39**(1), 61-76.

Demery, David and Lionel Demery (1992), 'Adjustment and Equity in Malaysia', in Christian Morrisson (ed.), *Adjustment and Equity in Developing Countries*, Paris, France: Organisation for Economic Cooperation and Development.

Devarajan, Shantayanan (1997), 'Real Exchange Rate Misalignment in the CFA Zone', *Journal of African Economies*, **6**(1), 35-53.

Devarajan, Shantayanan and Lawrence E. Hinkle (1994),'The CFA Franc Parity Change: An Opportunity to Restore Growth and Reduce Poverty', *Africa Spectrum*, **29**(2), 131-51.

Dollar, David (1992), 'Outward-Oriented Economies Really Do Grow More Rapidly: Evidence from 95 LDCs, 1976-1985', *Economic Development and Cultural Change*, **40**(3), 523-44.

Dornbusch, Rudiger and Sebastian Edwards (1994), 'Exchange Rate Policy and Trade Strategy', in Barry P. Bosworth, Rudiger Dornbusch, and Raúl Labán (eds) (1994), pp. 81-104.

Dornbusch, Rudiger and Sebastian Edwards (eds) (1995), *Reform, Recovery and Growth: Latin America and the Middle East*, A National Bureau of Economic Research Project Report, Chicago, US: The University of Chicago Press.

Edwards, Sebastian (1988), *Exchange Rate Misalignment in Developing Countries*, Occasional Paper Number 2/New Series, Baltimore, US and London, UK: The Johns Hopkins University Press, (for the World Bank).

Edwards, Sebastian (1989), 'Exchange Rate Misalignment in Developing Countries', *The World Bank Research Observer*, **4**(1), 3-21.

Edwards, Sebastian (1993), 'Openness, Trade Liberalization and Growth in Developing Countries', *Journal of Economic Literature*, **31**, 1358-93.

Elbadawi, Ibrahim and Nader Majd (1996), 'Adjustment and Economic Performance Under a Fixed Exchange Rate: A Comparative Analysis of the CFA Zone', *World Development*, **24**(5), 939-51.

Faini, Riccardo and Jaime de Melo (1990), 'Adjustment, Investment and the Real Exchange Rate in Developing Countries', *Economic Policy*, 492-519.

Finger, J. Michael (1991), 'Trade Policy in the United States', in D. Salvatore (ed.), *A Handbook of Trade Policies*, Westport Connecticut, US: Greenwood Publishing Group.

Finger, J. Michael (1996), 'Legalized Backsliding: Safeguards Provisions in GATT', in Will Martin and L. Alan Winters (eds), *The Uruguay Round and the Developing Countries*, Cambridge, UK: Cambridge University Press.

Foroutan, Faezeh (1997), 'Preconditions and Sustainability of Reforms', in John Nash and Faezeh Foroutan (eds) (1997), pp. 104-40.

Ghei, Nita and Lawrence E. Hinkle (1999), 'A Note on Nominal Devaluations, Inflation and the Real Exchange Rate', in Lawrence E. Hinkle and Peter J. Montiel (eds) (1999), pp. 539-85.

Ghei, Nita and Steven B. Kamin (1999), 'The Use of the Parallel Market Rate as a Guide to Setting the Official Exchange Rate', in Lawrence E. Hinkle and Peter J. Montiel (eds) (1999), pp. 497-538.

Ghei, Nita and Lant Pritchett (1999), 'The Three Pessimisms: Real Exchange Rates and Trade Flows in Developing Countries', in Lawrence E. Hinkle and Peter J. Montiel (eds) (1999), pp. 467-96.

Ghura, Dhaneshwar and Thomas J. Grennes (1993), 'The Real Exchange Rate and Macroeconomic Performance in Sub-Saharan Africa', *Journal of Development Economics*, **42**(1), 155-74.

Global Currency Report (1999), **44**(1), January-February-March, Brooklyn, NY, US: Currency Data & Intelligence, Inc.

Hernández-Catá, Ernesto (1999), 'Sub-Saharan Africa: Economic Policy and Outlook for Growth', *Finance and Development*, **36**(1), 10-12.

Hinkle, Lawrence E. and Peter J. Montiel, (eds) (1999), *Exchange Rate Misalignment: Concepts and Measurement for Developing Countries*, A World Bank Research Publication, New York, US: Oxford University Press.

International Monetary Fund (1999), *Annual Report on Exchange Arrangements and Exchange Restrictions, 1999*, Washington, DC, US: International Monetary Fund.

Jones, Christine and Miguel Kiguel (1994), 'Africa's Quest for Prosperity: Has Adjustment Helped?', *Finance and Development*, **31**(2), 2-5.

Keynes, John M. (1925), 'The Economic Consequences of Mr. Churchill', in *Essays in Persuasion* (The Norton Library, 1963), New York, US: WW Norton & Company, Inc., pp. 244-70.

Klau, Marc (1998), 'Exchange Rate Regimes and Inflation and Output in Sub-Saharan Countries', Working Papers No. 53, Basel: Bank for International Settlements, Monetary and Economic Department, March.

Krueger, Anne O. (1995), 'Partial Adjustment and Growth in Turkey', in Rudiger
  Dornbusch and Sebastian Edwards (eds) (1995), pp. 343-67.
Krugman, Paul A. (1989), 'Is Free Trade Passe', *Journal of Economic Perspectives*, **1**,
  131-44.
Krugman, Paul A. (1992), 'Does the New Trade Theory Require a New Trade Policy',
  World Economy, **15**, 423-42.
Labán, Raúl and Felipe Larraín (1995), 'Continuity, Change, and the Political
  Economy of Transition in Chile', in Rudiger Dornbusch and Sebastian Edwards
  (eds) (1995), pp. 115-48.
Lieberman, Ira (1990), *Industrial Restructuring: Policy and Practice*, Policy and
  Research Series No. 9, Washington, DC, US: The World Bank.
Lewis, Jeffrey D. and Malcolm F. McPherson (1994), 'Macroeconomic Management:
  To Finance or Adjust?' in David L. Lindauer and Michael Roemer (eds), *Asia and
  Africa: Legacies and Opportunities in Development*, San Francisco, US: ICS Press,
  A Co-publication of the International Center for Economic Growth and the
  Harvard Institute for International Development, pp. 99-149.
Murphy, Kevin, Andrei Shleifer and Robert Vishny (1991), 'The Allocation of Talent:
  Implications for Growth', *Quarterly Journal of Economics*, **106**(2), 503-30.
Nam, Chong-Hyun (1995), 'The Role of Trade and Exchange Rate Policy in Korea's
  Growth', in Ito Takatoshi and Anne O. Krueger (eds), *Growth Theories in Light of
  the East Asian Experience*, National Bureau of Economic Research – East Asia
  Seminar on Economics, **4**, Chicago, US: The University of Chicago Press, pp. 153-
  77.
Nash, John (1997), 'Two Steps Forward, One Back', in John Nash and Faezeh
  Foroutan (eds) (1997), pp. 9-39.
Nash, John and Faezeh Foroutan (eds) (1997), *Trade Policy and Exchange Rate
  Reform in Sub-Saharan Africa*, Development Issues Number Six, Canberra,
  Australia: National Centre for Development Studies.
Nashashibi, Karim and Stefania Bazzoni (1994), 'Exchange Rate Strategies and Fiscal
  Performance in Sub-Saharan Africa', *IMF Staff Papers*, **41**(1), 76-122.
Nowak, Michael, Rifaat Basanti, Balazs Horvath, Kalpana Kochhar and Roohi Prem
  (1996), 'Ghana, 1983-91', in Michael T. Hadjimichael, Michael Nowak, Robert
  Sharer, Amor Tahari, and a Staff Team from the African Department (eds),
  Adjustment for Growth: The African Experience, Washington, DC, US:
  International Monetary Fund, pp. 22-47.
Pritchett, Lant (1997), 'Economic Growth: Hills, Plains, Mountains, Plateaus and
  Cliffs', mimeo, The World Bank, (9 October).
Roemer, Michael (1994), 'Asia and Africa: Towards a Development Policy Frontier',
  Development Discussion Paper No. 485, Cambridge, Mass, US: Harvard Institute
  for International Development.
Sachs, Jeffrey and Felipe Larrain (1999), 'Why Dollarization Is More Straitjacket
  Than Salvation', *Foreign Policy*, 80-92.
Sachs, Jeffrey D. and Andrew Warner (1995), 'Economic Reform and the Process of
  Global Integration', in William C. Brainard and George L. Perry (eds), *Brookings
  Papers on Economic Activity*, Washington, DC, US: Brookings Institution, pp. 1-
  118.
Sekkat, Khalid and Aristomène Varoudakis (1998), 'Exchange-Rate Management and
  Manufactured Exports in Sub-Saharan Africa', Development Center Technical

Papers No. 134 (March), Paris, France: Organisation for Economic Cooperation and Development.

Summers, Robert and Alan Heston (1991), 'The Penn World Table (Mark 5): An Expanded Set of International Comparisons, 1950-1988', *Quarterly Journal of Economics*, **106**(2), 327-68.

Tarr, David G. (1990a), 'Quantifying Second Best Effects in Grossly Distorted Markets: The Case of the Butter Market in Poland', *Journal of Comparative Economics*, **14**, 105-19.

Tarr, David G. (1990b), 'Second-Best Foreign Exchange Policy in the Presence of Domestic Price Controls and Export Subsidies', *The World Bank Economic Review*, **4**(2), 175-93.

Tarr, David G. (1994), 'The Welfare Costs of Price Controls for Cars and Color Televisions in Poland: Contrasting Estimates of Rent-Seeking from Recent Experience', *The World Bank Economic Review*, **8**(3), 415-43.

Tarr, David G. (1999), 'The Design of Optimal Tariff Policy for Russia', in Harry G. Broadman (ed.), *Russian Trade Policy: Reform for WTO Accession*, Washington, DC, US: The World Bank, pp. 7-29.

Torres, Craig (1999), 'Chile Suspends Trading Band on its Peso: New Free-Floating System is Intended to Stimulate Export-Led Expansion', *Wall Street Journal*, 7 September 1999, p. A21.

United States Bureau of the Census (1975), *Historical Statistics of the United States: Colonial Times to 1970, Part I, Bicentennial Edition*, Washington, DC, US: United States Department of Commerce, Bureau of the Census.

Westphal, Larry E. (1990), 'Industrial Policy in an Export-Propelled Economy: Lessons from South Korea's Experience', *Journal of Economic Perspectives*, **4**, 41-60.

World Bank (1995), *Ghana: Growth, Private Sector, and Poverty Reduction. A Country Economic Memorandum*, Washington, DC, US: World Bank, Country Operations Division, West Central Africa Department (May 15).

World Bank (1999), *World Development Indicators*, Electronic Database, Washington, DC, US: The World Bank.

2. Macroeconomic Conditions and Import Surcharges in Selected Transition Economies

Piritta Sorsa

1. INTRODUCTION

Trade policy reversals have become part of the macroeconomic policy mix in many transition economies in the 1990s. Bulgaria (1993, 1996), the Czech Republic (1990, 1997), Hungary (1995), Poland (1992), Romania (1998), and the Slovak Republic (1990, 1994, 1997) all introduced import surcharges over the decade to deal with balance of payments problems. This has taken place despite the generally recognised ineffectiveness of increased import protection in achieving the external balance[1] in the long run. While surcharges under fixed exchange rates may reduce imports and thus improve the current account deficit in the short run, their long-run implications for the balance of payments are uncertain as taxes on imports also tax exports. Under flexible exchange rates, the effect of surcharges on the balance of payments is even more uncertain and depends on their impact on the savings-investment balance. The use of second-best trade policies for stabilisation can have large distortion costs created by increased protection. The efficiency of domestic resource allocation is reduced, which in turn affects growth. In transition economies, trade policy reversals not only slow down required transition in the real sector to changes in relative prices by sustaining uncompetitive activities, but also encourage protectionist lobbies to continue to resist adjustment. Further inefficiencies are created by resources spent in lobbying for rent seeking.

---

1. See Corden (1997).

The frequent use of the second-best trade policies for stabilisation in transition countries raises questions on the appropriateness of the macroeconomic policy mix used in these countries at the time of imposing the surcharges. The use of trade measures may suggest that first-best policies were not available or were judged not to work in a given macroeconomic environment to deal with external imbalances. This can arise, for example, if the government is unwilling to temporarily adjust a nominal anchor such as the exchange rate. Monetary policy effectiveness may also be compromised with exchange rate pegs with open capital accounts, or adjustments in fiscal policy may be judged to take too long to take effect or may be undesirable in a given cyclical position. In transition economies, effectiveness of fiscal policy in reducing imports may also be compromised at early stages of transition if import demand is driven by fundamental changes in tastes and preferences. Import surcharges have at times been justified to improve the fiscal balance if no other revenue sources are available. On the other hand, macroeconomic conditions may also be used as an excuse to increase protection on microeconomic grounds against permanent loss of competitiveness.

This chapter analyses the role of macroeconomic conditions and policies in the demand for protection expressed in trade policy reversals in selected transition economies. First, it briefly discusses the literature on macroeconomics and protection and the various interlinkages between trade and macroeconomic policies. It then examines the potential macroeconomic determinants of trade policy reversals in four transition countries – the Czech Republic, Hungary, Poland, and the Slovak Republic.[2] The empirical analysis, although subject to many caveats, suggests that appreciation of the real exchange rate was the main explanation for trade policy reversals, while overall demand conditions or the fiscal-monetary policy mix in terms of real interest rates were less important. In terms of the policy mix, this may suggest that balance of payments difficulties may have been used as an excuse for increased protection. To deal with problems with the external balance, either exchange rate policies could have been more flexible or the fiscal policy tighter to contain demand instead of resorting to increased import protection. The latter may only have aggravated the external balance by slowing down exports and restructuring of production.

---

2. Bulgaria was left out of the sample due to poor data and Romania's import surcharge is too recent to have adequate data for the analysis.

2. MACROECONOMICS AND PROTECTION

2.1 Macroeconomics and Protection in the Literature

Macroeconomic conditions can be important determinants of protection. They have been much less analysed in the trade policy literature than structural or political economy factors.[3] Macroeconomic factors such as exchange rate and relative price fluctuations can make resource allocation according to comparative advantage more difficult and cause producers to lobby for protection (Eichengreen, 1997).

Changes in the business cycle have also been observed to lead to increased protectionist pressures against imports (Leidy, 1996) as activity declines. Demand for protection may also be pro-cyclical, if increased demand increases imports substantially (Dornbusch and Frankel, 1987) causing lobbying for protection. The fluctuations in prices or demand shifts can result from changes in world market conditions, changes in fundamentals in the economy or from uncoordinated domestic macroeconomic policies.

A number of empirical studies have reviewed the linkages between trade and macroeconomic policies. Eichengreen (1997) reviews both theoretical and empirical literature on macroeconomic policy stability and trade, and concludes that, for a range of plausible model specifications, policy instability may prevent the gains from trade from being fully realised. For example, in recent studies policy-induced exchange rate instability is shown to discourage trade although the magnitude is small. He notes that more needs to be done to establish the channels through which this effect operates, and in particular whether the related relative price instability is a source of protectionist pressures. An analysis of several countries' experience with external imbalances and trade policy concluded that large fiscal deficits have often been at the heart of major inflation and balance of payments crises in developing countries (Thomas *et al.,* 1991). An expansionary monetary policy which was often a consequence of money financing of deficits also contributed to the problems. Furthermore, the study notes that overvalued real exchange rates arising from expansionary fiscal and monetary policies

---

3. See, for example, Corden (1997); Krueger (1993); and Winters (1995). Most important of the arguments used have been political economy factors, for example, rent seeking and infant or sunset industry arguments for protection. Demand for protection may also arise from loss of competitiveness due to changes in productivity, intersectoral misalignments of production, and wage and transfer problems (Dornbusch and Frankel, 1987).

inconsistent with the nominal exchange rate policy have frequently led to generalised increases in restrictions on imports and capital movements intended to reduce the loss of international reserves. Another study by Little *et al.* (1993), notes that countries with flexible exchange rates may have been less likely to impose tight trade restrictions in response to balance of payments problems than those with fixed regimes. Drabek and Brada (1998) discuss the relationship of exchange rate regimes and protection in transition countries, and conclude that more flexible exchange rates might have avoided resort to protection to deal with real appreciation. All these studies point to important linkages between trade and macroeconomic policies and protection.

2.2   Trade and Macroeconomic Determinants of Protection

Trade flows are generally affected by two main macroeconomic variables: relative levels of activity and international competitiveness. Developments in trade flows, in turn, can affect the demand for protection. Key determinants of the level of aggregate demand for domestic production and imports are the business cycle and the real exchange rate. In addition, real interest rates, which are influenced by the overall monetary-fiscal policy mix, can have an important impact on overall demand.

The impact of the business cycle on demand for protection can be ambiguous. On the one hand, domestic producers faced with declining demand may request protection against imports to shift more demand for their goods. On the other hand, a recession by reducing overall demand will also reduce imports, which can make it harder to sustain a case for protection against increases in imports. This may also suggest that demand for protection on these grounds can be countercyclical. Thus, the sign of the coefficients for this variable as a determinant of trade policy reversals can be positive or negative.

An appreciating real exchange rate clearly makes it more difficult for domestic firms to compete with imports, and thus can be a major source of demand for protection. The sign of this coefficient is likely to be positive. Exchange rate appreciation also affects overall demand by making export development more difficult. The appreciation, which can reflect changes in long-run equilibrium rate or deviations from it, can result from a number of factors.[4] With an open capital account, large capital inflows can appreciate the real exchange rate with fixed rates. Real exchange rate appreciation can

---

4.   Real exchange rate dynamics in transition countries have been analysed by Halpern and Wyplosz (1997) and Krajnyak and Zettelmeyer (1998).

also result from differential productivity growth in traded and non-traded goods sectors, or from price arbitrage as administratively controlled prices are gradually liberalised or adjusted to reflect costs. Real appreciation may also result from changes in macroeconomic policy mixes such as loose monetary or fiscal policies.

Another important determinant of overall demand, and thereby of demand for protection, can be the real interest rate. High real interest rates would tend to reduce interest-sensitive components of overall demand of both domestic production and imports. Their impact on demand for protection, as in the case of cyclical factors, can depend on how various components of demand are affected. If, for example, imports contain a large share of capital goods, their demand should go down. If high real interest rates lead to real appreciation, the external balance may deteriorate. Thus, their impact on the demand for protection can be positive or negative.

Real interest rates, apart from conditions in external supply of funds and capital account openness, can be influenced by the fiscal-monetary policy mix. The impact of monetary policy on overall demand and real interest rates can depend on the fiscal stance. If tight monetary policy is accompanied by loose fiscal policy, the impact of the policy mix on real interest rates can be reduced depending on how deficits are financed (money creation or domestic credit). Financing the deficit by printing money would tend to increase inflation and reduce real interest rates. Financing by domestic credit could further increase real interest rates by increasing overall demand for credit. Tight fiscal policies would tend to reduce overall demand, real interest rates and inflation. Depending on the exact policy mix, demand for imports could increase or decrease.

2.3   Trade Policy and Stabilisation

The above indicates that the macroeconomic determinants of demand for protection can be diverse. In general, they are related to demand conditions or loss of competitiveness, which can result from a number of factors including the applied macroeconomic policies. In determining various policy responses to external imbalances, the authorities, in principle, should find the source of the excess demand and address the problem accordingly. Depending on the situation and the temporary or permanent nature of the demand change, this may imply reducing aggregate demand by an appropriate monetary-fiscal policy mix or changing the level of the exchange rate.

It is clear that trade policies are second-best to deal with external imbalances. The use of trade measures to deal with balance of payments problems as second-best policies has been discussed by Corden (1997). If exchange rates are fixed, an increase in protection may improve the current account in the short run by shifting demand and resources into import-competing industries. However, the tax on imports by changing relative prices will also attract resources from exporting, which eventually will worsen the current account. Thus, one could argue that, in very limited circumstances with a fixed exchange rate and no possibility to change the fiscal-monetary-exchange rate policy mix, a surcharge could help the current account in the short run. However, these circumstances are likely to be very rare and should be weighed against the costs of the surcharge on trade policy credibility, resource allocation, and rent seeking. With flexible exchange rates, the impact of increased protection on the current account is more complex. An increase in protection would lead to an appreciation of the exchange rate, offsetting its initial impact on the current account, unless demand is reduced at the same time. The impact on the current account would also depend on how the savings-investment balance is affected. Higher fiscal revenues may increase public savings and improve the savings-investment balance. On the other hand, higher protection may attract resources to import-competing industries. If private investment goes up, the current account can deteriorate. Thus, increases in tariffs are not a first-best policy to deal with excess demand and external imbalances. If they are used as a second-best instrument to deal with macroeconomic imbalances, they should at least be uniform and time bound. Depending on the source of the problem for excess demand for imports, more restrictive monetary and fiscal policies or appropriate adjustments in the exchange rate should work better to bring a sustainable improvement to the balance of payments than trade restrictions.

Taxing trade for fiscal reasons is also inefficient, as general consumption taxes are likely to raise the same revenue, with fewer production distortions created than tariffs. Import taxes raise prices of both domestic and imported goods and collect revenue only on imported goods. Trade taxes, however, tend to have lower collection costs than broader-based consumption taxes. But given their distortion costs, trade taxes should only be used if no less distortionary taxes can be applied. The latter is likely to be rare in practice.

Any use of trade policies for stabilisation should also consider their costs in terms of efficiency of resource allocation and resources lost in rent seeking. The traditional costs of protection are well known (Corden, 1997). In a dynamic context, higher protection of imports will also slow down structural adjustment and restructuring of industries, which in transition economies are essential to attain sustainable long-term growth. Policy reversals also create incentives for lobbying for further protection, which will further slow down incentives for restructuring.

3. MACROECONOMICS AND TRADE POLICY REVERSALS IN TRANSITION COUNTRIES

Before discussing empirical estimates on the interaction of macroeconomic conditions and trade policies in the four transition economies, this section will first discuss briefly trade and macroeconomic developments in these countries in the 1990s.

3.1 Trade Policy Developments

Trade policy stances are measured by an index of trade restrictiveness. It is a composite measure of the restrictiveness of a country's trade policies, taking into account both tariff and non-tariff barriers (NTBs).[5] The index takes values between '1' (open) and '10' (restrictive). Tariffs fall into five categories[6] and NTBs into three.[7] The index is a weighted average of these two measures of protection with a higher weight assigned to NTBs due to their assumed higher distortion costs. While the index captures mainly large changes in countries' trade policies, it is subject to a number of caveats – the weight assigned to NTBs in the index is arbitrary, and no account is taken of tariff dispersion or exemptions in increasing the distortiveness of a country's trade regime. Despite these caveats, the index seems to capture well changes in trade policies in the four transition countries. The dismantling of central planning resulted in large changes in trade policy stances and thus in movement on the index. Furthermore, the impact of distortions and exemptions on tariff dispersion in these countries is moderate.

Although all four transition countries liberalised substantially their trade regimes over the 1990s, the process has been subject to a number of reversals.[8] Figure 2.1 shows developments in trade policies in the four countries since the early 1990s, measured by the index of trade restrictiveness. Initially, in the early 1990s, the four transition countries had quite restrictive trade regimes, reflecting centrally planned trading arrangements in the framework of the Council of Mutual Economic

---

5. For details, see Sharer *et al.* (1997).
6. These are below 10 percent; 10-15 percent; 15-20 percent; 20-25 percent; and above 25 percent.
7. NTBs cover less than 1 percent, between 1 percent and 25 percent, or above 25 percent of imports and exports.
8. Drabek and Brada (1998) discuss in detail trade policy developments in the four countries.

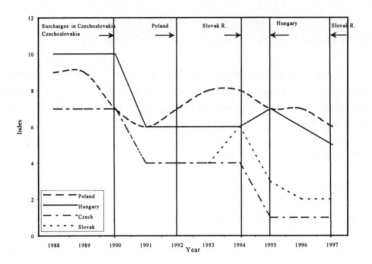

Source: IMF staff estimates.

Figure 2.1 Evolution of Trade Policy Stance with the Trade Restrictiveness Index

Assistance (CMEA). They ranked between '7' and '10' on the index. NTBs were especially high, reflecting total controls on trading transactions.

Over the decade the Czech Republic became very open by removing all NTBs and lowering its tariffs to below 10 percent, ranking it '1' in 1997 on the index. It briefly reintroduced an import deposit requirement in 1997, but this was eliminated within a few months. The other three countries, after an initial liberalisation with the removal of the CMEA-related quantitative restrictions, have experienced several trade policy reversals. In most cases, this has taken the form of import surcharges, but general tariffs have also been increased. Poland, in the early 1990s, initially lowered tariffs drastically from an average of 18 percent to 6 percent. Tariff liberalisation was seen as an element of its anti-inflation policy. This was, however, reversed rapidly with the introduction of an import surcharge of 6 percent in 1992, when tariffs were also increased back to an average of 18 percent. The surcharge was maintained for about four years, whereupon tariffs were also slightly reduced in the context of Poland's Uruguay Round commitments. In 1997 Poland ranked '6' on the index. The Slovak Republic gradually removed all NTBs by 1995. Reductions in tariff protection have been slower, and since 1994 a surcharge of 10 percent (that gradually declined to 7 percent) was levied on imports until early 1997. However, another surcharge was introduced in the second half of 1997, which was later removed in 1998.

After the removal of the surcharge, the Slovak Republic ranked '1' on the index in 1998. Hungary gradually lowered protection, especially NTBs, but tariffs have also been reduced. However, in 1995 an import surcharge of 8 percent was introduced, which was only eliminated in 1998, ranking Hungary '5' on the index.

All the surcharges have been introduced in compliance with World Trade Organization (WTO) rules.[9] These rules are weak in preventing the introduction of surcharges as their justification is in general examined only several months after their introduction. In recent years the WTO has taken a tougher stance in asking countries to gradually eliminate the surcharges making the rules stricter against longer term maintenance of surcharges. All four countries invoked the balance of payments exemptions of the GATT/WTO rules to justify the surcharges. This implicitly suggests that the motivation for the policy reversals was the countries' macroeconomic situation.

3.2   Macroeconomic Developments

To give background to the analysis of import surcharges, this section briefly examines the macroeconomic situation in the four transition countries prior to the introduction of the surcharges and looks at whether the trade measures may have made sense at the time of their introduction. The first experience with a surcharge in the Czech Republic was in 1990 when a surcharge of 20 percent was introduced by the then Czechoslovakia. Available statistics suggest that at the time there did not seem to be a large current account problem (Figure 2.2). The current account deficit in 1990 was about one percent of GDP. Between 1990 and 1992, output declined substantially reaching –20 percent in 1991, which is also likely to have contributed to lower imports and the subsequent current account surplus of nearly five percent of GDP in 1991. The fiscal account in 1990 was in rough balance.

---

9. This means that the surcharge is notified to the WTO, and justified on balance of payments grounds and/or to protect foreign exchange reserve levels. A WTO committee examines the case ex-post (often more than six months after the notification of the surcharge) and approves the restrictions generally for a given period.

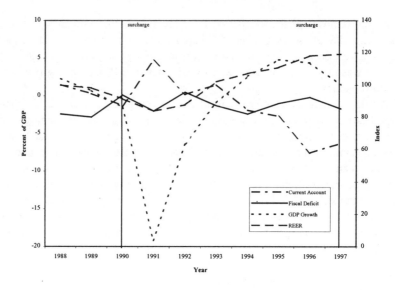

Source: IMF

Figure 2.2 Developments in Key Macroeconomic Aggregates: The Czech Republic

The above would suggest little macroeconomic justification for an import surcharge on balance of payments grounds. One motivation for the surcharge may have been avoidance of a larger devaluation and possibly protection of domestic industries. The latter is more likely as the surcharge applied only to a small part of imports. The surcharge is likely to have slowed down transition in the real sector to changes in market conditions. The initial undervaluation of the exchange rate (Halpern and Wyplosz, 1997) should have had a favourable impact on competitiveness and thus reduced the need for surcharges. Subsequently, the Czech Republic continued to liberalise trade.

An import deposit requirement was, however, again introduced between April and August 1997 which increased the cost of importing – comparable to the effect of a corresponding increase of tariff. In 1996 and 1997 the current account deficit was worsening and reached 6-8 percent of GDP. In 1997, growth had started to slow down (from just under 4 percent in 1996 to about 2 percent in 1997), the fiscal deficit to increase (from 1 percent in 1996 to about 2 percent of GDP in 1997) and the real exchange rate continued to appreciate with the fixed peg. The deposit/surcharge in 1997 was imposed in a deteriorating balance of payment situation. At the same time the fiscal deficit was widening, real interest rates increased and the real exchange rate continued to appreciate. In the end, the authorities adjusted the exchange rate in mid-1997 by introducing a more flexible managed float (Box 2.1). The motivation for the surcharge was the deteriorating balance of payments situation, but it seems that the surcharge might have been avoided by more and earlier fiscal tightening and earlier action in increasing exchange rate flexibility.

Box 2.1 Exchange Rate Arrangements

Czech Republic: until May 1997 peg to a basket, thereafter managed float.
Hungary: until March 1995 fixed peg with irregular adjustments, thereafter crawling peg.
Poland: since 1991 a crawling peg to a basket of currencies.
Slovak Republic: fixed peg to a basket of currencies, since October 1998 free float.

In Hungary, a surcharge was introduced in 1995. The current account deficit had deteriorated sharply in 1993 to over 10 percent of GDP, but recovered in 1994 and 1995 to about 7-8 percent of GDP (Figure 2.3). Growth of GDP was relatively strong in 1994 and 1995 (2-3 percent), compared to the negative rates in the previous years. Fiscal deficits in the preceding years had reached 7-8 percent of GDP and they seemed to stay at this level between 1992 and 1995. Thus, the statistics suggest that the current account situation in Hungary was already improving at the time of the surcharge, while the fiscal deficit was persistently high, suggesting a loose fiscal policy. Real interest rates were also coming down from about 8-9 percent in 1994 to about 3-4 percent in 1995-1997, suggesting either a looser monetary stance or improvement in the country's creditworthiness, or both. The balance of payments motivation for the surcharge in this situation can be questionable, and its true motivation is likely to have been fiscal reasons or protection. The fact that it was not uniformly applied to all industry (energy and capital goods were exempt) also undermines its balance of payments motivation. It is doubtful whether no other fiscal revenue sources could have been found. In 1995 the authorities also adjusted the exchange rate, from a fixed peg with periodic adjustments to a more flexible managed float. Again, one could ask whether a search for other fiscal revenues, or more and earlier adjustments in the exchange rate policy, could have prevented the resort to the import surcharge.

Trade and Macroeconomic Policy

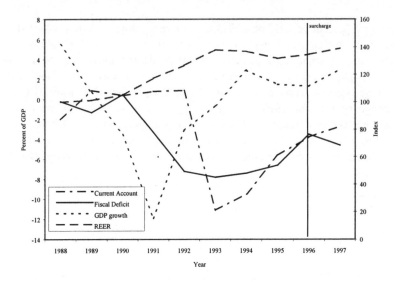

Source: IMF staff estimates

Figure 2.3 Developments in Key Macroeconomic Aggregates: Hungary

In Poland, when the 6 percent surcharge was imposed in 1992, the current account deficit was relatively low (Figure 2.4). In the preceding year it stood at about 2-3 percent of GDP. In 1992 there was a large increase in growth (from –7 percent in 1991 to 3 percent in 1992) which may have put more pressure on the current account. At the same time, despite the increase in growth, fiscal policy remained expansionary and the deficit stood at 6-7 percent of GDP in 1991 and 1992. Real interest rates were negative, suggesting a loose monetary policy. The current account situation does not seem to justify the imposition of the surcharge. It is likely to have been influenced by the fiscal situation or the loss of competitiveness following the sharp real appreciation of the currency between 1990 and 1992. The fact that the surcharge was not uniformly applied (alcohol, tobacco, fuels, cars, and medical equipment was exempt) to all imports again undermines its macroeconomic effectiveness. In these circumstances, one could again ask whether fiscal and monetary policies could not have been tightened to reduce demand to deal with any pressures on the current account or the fiscal deficit and to avoid the resort to the import surcharge.

In the Slovak Republic, in addition to the 1990 imposition of the surcharge, another one was imposed in 1994 and again in 1997. In 1993 the current account had deteriorated to over 5 percent of GDP, but it improved in

1994 to a surplus of about 5 percent (Figure 2.5). The large fiscal deficit of 1992 and 1993 of about 7-10 percent of GDP had also started to improve. The GDP growth was strong between 1994 and 1997, which is likely to have contributed to the worsening of the current account deficit in 1996 and 1997 to about 10 percent. Despite growth pressures, fiscal policy seemed to remain loose (the deficit increased from about 1 percent to nearly 4 percent between 1996 and 1997), and the real exchange rate was appreciating. The low level of real interest rates in 1994 also suggests that monetary policy may have been loose as well. But instead of tighter demand management, the policy makers chose an import surcharge to constrain demand for imports, in order to deal with the current account deficit. No adjustment was made to the exchange rate. Again the surcharge was not uniformly applied (it applied to 75 percent of imports), which undermines its macroeconomic motivation.

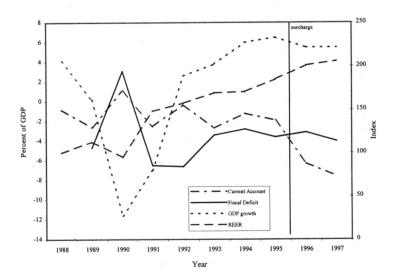

Source: IMF staff estimates.

Figure 2.4 Developments in Key Macroeconomic Aggregates: Poland

In sum, it seems that in all cases, although the official motivation for the surcharges was a dire balance of payments situation, other policies such as fiscal tightening or an earlier adjustment of the exchange rate (which in many cases was undertaken subsequently) could have avoided the imposition of surcharges. Furthermore, in many cases the imposition of the surcharge is likely to reflect giving in to protectionist pressures from industries losing competitiveness.

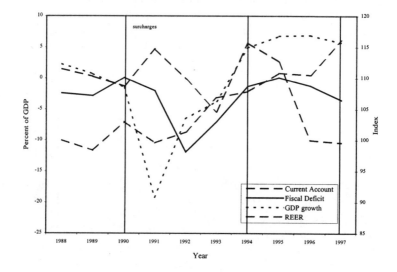

Source: IMF staff

Figure 2.5 Developments in Key Macroeconomic Aggregates: Slovak Republic

3.3   Estimation Results

To test the hypothesis of the impact of the various macroeconomic conditions discussed in section 2.2 on trade policy reversals, some econometric estimation was undertaken. In the literature the difficulty of measuring the restrictiveness of a country's trade policies has been discussed widely and it has been a significant obstacle for empirical work (Edwards, 1997;

Dornbusch and Frankel, 1987). Many studies have proxied changes in trade policies by a measure of openness related to the share of trade in GDP. This is unsatisfactory as the trade share tends to decrease with country size and can be sensitive to terms-of-trade movements or deflators used. Others have constructed complex indexes, which require much data that is hard to get across countries (Anderson and Neary, 1994), especially across time. To overcome these difficulties this study used an index of trade policy that combines developments in both tariff and NTBs and captures changes in trade policies (see above).

Changes in the index were regressed on changes in the real exchange rate (REER), relative level of activity (GDP), and real interest rates (RR) following the methodology used in Dornbusch and Frankel (1987). The real exchange rate reflects changes in competitiveness, while changes in GDP reflect overall demand conditions[10] and those in the real interest rate the overall monetary-fiscal policy mix. The expected signs of the coefficients are noted below.

$$\log (\text{Index}) = F (\log(\text{REER}), \text{GDP}, \text{RR})$$
$$+ \qquad +/- \quad +/-$$

The regressions were run for 1988-97, and the equation including the real interest rate was only run for Poland and Hungary (Table 2.1). Despite the serious estimation problems (see below), the results give support for the role of real exchange appreciation in explaining trade policy reversals. The t-statistics of the lagged REER variable are significant in both regressions and the sign correct. The estimation does not differentiate between changes in the equilibrium real exchange rate and deviations from this. No matter what the source of the real appreciation, it seems to have affected competitiveness of some industries, which would have lobbied for protection. The t-statistics of the GDP are also significant and positive indicating a small impact on trade policy reversals from changes in overall economic activity. This suggests that demand for protection in the transition economies would not have been countercyclical. Increased growth would increase imports, which could have a small impact on demand for protection. The t-statistic of the lagged real interest rate (RR) is not significant, suggesting that real interest rates do not have a large impact on demand for protection and trade policy reversals. The country-specific dummies suggest that institutional factors in each country explain a certain part of demand for protection especially in the Czech and

---

10. The regression was also run with fiscal and current account deficits, but they were not significant.

Table 2.1 Regression Results

Equation 1

GLS (Cross Section Weights) // Dependent Variable is _log(INDEX)

Sample: 1990 1997
Included observations: 8
Total panel observations: 32
Convergence achieved after 3 iteration(s)

Variable	Coefficient	Std. Error	t-Statistic	Prob.
ΔLog(REER)$_{t-1}$	0.875078	0.247879	3.530268	0.0012
ΔGDP	0.018433	0.003764	4.897254	0.0000

Fixed Effects

POL--C	-0.133176
HUN--C	-0.124145
CZ--C	-0.263832
SLO--C	-0.186124

Weighted Statistics

R-squared	0.560217	Mean dependent var	-0.177095
Adjusted R-squared	0.475644	S.D. dependent var	0.441054
S.E. of regression	0.319378	Sum squared resid	2.652062
Log likelihood	32.33484	F-statistic	33.12009
Durbin-Watson stat	2.626839	Prob(F-statistic)	0.000005

Unweighted Statistics

R-squared	0.194427	Mean dependent var	-0.134290
Adjusted R-squared	0.039509	S.D. dependent var	0.325881
S.E. of regression	0.319378	Sum squared resid	2.652062
Durbin-Watson stat	2.570869		

Table 2.1 (continued)

Equation 2

GLS (Cross Section Weights) // Dependent Variable is _ log(INDEX)

Sample: 1990 1997
Included observations: 8
Total panel observations: 16
Convergence achieved after 2 iteration(s)

Variable	Coefficient	Std. Error	t-Statistic	Prob.
ΔRR	0.000207	0.000884	0.233978	0.8182
ΔGDP	0.019277	0.006121	3.149505	0.0066
Δlog(REER)$_{t-1}$	0.908298	0.279131	3.254015	0.0053

Fixed Effects

POL--C	-0.141288
HUN--C	-0.125424

Weighted Statistics

R-squared	0.703504	Mean dependent var	-0.082776
Adjusted R-squared	0.595687	S.D. dependent var	0.223248
S.E. of regression	0.141954	Sum squared resid	0.221659
Log likelihood	23.25926	F-statistic	13.04998
Durbin-Watson stat	2.689524	Prob(F-statistic)	0.001248

Unweighted Statistics

R-squared	0.492047	Mean dependent var	-0.068663
Adjusted R-squared	0.307337	S.D. dependent var	0.170564
S.E. of regression	0.141954	Sum squared resid	0.221661
Durbin-Watson stat	2.342698		

Slovak Republics. The relatively low R-square statistics can suggest that microeconomic determinants of protection are also important. The results would suggest that loss of competitiveness is the main determinant of protection. Dornbusch and Frankel (1987) also found that that the real exchange rate was the most important macroeconomic determinant of demand for protection.

Given the sample problems, the results may not be very robust and should be interpreted with caution. One problem is the very small number of observations available for transition economies as data especially prior to 1990 is unreliable. To overcome this problem the study used pooled cross-section estimation with data from the four countries between 1988 and 1997, which is a balanced panel. The small sample size (40) also renders tests for stationarity of the variables or co-integration between the variables difficult.[11] The REER and GDP are generally known to have unit roots. The estimation method used was weighted Generalized Least Squares (GLS) estimated in logs and first differences to ensure stationarity of the variables. The model was estimated with fixed effects (common slopes but country-specific intercepts). Dummies in the fixed effects model capture country-specific institutional effects on the demand for protection. To correct for possible simultaneity bias between the Index and the REER, the latter was estimated using RR and GDP as instruments.

Another estimation problem is the poor quality and availability of data especially in the pre-1990-1992 period for transition countries. A problem is also raised by the fact that the Czech and Slovak Republics only became separate countries in 1993. Furthermore, although estimates of trade policy developments, the real exchange rate, and GDP are available for 1988-1997 for all four countries, data for real interest rates is not available for the Czech and Slovak Republics until 1993.

3.4 Policy Issues

The results naturally raise questions on the macroeconomic policy mixes in the respective countries and how they may have or should have contributed to the real appreciation and thereby to trade policy reversals. Most countries at the time of the policy reversals had relatively fixed exchange rate regimes with pegs or crawling pegs to one or more currencies and gradually opening capital accounts. The use of the exchange rate as a nominal anchor for stabilisation may have constrained the use of the exchange rate instrument to

---

11. Stationarity of the series was tested, but the values for most variables were below the critical values. The sample did not have enough observations to run the test for co-integration.

deal with current account problems. This put pressure on other macroeconomic policies or trade policy to deal with potentially volatile or excessive real exchange rate movements or macroeconomic imbalances. However, it is interesting that in two of the countries (Hungary and the Czech Republic) the exchange rate regime was changed subsequent to the imposition of the import surcharges. In the Slovak Republic the regime was eventually changed one year after the third surcharge was imposed. But only the Czech Republic repealed the surcharge subsequently, while the others maintained it. This raises the question that had the exchange regimes been made more flexible earlier, the countries could have been spared the distortion costs from trade policy reversals and higher protection, which are likely to have affected especially export competitiveness and the attractiveness of the foreign investment climate.

However, in transition countries much of the movement in the real exchange rate is likely to reflect shifts in the long-run equilibrium rate, to which the economy should be adjusting. One source of the appreciation is likely to be increased productivity growth in the traded goods sector compared to the non-traded one discussed above (Halpern and Wyplosz, 1997). As all four countries have undergone substantial structural transformation over the decade, this effect can be large. Although data on productivity growth (measured by output per employee) is relatively poor, Figure 2.6 does indicate that productivity increased, especially in Hungary and Poland, in which the real appreciation was also the largest. Another source of appreciation of the equilibrium exchange rate can be large capital inflows. Net inflows of capital into all four countries have been large, especially up until 1995 with the capital and financial account reaching 17-18 percent of GDP in the Czech Republic and Hungary. Although the amounts have fluctuated widely from one year to another, they are likely to have had an impact on the equilibrium exchange rate. In some countries such as the Czech Republic, these inflows may have been aggravated by high real interest rates. A further source of real appreciation may have been price arbitrage as previously controlled prices have gradually been adjusted to market levels. In these cases, the countries should adjust to the new relative prices. Trade policy reversals will only retard the adjustment process.

The above also raises the question of whether fiscal and monetary policy mixes could or should have been different in dealing with the real appreciation and current account deficits in the framework of relatively fixed exchange rates. This would apply especially to the part of the real appreciation that does not reflect changes in the long-run equilibrium rate. The above discussion on macroeconomic developments shows that fiscal policy in most of the countries prior to the imposition of the surcharges was loose or expansionary. As discussed above, in Poland real interest rates were negative prior to the imposition of the surcharge, which may also suggest an expansionary monetary policy. Since the surcharge, real interest rates in Poland (Figure 2.7) have increased, and fiscal policy was tightened, although overall deficits have remained relatively large. Thus a further tightening of fiscal policy could have slowed down some of the real appreciation. In Hungary, fiscal policy was tightened after the surcharge in 1996 but it became more expansionary again in 1997. Both the Czech Republic and especially the Slovak Republic have tightened monetary policy after the surcharges. However after initial tightening, fiscal policy has become more expansionary in 1997 in the Czech Republic, and in 1996 and 1997 in the Slovak Republic. In all four, the gradual opening of the capital account may have influenced the effectiveness of monetary policy, which puts even more pressure on fiscal policy (or exchange rate policy). This suggests, as discussed above, that had the tighter monetary policy been accompanied by tighter fiscal policy, real appreciation might have been slower. This in turn could have reduced pressure on the current account and on the demand for protection. The other alternative could have been the introduction of a more flexible exchange rate regime earlier in the process.

Overall, apart from Hungary, the policy mixes including the surcharges do not seem to have prevented the deterioration of current account deficits over the decade. One explanation for this can be the impact of the increase in protection on export development.

4.   CONCLUSIONS

The discussion in the chapter suggests that the main determinant of demand for protection and trade policy reversals in the four transition countries has been the appreciation of the real exchange rate. All four countries' trade regimes were subject to reversals over the decade in response to macroeconomic imbalances. While much of the appreciation is likely to be related to changes in fundamentals and structural factors such as productivity growth, price adjustments and capital inflows to which the economy should adjust, some of it may be explained by the macroeconomic policy mix in these countries.

An analysis of the macroeconomic conditions in the four countries suggests that surcharges might have been avoided had macroeconomic policies, especially in terms of fiscal and exchange rate policies, been adjusted more appropriately in response to current account imbalances. A tighter fiscal policy, without the surcharges, might have slowed down the real

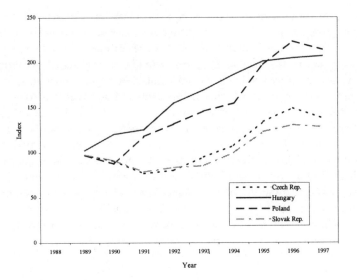

Source: IMF (output per employee).

Figure 2.6 Productivity in the Four Transition Economies

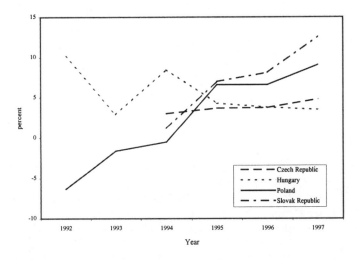

Source: IMF (lending rate less consumer prices)

Figure 2.7 Real Interest Rates in the Four Transition Countries

appreciation and improved the competitiveness of exports and import competing industries. While the exchange rate, as a nominal anchor, is likely to have helped in stabilisation in the early stages of transition, a more flexible exchange rate policy later in the process might have changed the terms of trade in favour of tradeable goods and reduced pressures for protection. The present policy mix, coupled with the reversals in trade openness, is likely to have sustained uncompetitive industries and slowed down export development and structural change in the economies. Thus more open trade policies, especially in Poland and Hungary, could have helped faster adjustment and thus a more sustainable current account. Fiscal adjustment may have been partly postponed by slower trade liberalisation. What this may also suggest is that the external imbalances have also been used as an excuse for increased protection on microeconomic grounds. In sum, in all four countries import surcharges and their potential negative side effects could have been avoided by a better macroeconomic policy mix.

REFERENCES

Anderson, James and Peter Neary (1994), 'Measuring the Restrictiveness of Trade Policy', *World Bank Economic Review*, **8**(1), 151-69.

Corden, W. Max (1997), 'Trade Policy and Economic Welfare', Oxford, UK: Clarendon Press.

Dornbusch, Rudiger and Jacob Frankel (1987), 'Macroeconomics and Protection', in Richard Stern (ed.), *U.S. Trade Policies in a Changing World*, Cambridge, MA, US: MIT Press, pp. 77-143.

Drabek, Zdenek and Joe Brada (1998), 'Exchange Rate Regimes and the Stability of Trade Policy in Transition Economies', mimeo.

Edwards, Sebastian (1997), 'Openness, Productivity and Growth: What Do We Really Know?' NBER Working Paper 5978, Cambridge, MA, US: National Bureau of Economic Research.

Eichengreen, Barry (1997), 'Free Trade and Macroeconomic Policy', mimeo, Berkeley, US: University of California.

Halpern, Laszlo and Charles Wyplosz (1997), 'Equilibrium Exchange Rates in Transition Economies', *IMF Staff Papers*, International Monetary Fund, **44** (March), 430-61.

Krajnyak, Kornelia and Jeromin Zettelmeyer (1998), 'Competitiveness in Transition Economies: What Scope for Real Appreciation', *IMF Staff Papers*, International Monetary Fund, **45** (June), 309-62.

Krueger, Anne O. (1993), *Political Economy of Policy Reform in Developing Countries*, Cambridge, MA, US: MIT Press.

Leidy, Michael (1996), 'Macroeconomic Conditions and Pressures for Protection Under Anti-dumping and Countervailing Duty Laws: Empirical Evidence from the United States', IMF Working Paper WP/96/88, Washington, DC, US: International Monetary Fund.

Little, Ian, Richard Cooper, W. Max Corden and Sarath Rajapatirana (1993), *Boom, Crisis and Adjustment: The Macroeconomic Experience of Developing Countries*, New York, US: Oxford University Press for the World Bank.

Sharer, Ron, Piritta Sorsa, Nur Calika, Paul Ross, Clinton Shiells and Thomas Dorsey (1997), *Trade Liberalization in IMF-Supported Programs*, World Economic and Financial Surveys, Washington, DC, US: International Monetary Fund.

Thomas, Vinod, John Nash, with Sebastian Edwards *et al.* (1991), *Best Practices in Trade Policy Reform*, New York, US: Oxford University Press.

Winters, L. Alan (ed.) (1995), *Foundations of an Open Economy: Trade Laws and Institutions for Eastern Europe*, London, UK: Centre for Economic Policy Research.

PART TWO

TRADE AND LABOUR

3. Trade-Labour Link: A Post-Seattle Analysis

Arvind Panagariya

1. INTRODUCTION

The first Ministerial Conference of the World Trade Organization (WTO), held in Singapore during 9-13 December 1996, had a rough start. The United States (US) had wanted to create a WTO working group on labour standards, which developing countries bitterly opposed. In the end, developing countries prevailed and the US effectively agreed to delegate the subject to the International Labour Organization (ILO). In the only paragraph on the subject, the Singapore Ministerial Declaration stated:

> We renew our commitment to the observance of internationally recognized core labor standards. The International Labour Organization (ILO) is the competent body to set and deal with these standards, and we affirm our support for its work in promoting them. We believe that economic growth and development fostered by increased trade and further trade liberalization contribute to the promotion of these standards. We reject the use of labor standards for protectionist purposes, and agree that the comparative advantage of countries, particularly low-wage developing countries, must in no way be put into question. In this regard, we note that the WTO and ILO Secretariats will continue their existing collaboration.

Most readers, including legal experts, will agree that this statement conclusively designates the ILO as the competent body to 'set and deal' with labour standards and leaves little room for the WTO to take lead. So as not to leave any doubt about the validity of this interpretation, Trade and Industry Minister of Singapore Mr. Yeo Cheow Tong, who also chaired the Ministerial Conference, went on to note in his concluding speech, 'Some delegations had expressed the concern that this text may lead the WTO to acquire a competence to undertake further work in the relationship between

101

trade and core labour standards. I want to assure these delegations that this text will not permit such a development'.

For two years following the Singapore Ministerial no WTO Member, including the US, questioned this understanding and interpretation of the Singapore Declaration. But beginning in January 1999, the US began to place proposals before the WTO for the establishment of a work programme in the WTO that would address trade issues relating to labour questions.[1] Later, as the preparations for the Seattle Ministerial got under way, it became increasingly clear that the US would return to its original demand for a working party on labour standards in the WTO. By 13 October 1999, the *Financial Times* had reported that the US was set to call for such a working party. In early November, the US did table a formal proposal at the WTO.[2]

The opposition to a WTO working party on labour standards by the major developing countries such as Brazil, Egypt, India and Malaysia, had been well known. At Singapore, these countries had fought hard to have the matter delegated to the ILO and had even given up their opposition to a working party on investment in return. Given the intellectual merit of the case, they had also been supported in their endeavour by some key developed countries, most notably Australia and Great Britain but also Germany and Switzerland. Therefore, the decision by the US in early November to go back on the letter and spirit of the Singapore Declaration immediately cast a shadow of doubt on the success of the Seattle Ministerial.[3]

Initially, the US attempted to soften the impact of its demand by arguing that the sole purpose of the WTO working party would be to generate discussion on how labour standards impact trade and development. But later, while the Seattle Ministerial Conference was in progress, President Clinton went on to tell the Seattle Post-Intelligencer that he would like the working party to define core labour standards, which should then be incorporated into all trade agreements and subject to trade sanctions. This explicit acknowledgement by the US of its ultimate goal behind the demand for the working party instantly united the major developing countries in their opposition to the US proposal and sealed the fate of the Seattle conference.

---

1. Two such proposals were made, one in January and the other in July 1999. See the document 'US Proposal on Labor Rights' in Jenkins (1999).
2. See *Financial Times* (1999).
3. For example, in a letter published in the *Financial Times*, 10 November 1999, I had already stated that 'if the US persists in its demand, developing countries, which are bound to bear the brunt of the link [between trade and labour standards], will be fully justified in walking away from the Seattle talks'. See Panagariya (1999a). In Panagariya (1999b), I offered a comprehensive discussion of the agenda for a possible Seattle Round and argued that developing countries should make every effort to limit the agenda to trade liberalisation and the Uruguay Round built-in agenda.

The demand for a WTO working party on labour standards by the US, though unsuccessful in Seattle, has returned the contentious issue of the link between trade and labour standards to the centre stage of multilateral trade negotiations. Motivated by this fact, I undertake a detailed and systematic analysis of the subject in this chapter. I begin first by dissecting the intellectual case for the link in section 2. In section 3, I describe the so-called 'core' ILO Conventions. In section 4, I identify the sources of pressures for higher labour standards that led to the failure in Seattle as also the pressure being exerted within the current system on some developing countries to raise labour standards to preserve their privileges under the Generalized System of Preferences (GSP). Finally, in section 5, I conclude the chapter with suggestions for future progress towards the resolution of the current impasse.

2. EVALUATING THE CASE FOR LINKING TRADE AND LABOUR STANDARDS

The case for labour standards was originally subject to a critical examination by Bhagwati (1995, 1997). Here I offer an updated discussion of the subject, though it may be acknowledged at the outset that Bhagwati's original arguments and critique remain valid today. The advocates of the linkage have offered few new arguments that would seem persuasive.

2.1 The Efficiency Issue

With respect to efficiency, two simple analytic points may be made. First, in general, optimal labour standards are not uniform over time or across countries, either from the national or global welfare standpoint. The changes in marginal benefits and costs of labour standards as, for example, due to changes in income or productivity in 'supplying' labour standards, cause optimal labour standards to vary over time as well as across nations. Therefore, there is no presumption that the differences in observed labour standards between two countries necessarily imply deviations from optimal standards in at least one of them. Nor is there a case for the harmonisation of labour standards internationally (or over time) on the ground that it promotes efficiency at the global or national level. Equally, the observed labour standards can be below the optimal level both in developed and developing countries; just because labour standards are higher in developed countries does not mean that they are optimal.

Second, the targeting literature, pioneered by Bhagwati and Ramaswami (1963) and Bhagwati (1971), tells us that when an economy is in a sub-optimal equilibrium, the first best policy is to correct the underlying distortion at its source. Once this is done, there is no need to intervene elsewhere in the economy. Thus, if the market happens to produce sub-optimal labour standards, we should correct this distortion directly rather than through an indirect instrument such as trade sanctions. Under the direct approach, once labour standards have been set at the optimal level, free trade remains the optimal trade policy in the traditional sense. Purely from an efficiency standpoint, a case cannot be made for linking trade and labour standards.

2.2 Evaluating the Appropriateness of Pursuing Labour Standards in the WTO

As argued above, if labour standards were set at their optimal levels everywhere, the discussion of raising them through the WTO instrumentality will be moot. Instead, we will only need the WTO to promote further trade liberalisation. To proceed, therefore, we must assume that the existing labour standards are sub-optimal, possibly in developing as well as developed countries. The question then is whether the WTO is the right institution to achieve this goal. Subsumed within this question, of course, is the issue of linkage itself since the key feature that distinguishes the WTO from the alternative institution, the ILO, is its ability to back up agreements on labour standards by trade sanctions. But in this sub-section, I will only touch on this issue, leaving its detailed discussion to the following sub-section.

There are at least three criteria on which we can judge the appropriateness of the inclusion of areas such as labour standards, intellectual property rights, competition policy or investment policy into the WTO. First, is the area sufficiently closely related to trade? That is to say, do countries choose the policies in that area principally to influence trade or to fulfil other objectives? Second, will the inclusion of the subject improve world welfare? And third, will the inclusion improve the welfare of each WTO Member? The second criterion is, of course, necessarily fulfilled if the third one is. As such, the second criterion is weaker and is not likely to be accepted by countries that stand to lose, unless the beneficiaries of the discipline compensate them.

It is immediately clear that trade policy, which the WTO has been designed to oversee, meets all these criteria. The principal objective behind trade barriers is to restrict trade flows.[4] Trade liberalisation is beneficial to the world and it is also beneficial to individual countries that engage in reciprocal bargains under the auspices of the WTO. Trade liberalisation is a win-win activity.

By contrast, the trade-labour link fails to meet any of these criteria with a reasonable degree of confidence. Rarely do countries set labour standards to influence trade flows. There is no doubt that these standards have an influence on trade flows but no one will argue that this is reason enough to subject them to the WTO discipline. After all, exports equal domestic output minus domestic consumption so that any change affecting either of these quantities must affect trade unless the good happens to be non-tradeable!

Countries choose labour standards based on the prevailing socio-politico-economic conditions. In developing countries such as India, child labour existed long before trade acquired any significance at all. Likewise, much of the labour legislation in the country was enacted to fulfil the perceived needs of labour rather than to fulfil the needs of the industry to be competitive *vis-à-vis* foreign sources, either at home or abroad. Quite the contrary, the prevailing political economy led to such high labour standards in some dimensions that many domestic firms could only survive behind a high protective wall.[5] In the view of many economists, today, these labour laws constitute a barrier to successful trade liberalisation. In effect, we have a case of labour standards driving trade policy rather than the other way around.

Turning to the other two criteria, the link between trade and labour is not a win-win policy and may very well lead to a decline in world welfare. Chances are that the trade-sanctions bullet will miss its target. Consider child labour. One possibility is that countries will fail to meet the WTO standards leading to the imposition of trade sanctions. If so, no improvement in labour standards will be achieved and the gains from trade will be reduced. World welfare will necessarily be reduced. Alternatively, child workers may simply be shifted from producing exports into alternative activities. Again, there will be no net reduction in the aggregate volume of child labour while the wages

---

4. Interestingly, when the principal objective is viewed to be different from protection, the WTO often accommodates trade restrictions. Thus, it permits temporary quantitative restrictions when the objective is to overcome temporary balance of payments difficulties. Likewise, in the past, when economic thinking (now largely discredited) admitted a role for trade restrictions to achieve the development objective, the General Agreement on Tariffs and Trade (GATT), the predecessor institution of the WTO, readily permitted permanent quantitative restrictions in developing countries.

5. In the organised sector, workers are paid wages that are substantially higher than elsewhere in the economy, and cannot be fired. This means that even when a firm becomes unprofitable, it cannot exit. Often such firms are declared 'sick', with the government taking charge of them and paying the high wages at the taxpayer's expense.

received by the children in alternative employments will be lower or the working conditions worse. Once again, world welfare will be reduced.

What the trade-labour link tries to accomplish is to kill two birds with one stone; use the WTO to achieve both free trade and higher labour standards. In technical terms, the link seeks to hit two targets with one instrument. But as the first Nobel laureate in economics, Jan Tinbergen, demonstrated, in order to be successful, one would normally require at least as many instruments as targets. Taking advantage of this insight, a recent statement entitled 'Third-World Intellectuals and NGOs: Statement Against Linkage' (TWIN-SAL) argued that the best course to promote labour standards is to pursue them through an alternative institution, the ILO, and leave the WTO the task to promote free trade. This is also consistent with the Singapore Declaration.

2.3   Preserving One's Moral Values

The trade-labour link effectively requires countries to raise standards to a pre-specified level or face trade sanctions from other countries. One argument offered in defence of this policy is that a country that adheres to higher labour standards within its national boundaries has the moral right to suspend trade with another country that does not adhere to equally high labour standards. For instance, if the US subscribes to values that do not admit child labour and has itself outlawed the practice, it should also have the right to suspend imports made by child labour in other countries. Why should US citizens have to compromise their values to accommodate the imports from abroad?

There are two problems with this line of reasoning. First, when the US chooses to outlaw child labour from its territory, it also chooses to pay the cost of the change by foregoing the output produced by potential child workers and by committing resources to educational facilities for them. But when it asks other countries also to abandon the practice *because it will help promote a value held dear by its own citizenry*, the cost, in terms of the output foregone and additional resources spent on education, is borne by the trading partners. These costs are not trivial. According to a study undertaken by Consumer Utility and Trust Company (CUTS), a non-governmental organisation (NGO) based in India, it will cost anywhere between US$12 billion to US$18 billion per annum in India alone to send all existing child workers to schools. It is unlikely that the US and other developed countries would be willing to bear even a tiny fraction of this cost.

Second, if a common set of labour standards is to be adopted at the WTO to promote higher moral values, Member countries must share these values with sufficient conviction that they are voluntarily willing to subject themselves to trade sanctions as an instrument of enforcement. But there are few moral values that are shared universally with such conviction. Proponents of the trade-labour link often give the impression that there is a general agreement on the so-called 'core' labour standards among the WTO Members. To substantiate the argument, they refer to the ILO Conventions on 'core' labour standards that many countries have ratified.[6] Quite apart from the fact that the ratification may simply be a feel-good act or an expression of philosophical belief in the values embedded in the Conventions, the latter are quite far from being universally ratified. For example, the US itself has ratified only one of the seven 'core' ILO Conventions.[7] Only 73 out of 175 ILO members have ratified all seven Conventions. At 101 countries, the Minimum Age Convention remains the least ratified. Thus, even in the absence of trade sanctions, countries show very different preferences with respect to what are supposedly 'universally agreed' standards.

Recently, Rodrik (1997) has questioned the logical consistency of the position taken by the critics of the 'preservation of moral values' argument. To explain his argument, consider a US corporation, which must find a cheaper source of supply of some of its labour-intensive components if it is to survive. Suppose further that it has two options. Under the first option, it can outsource the components to a local Honduran firm that runs a sweatshop operation. Under the second option, it can open a domestic sweatshop at the Mexican border and employ the same Hondurans as migrant workers. The costs of production, the wages received by Hondurans workers (net of migrations costs) and working conditions are identical in both cases. Therefore, if one approves of one option, one necessarily approves of the other option. Rodrik notes, however, that this is not so:

> Interestingly, the vast majority of the economists who have no difficulty with the outsourcing example would also accept that it is not good public policy to

---

6. Though a more detailed discussion of the ILO Conventions appears in Section 3, it may be noted here that the seven conventions are: Forced Labour Convention, 1930 (No. 29), Abolition of Forced Labour Convention 1957 (No. 105), Freedom of Association and Protection of the Right to Organize Convention, 1948 (No. 87), Right to Organize and Collective Bargaining Convention, 1949 (No. 98), Equal Remuneration Convention, 1951 (No. 100), Discrimination (Employment and Occupation) Convention, 1958 (No. 111) and Minimum Age Convention, 1973 (No. 138). Of these, the US has only signed the Convention on Abolition of Forced Labour, 1957 (No.105). In 1999, a new convention called the Convention on the Worst Forms of Child Labour (No. 182) was signed. The ILO now lists this convention along with the other seven as well, and presumably includes it among the 'core' standards.
7. These do not include the Convention on the Worst Forms of Child Labour (No. 182) mentioned in footnote 6. This convention had been ratified by 41 countries at the time of writing.

relax labor standards for migrant workers to the point of allowing sweatshop conditions. Clearly, there is an inconsistency between these two positions. There seems to be a greater coherence in the behavior of the lay public, which reacts with equal outrage to the two versions of the parable – outsourcing versus migration – than in the perception of the economists.[8]

On the surface, this appears to be a compelling critique of the position taken by the opponents of trade sanctions against countries with low labour standards. Yet, upon closer examination, contrary to Rodrik's contention, it is the position of the 'lay public' that is logically inconsistent and the view of the 'vast majority of the economists' that is consistent. Thus, when the 'lay public' shows outrage against the poor treatment of migrant workers, it wants them to be treated on a par with US workers with the cost of such treatment falling on the corporation and hence the US economy. But when the 'lay public' shows outrage against sweatshops in Honduras, it wants trade sanctions that place the burden of upholding their moral values on the Hondurans! Logical consistency would require that the 'lay public' be willing to offer the Honduran government the cost of bringing the working conditions in Honduras to the US level as well.

Likewise, the apparent contradiction in the position of the 'vast majority of economists' is resolved once we recognise that when foreigners come in the midst of post-Renaissance societies, especially the US, the local population begins to view them as one of their own. The willingness to confer the same rights on migrant workers as those available to local workers is an outcome of this empathy. Moreover, the acceptance of sweatshops abroad is a vote not against the rights and well-being of the workers employed therein, but against trade sanctions that will bring an even worse alternative. Thus, there is no contradiction between the advocacy of equal rights for migrant workers and the opposition to trade sanctions when the same workers are employed in their own country under sweatshop conditions.

Indeed, the position attributed by Rodrik to the 'lay public' appears more coherent and understandable when considered from the viewpoint of the US labour groups. Within the framework of his parable, weaker labour standards in Honduras mean greater competition through trade in labour-intensive industries in the US. Likewise, permitting sweatshop conditions for migrant labour on US soil gives greater incentive to US firms to employ the latter. Both policies put pressure on the wages paid to local workers.

8. Rodrik (1997) p. 34.

2.4 The Fair Trade Issue

Yet another argument offered by the proponents of the trade-labour link is that lower labour standards in developing countries give them 'unfair' competitive advantage over their developed country counterparts. Deep down, this is essentially the age-old 'pauper-labour' argument that labour unions have repeatedly used to seek protection for labour-intensive industries in developed countries. Traditionally, the argument has relied primarily on the existence of low wages in labour-abundant countries as the source of 'unfair' advantage. In its current incarnation, the reach of the argument has been widened by including a whole host of labour standards among the sources of unfair advantage.

As has been pointed out repeatedly by economists in textbooks and op-ed articles alike, this argument is in direct conflict with the basic principle of comparative advantage. Virtually every textbook on international trade describes the pauper-labour argument as a common fallacy. The simple point is that high wage countries are perfectly capable of competing against low wage countries due to their higher productivity. What they cannot do is to compete against the latter in goods in which they have a *comparative disadvantage.*

The contention that lower labour standards give poor countries an 'unfair' advantage begins to look even sillier when we consider the enormous advantages enjoyed by developed countries in the areas of technology and capital. Thus, for instance, if we were to poll individuals in New Delhi on whether the superior access to technology and capital gives *developed* countries unfair competitive advantage, almost all of them will say 'yes'; they will also overwhelmingly support provisions in the WTO that will require developed countries to share technology with developing countries at low or no cost. But does that make good economic sense? The very essence of the gains from trade is that, due to differences in underlying fundamentals, countries differ in their abilities to produce different products. Developing countries have a comparative advantage in labour-intensive goods and developed countries in capital- and technology-intensive goods.

A slightly different twist to the fair trade argument is that trading freely with countries with lower labour standards may lead to a decline in one's own standards. This is the so-called 'race-to-the-bottom' argument. As commonly made, the argument states that competition for capital and jobs may lead countries to adopt ever-declining labour standards. Therefore, there is a need to set labour standards cooperatively. While this theoretical possibility exists, its empirical relevance depends on two key factors: (1)

responsiveness of capital to labour standards and (2) degree to which countries compete for capital by lowering labour standards. These are both empirical questions on which, to date, the proponents of the 'race-to-the-bottom' argument have provided little evidence. Levinson (1996) looked at the first of these two questions in the context of environmental standards and found very weak evidence, at best, in favour of capital mobility in response to differences in standards. Though no direct evidence is available on the second question, it is unlikely that countries set labour standards so as to make them attractive to capital. As already argued earlier with the help of the Indian example, dominant considerations in setting labour standards are domestic. Moreover, as Bhagwati (1995) argues, governments typically play the game of attracting capital through tax breaks, land grants at highly subsidised prices, cheap electricity and so forth.

2.5   Ineffectiveness of Trade Sanctions in Raising Labour Standards

Many developing countries do recognise the need for raising labour standards. Child labour in India is a case in point. To begin with, poor parents love their children just as much as rich parents do. They send their children to work not out of wickedness, but out of sheer economic necessity. Moreover, there are numerous NGOs in the country working towards alleviating the child labour problem and the government is under continuous pressure from them. Finally, there are also laws against the employment of children in hazardous industries, but their enforcement remains beyond the means and ability of the government.[9] It is unlikely that trade sanctions can significantly change this reality.

Indeed, there are reasons to believe that trade sanctions will have the opposite effect to the desired impact. This is evidenced by the experience of Bangladesh in 1993, when merely the threat of US sanctions led the terrified owners of garment factories in Dhaka to dismiss from work all children below the age of 16. According to a recent article by Jeremy Seabrook in the *Financial Times*, anecdotal evidence suggests that many of these children

---

9. Developing countries are not alone in the inability to enforce laws in this sphere. Thus, consider the following statement in de Gray (1994): 'Recent reports about labor conditions in the US, for example, indicate that there is significant illegal employment of children and that many such children work in unsafe, dangerous conditions. A spokesman for the US National Child Labor Committee is reported as saying recently, "We have no compunction in saying that there are over two million child labor violations each year in the US". As for enforcement, it is reported that an establishment employing adolescents can anticipate a federal inspection once every 50 years'. The quotation by de Gray is from Holloway (1993), which itself appeared in the magazine *Scientific American*.

met a fate worse than in the factories, ending up in workshops and factories not producing for export, or as prostitutes and street vendors.

More broadly, few advocates of trade sanctions against child labour realise that, world-wide, only five percent of the working children are employed in export industries. This percentage can be reduced to zero simply by moving the children to produce similar goods sold domestically and having adults produce the goods sold in foreign markets. The resulting increase in the costs of exports will provide some additional protection to the corresponding US and European industries, but do nothing at all to lower the aggregate level of child labour.

Likewise, export-processing zones employ a tiny fraction of the labour force, well below one percent. A stricter enforcement of labour rights will do little for labour rights in general. The bulk of the labour force in developing countries is employed in the informal sector that hardly engages in international trade. The inevitable conclusion is that the proposed link will do virtually nothing to improve labour's fate, whether in relation to children or adults.

2.6 Selectivity in the Developed Country Agenda

A key problem with the manner in which developed countries have pursued the demand for higher labour standards – regardless of whether it is dealt with at the WTO or the ILO – is the asymmetry of the proposed agenda. Independently of whether the objective is the preservation of moral values or pursuit of fair trade, the issues proposed for negotiation are exclusively those in which developing countries must give one-way concessions. Thus, only issues such as child labour and labour rights in export processing zones, where developing countries will be defendants rather than plaintiffs, are included. Enforcement against sweatshops in the apparel industry or the rights of migrant labour which is subject to quasi-slavery conditions in parts of the industrial world, are not on the proposed agenda.

One suspects that if the issue of child labour is brought into the WTO, the US will eventually want to set annual targets for its reduction much along the lines it once sought to expand the Japanese imports from the US. Why then should we also not have similar targets for unionisation? After all, in the US, less than 14 percent of the labour force is currently unionised and is, thus, able to bargain collectively. Why should enforcement not be judged by outcomes in this area? Moreover, unionisation in the US has been handicapped, among several factors, by legislation on matters such as the right to hire replacement workers during a strike. Such legislation has blunted the unions' chief weapon – the ability to strike effectively. Why are the rules that make strikes a more effective tool of unionisation, not on the proposed agenda for the WTO?

Also missing from the social agenda proposed by developed countries at the WTO is the subject of union representation on boards of directors that exists in some European nations. If developing countries are to go along with conferring on workers, as they should, the right to unionise, mature democracies such as the US should also be willing to take on additional obligations that advance the rights of labour in these countries. Yet, no such move is on the horizon and, in any case, it is an academic issue since, at present, unions are absent from most US factories in the first place.

Yet another example of protectionist bias in the current labour standards agenda is the demand for the minimum wage. Why should minimum wage take priority over employment generation in poor countries where unemployment is high and employment insurance virtually absent? Will workers, as a whole, be better served by guarantees of minimum wages for those lucky enough to find jobs, or by greater employment opportunities? Surely, higher minimum wages in developing countries will provide industrial countries with greater protection against imports from those countries. Greater employment opportunities, by contrast, may bring more labour-intensive goods into industrial countries and hence intensify competition.

Finally, if the objective is to promote 'social' values, why should this be limited to the values related to labour? Why not also include issues such as drug trafficking? Those advocating the trade-labour link often complain that in the absence of such a link, countries such as India fail satisfactorily to enforce their own laws relating to child labour. But as Mohan (1996) notes, one can equally complain about the lax enforcement of the laws against drug trafficking in the US. Drug trade has been the cause of continued large overvaluation of the exchange rate and, hence, de-industrialisation in the neighbouring countries in Latin America. Should these latter countries then, not have the right to link the access to US exports in their markets with the effective enforcement of drug laws by the US?

3.   THE ILO CONVENTIONS[10]

Conceptually, labour standards include all norms and rules that govern working conditions and industrial relations. But in articulating their demands,

---

10. Unless otherwise noted, the information in this section has been drawn from various pages of the official ILO web site on the World Wide Web.

developed countries have focused on some specific standards that they have gone on to term the '"core" labour standards'. This term gives the impression that the standards encompassed by it must be so basic that there could hardly be any disagreement on their desirability. Yet, the matter is not so simple. As Bhagwati (1995) argues cogently, once we get past slavery, universally agreed labour standards simply do not exist. For instance, even the issue of child labour, which at first blush seems straightforward, is quite contentious. In many countries, the alternative to child labour may be starvation. Moreover, in the absence of educational facilities, abrupt abolition of child labour may produce social chaos. Not surprisingly, many countries are opposed to the abolition of child labour until they reach a level of development in which the income earned by children is no longer necessary as a contribution to the family income to avoid starvation, and sufficient educational facilities are available.

The term '"core" labour standards' has come to mean different things to different individuals and entities. One particular definition that has been at the centre of the discussion is that used by the ILO. This institution defines the 'core' standards as consisting of the following five norms (described in greater detail in the corresponding ILO Conventions):[11]

- Freedom of Association and Protection of the Rights to Organize Convention, 1948 (C87);
- Right to Organize and Collective Bargaining Convention, 1949 (C98);
- Forced Labour Convention, 1930 (C29) and Abolition of Forced Labour Convention, 1957 (C105);
- Equal Remuneration Convention, 1951 (C100), and Discrimination (Employment and Occupation) Convention, 1958 (C111); and
- Minimum Age Convention, 1973 (C138) and the Convention on the Worst Forms of Child Labour, 1999 (C182).

Convention 87 stipulates that workers have the right to establish and join the organisations of their own choosing. These organisations, in turn, have the right to draw their own constitutions and rules, to elect their

---

11. Informal agreement on which of the ILO Conventions are to be regarded as human rights standards dates at least as far back as 1960. Formal recognition was achieved when the Social Summit in Copenhagen in 1995 identified six ILO Conventions as essential to ensuring human rights in the workplace: Nos. 29, 87, 98, 100, 105 and 111. In addition, the United Nations High Commissioner for Human Rights now includes these conventions on the list of 'International Human Rights Instruments'. The Governing Body of the ILO subsequently confirmed the addition of the ILO Convention on Minimum Age, No. 138 (1973), in recognition of the rights of children.

representatives in full freedom, and to organise their administration and activities. Convention 98 is viewed as essential to making Convention 87 meaningful and is, therefore, frequently grouped with it. Convention 98 provides for protection against anti-union discrimination, for protection of workers' and employers' organisations against acts of interference by each other and for measures to promote collective bargaining.

Convention 29 requires the suppression of forced or compulsory labour in all its forms. It permits certain exceptions such as military service, convict labour properly supervised, and emergencies such as wars, fires and earthquakes. Convention 105 prohibits the use of any form of forced or compulsory labour as a means of political coercion or education, punishment for the expression of political or ideological views, workforce mobilisation, labour discipline and punishment for participation in strikes or discrimination.

Convention 100 provides for equal pay for work of equal value without discrimination based on sex. Convention 111 calls on the signatory governments to declare and pursue a national policy designed to promote, by methods appropriate to national conditions and practice, equality of opportunity and treatment in respect of employment and occupation. It calls for the elimination of any form of job discrimination based on race, colour, sex, religion, political opinion, national extraction or social origin.

Convention 138 establishes a minimum age for work. It states that children should not enter the labour market before completion of compulsory education or before having reached the age of 15. In case of work that is unhealthy or dangerous, the Convention sets a minimum age of 18. These provisions are waived in relation to work undertaken in training institutions. Likewise, light work by children aged from 13 to 15 years may be allowed so long as it is not prejudicial to their educational activities. Developing countries may lower the minimum age of employment to 14 years and of light work to 12 years.

Convention 182, which came into existence as recently as 1999, abolishes child slavery, child prostitution and pornography, use of children for illicit activities (for example, drug trafficking), and any work which is likely to harm the health, safety or morals of children. Included in the last category is the work that exposes children to abuse, work with dangerous machines and equipment, work involving heavy loads, work in unhealthy environments, work for long hours or during the night and work involving unreasonable confinement at the employer's premises.

In the context of the rights of children, it is important to mention the United Nations (UN) Convention on the Welfare of the Child, 1989. This Convention is the most comprehensive instrument pertaining to the protection of children. It is distinguished from the ILO Convention 138 in that it focuses on 'child welfare' rather than on 'child labour'. The UN Convention states that children have the right to survival, protection, care, development and participation. In Article 32, it stipulates that children shall be protected from economic exploitation and from work likely to be hazardous or harmful to their health, or to interfere with their education. Interestingly, the UN Convention does not stipulate a uniform minimum age for work. While many developing countries have ratified the Convention, the US has not done so.

Some interesting facts with respect to the ratification record of various countries may be summarised as follows.[12] First, the total membership of the ILO currently is 175. The number of countries that have ratified the Conventions are, respectively, 154 for C29, 147 for C105, 132 for C87, 132 for C98, 149 for C100, 145 for C111, 101 for C138, and 41 for C182. There are 73 countries, 36 in Europe, 15 in the Americas, 5 in Asia and 17 in Africa which have ratified all 'core' Conventions. Second, the conventions with respect to child labour remain the least ratified. Some of the key large, influential developing countries are yet to ratify C138 and C182. Finally, the US has signed only one of the seven traditional 'core' Conventions: Convention 105 with respect to the abolition of forced labour. Thus, the US has not signed the Convention on collective bargaining (No. 98) or that on child labour (No. 138).

Even if we view the ratification of the Conventions with scepticism, based on the lack of any requirement for enforcement, non-ratification by some developed countries, most notably the US, highlights the lack of agreement on 'core' labour standards. The presumption is that if the practice in a country is consistent with a particular convention, the country would ratify it. Applying this logic, one is forced to conclude that the practice and laws in the US fall short of meeting the standards contained in six of the seven 'core' ILO Conventions in some form or other. This is most surely the reason behind the highly selective approach taken by the US in its demands for the trade-labour link in the WTO.

4.   PRESSURE POINTS IN THE CURRENT SYSTEM

The discussion of current pressures can be divided into two categories. In the first category, we have pressures to *introduce* the trade-labour link. In the

---

12. The ratification status, as described in the following, is taken from the ILO web pages at the time of writing.

second category, we have pressures coming from the existing provisions in the policies of developed countries that permit such a link. Let us discuss each category in turn.

4.1   The Pressures to Introduce the Trade-Labour Link in the WTO[13]

At the governmental level, as opposed to the civil-society level, the pressure for the trade-labour link at Seattle came almost exclusively from the US. For instance, according to a 15 November 1999 statement by the Canadian Trade Minister Pierre Pettigrew, the Canadian objective at Seattle was to 'work for official observer status at the WTO for the International Labour Organization (ILO) and urge global compliance with the ILO's two main instruments on child labour and worker rights'.

According to the document, 'Preparation of the Third WTO Ministerial Conference: EU Council Conclusions', while the European Union (EU) Council agreed to strongly support the protection of 'core' labour rights, it explicitly distanced itself from a trade-labour link. The Council agreed that at Seattle the EU would advocate three measures for progress on the issue of trade and labour rights: (1) enhanced cooperation between the WTO and the ILO and their Secretariats; (2) support to the work of the ILO and its observership in the WTO; and (3) creation of a Joint ILO/WTO Standing Working Forum on trade, globalisation and labour issues to promote a better understanding of the issues involved through a substantive dialogue between all interested parties (including governments, employers, trade unions and other relevant international organisations).

The last of these measures may suggest the EU's acquiescence to the US position. But the Council went on to explicitly confirm the EU's firm opposition to any sanctions-based approaches. It also agreed to pursue international consensus through discussions and negotiations with its partners. The Council agreed to oppose and reject any initiative to use labour rights for protectionist purposes and went on to state that the comparative advantage of countries, particularly low-wage developing countries, must in no way be put into question.

Thus, at present, the demand for the trade-labour link is coming exclusively from the US, which has had a long history of making such a demand. In its 1987 submission to the GATT Council, the US had sought the establishment of a working party on labour standards with the following standards on its agenda: (a) freedom of association, (b) freedom to organise

---

13. The documents on which this section is based can be found in Jenkins (1999).

and bargain collectively, (c) freedom from forced and compulsory labour, (d) minimum age for employment, and (e) measures for setting minimum standards in respect of conditions of work. Because the GATT Council failed to reach an agreement, no working party was established. In 1990, the US renewed its request, but trimmed the list of standards to (a), (b), and (c). Again, there was no consensus.

Therefore, unlike on environment, the Uruguay Round did not provide for a committee on labour. The internal US response to this fact was to build the demand for seeking a future trade-labour link into the Uruguay Round implementing legislation. Thus, the Uruguay Round Implementing Bill, Language on the WTO Labor Working Party (H.R.5110), passed by the US Congress in November 1994, explicitly directs the President to

> seek the establishment in the GATT 1947, and, upon entry into force of the WTO Agreement with respect to the US, in the WTO, of a working party to examine the relationship of internationally recognized worker rights, as defined in section 502(a)(4) of the Trade Act of 1974, to the articles, objectives, and related instruments of the GATT 1947 and of the WTO, respectively.

The objectives of the working party in H.R.5110 are to

> (1) explore the linkage between international trade and internationally recognised worker rights, as defined in section 502(a)(4) of the Trade Act of 1974, taking into account differences in the level of development among countries; (2) examine the effects on international trade of the systematic denial of such rights; (3) consider ways to address such effects; and (4) develop methods to coordinate the work program of the working party with the International Labor Organization.

This legislation formed the basis of the US demand for a WTO working party at the Singapore Ministerial. As noted in the introduction, the offensive mounted by the developing country Members of the WTO foiled the US efforts at Singapore. Notwithstanding the decision there to delegate the subject of labour standards to the ILO, in November 1999 the US tabled before the WTO a proposal to create a working group on trade and labour.

In its proposal, the US asked that the working group cover the following areas:

1. Trade and Employment: examination of the effects of increased international trade and investment on levels and composition of countries' employment.
2. Trade and Social Protections: examination of the relationship between increased openness in trade and investment and the scope and the structure

of basic social protections and safety nets in developed and developing countries.

3. Trade and Core Labour Standards: examination of the relationship between economic development, international trade and investment, and the implementation of 'core' labour standards.

4. Positive Trade Policy Incentives and Core Labour Standards: examination of the scope for positive trade policy incentives to promote implementation of 'core' labour standards.

5. Trade and Forced or Exploitive Child Labour: examination of the extent of forced or exploitive child labour in industries engaged in international trade.

6. Trade and Derogation from National Labour Standards: examination of the effects of derogation from national labour standards (including in export processing zones) on international trade, investment and economic development.

As it stands, most developing countries oppose the introduction of *any* new provisions linking trade and labour. They also see the establishment of a WTO working group as the first step towards a formal link and, therefore, stand squarely opposed to it. For instance, it is not clear that the Government of India will even consider setting up a working group of the ILO and the United Nations Conference on Trade and Development (UNCTAD) that has been suggested recently by Bhagwati (1999) as a compromise solution.

4.2 The Trade-Labour Link within the Existing Policies

Some developing countries already face the prospect of actual trade policy action against their exports, based on labour standards. In the US, under the 1984 GSP amendment, the US Government may deny the right to preferential entry of exports of a beneficiary country that 'has not taken or is not taking steps to accord internationally recognised worker rights to workers in the country'. Since 1988, 'denial of workers' rights' has been defined as an unfair trade practice in section 301 of the US Trade Act of 1974 and may be subject to action if it harms US economic interests.[14]

In June 1990, the American Federation of Labor-Congress of Industrial Organization asked the United States Trade Respresentative for withdrawal of GSP privileges from Bangladesh on charges of violation of internationally

---

14. See Raychaudhuri (1996) who, in turn, refers to de Castro (1995) as the source of his information.

recognised labour rights.[15] The charges included the use of child labour in the garment industry, violation of the minimum wage legislation, denial of the right to form trade unions in export processing zones and poor working conditions. At the time the complaint was filed, 30 percent of Bangladesh's garment exports to the US were covered by GSP and were subject to either zero or less than MFN duty. The Export Promotion Board contested the case for the Bangladesh Government. Fortunately, the US GSP Subcommittee investigated the case and decided to defer the final decision in April 1991 for one year.[16]

The social clause in the EU's new GSP scheme for 1995-1997 also discriminates against countries that do not apply labour standards contained in specific ILO Conventions. But the EU decided to suspend, until 1997, actual implementation of any linkage between GSP and workers' rights, in order to take into consideration the outcome of discussions in international negotiations. It was agreed, however, that starting on 1 January 1998, GSP would be tied to effective implementation of 'core' ILO Conventions by a special incentive arrangement and a conditional arrangement. Under the first arrangement, the EU will grant an additional preference margin to countries introducing the prohibition of child labour and effective policies for the protection of workers' rights to organise and bargain collectively. Under the second arrangement, the EU will have the authority to withdraw temporarily some or all of a country's preferential entitlement if the country employs forced labour or exports goods made by prison labour.[17]

5.   CONCLUSIONS: WHAT ARE THE SOLUTIONS?

A close examination of various arguments in section 2 demonstrated that a logically consistent case for a link between trade and labour standards does not exist. Not surprisingly, an editorial in the *Financial Times* (1999) preceding the Seattle Ministerial offered the following diagnosis:

> The WTO is ill-equipped to tackle these problems, even if its members agreed to do so. Grafting social policy aims onto an institution designed to dismantle

---

15. Khan (1996) reports that, according to Pakistani newspapers*The News*, 10 March 1996, and *Dawn*, 11 April 1996, Pakistan has also received threats of withdrawal of GSP privileges from the US. The threat applied to three industries: surgical instruments, sporting goods, and carpets.
16. Reza *et al.* (1996), who document this case, do not report the final outcome.
17. Raychaudhuri (1996), who relies on de Castro (1995) for this information, notes that the current status of this linkage is not known.

economic barriers is a recipe for confusion. In any case, poor countries would reject such a move as disguised protectionism.

Western governments know this. So why are they renewing their demands, despite a 1996 WTO agreement to leave labour standards to the International Labour Organization? And why risk splitting the WTO over the issue, just when unity is needed to launch a new trade round?

Most admit privately that they lack a persuasive intellectual case. But they say that unless the WTO acknowledges the depth of concern in the west about labour rights, further trade liberalization will be politically impossible. That claim looks disingenuous.

The discussion in section 4.1 reveals that even among developed countries, only the US is seeking a link between trade and labour. The demand for a WTO working group was tabled by the US alone. Canada did not support this demand. The EU was willing to go as far as a joint WTO/ILO Forum, but explicitly ruled out forging a link between labour standards and market access. Developing countries are outright opposed to a WTO working group with or without the involvement of the ILO.

Therefore, the solution must be sought in diffusing the pressures for a link between trade and labour in the US. Given the current mood of civil society, particularly of labour groups, this is a tough task and may require action on several fronts. There are no easy options, but three suggestions can be made.

First, one of the arguments that civil society groups have made with some justification recently is that the WTO looks after corporate interests while ignoring the interests of labour and environment. Two events that have given substance to this complaint are the inclusion of the Agreement on Trade-Related Aspects of Intellectual Property Rights (TRIPS), which makes intellectual property protection a central plank of the WTO, and the Organisation for Economic Cooperation and Development (OECD) push for a Multilateral Agreement on Investment (MAI). The civil society was successful in defeating the latter, but resents the former. It demands that the WTO must now do for nature and workers what it has already done for corporate interests. For instance, consider the following excerpt from a recent article by Bernard (1999) in the *Washington Post*:

> For example, the WTO says its purview does not include social issues – only trade. So it claims to be powerless to do anything about a repressive regime selling the products of sweatshops that use child labour. Yet let the same regime use the same children to produce 'pirated' CDs or fake designer T-shirts, and the WTO can spring into action with a series of powerful levers to protect corporate 'intellectual property rights'.

A possible response to this critique is to either take TRIPS out of the WTO and place it into the World Intellectual Property Rights Organization

(WIPO), or weaken its enforcement provisions. Rather than add to the existing distortion to achieve equality between corporate and labour interests, the economically superior option is to reverse the mistake that has been made.

As far as the environment is concerned, the leadership in the US and elsewhere in the developed world needs to articulate better the message that this subject is already under discussion at the WTO. The WTO Committee on Trade and Environment was created following a Ministerial Decision in Marrakesh in April 1994. This committee had been given both analytical and prescriptive functions: to identify the relationships between trade and environmental measures in order to promote sustainable development, and to make recommendations on whether any modifications to the provisions of the multilateral trading system are required. The work of the Committee is in progress. In addition, environmental concerns have also been aired at the WTO Dispute Settlement Body with the US environmental laws to achieve domestic objectives upheld in both the gasoline and shrimp-turtle cases.[18]

Second, we can strengthen the ILO and begin to promote more effectively labour standards through this institution. Many developed country WTO Members including the EU, Canada and Australia already favour this approach. What is needed is to convince the US Government and civil society groups that this is a feasible approach. Once TRIPS is weakened, this task may become easier. Bhagwati (1999) has recently proposed the creation of a joint ILO-UNCTAD Expert Group consisting of trade and labour scholars. He argues that if the agenda of such a group is symmetric, such that it is charged with studying egregious labour practices in both developed and developing countries, progress towards higher labour standards world-wide is feasible. At the moment, many developing countries are unwilling to go along with any kind of working group that brings a trade institution in the game, while the US wants such a group in the WTO. Therefore, an ILO-UNCTAD group may be the compromise on which both sides may agree.

Finally, some action can be taken directly by developed countries themselves. To the extent that they fear capital flight on account of low labour standards in developing countries, they can require their own corporations to adhere to the same labour standards abroad as at home. As Bhagwati (1995) puts it – do in Rome as you do in New York, not as the Romans do. Such an approach may eliminate a key source of concern on the part of labour groups.

---

18. There has been a clear public relations failure in explaining to the public that in each of these cases, the US law was upheld. The WTO only questioned the implementation that was ruled unduly discriminatory.

REFERENCES

Bernard, Elaine (1999), 'A New Society will be Heard', *Washington Post*, 5 December, pp. B1 and B5.

Bhagwati, Jagdish N. (1971), 'The Generalized Theory of Distortions and Welfare', in Jagdish N. Bhagwati, Ronald W. Jones, Robert A. Mundell and Jaroslav Vanek (eds), *Trade, Balance of Payments and Growth: Papers in International Economics in Honor of Charles P. Kindleberger*, Amsterdam, The Netherlands: North-Holland, pp. 69-90.

Bhagwati, Jagdish N. (1995), 'Trade Liberalization and Fair Trade Demands: Addressing the Environmental and Labour Standards Issues', *World Economy*, **18**, 745-59.

Bhagwati, Jagdish N. (1997), 'The World Trading System: The New Challenges', in Arvind Panagariya, M.G. Quibria, and Narhari Rao (eds) (1997), pp. 49-79.

Bhagwati, Jagdish N. (1999), 'Let the Millennium Round Begin in New Delhi', interview in the *Economic Times*, 25 January 1999.

Bhagwati, Jagdish N. and V.K. Ramaswami (1963), 'Domestic Distortions, Tariffs, and the Theory of Optimum Subsidy', *Journal of Political Economy*, **71**(1), 44-50.

de Castro, Juan A. (1995), 'Trade and Labor Standards: Using the Wrong Instrument for the Right Cause', Discussion Chapter No. 99, Geneva, Switzerland: UNCTAD.

de Gray, Rodney (1994), 'The International Trading System and Labor Standards', Document UNCTAD/MTN/RAS/CB.11, Project RAS/92/034, Geneva, Switzerland: UNCTAD.

Financial Times 1999, 'Trade and Labor', 13 October 1999.

Holloway, Margarite (1993), 'Hard Times/Occupational Injuries Among Children are Increasing', *Scientific American*, **269**(4).

Jenkins, Kristen (1999), 'Dueling Agendas: Documents on Labor and the WTO', New Economy Information Service, 1 November 1999.

Khan, Ashfaque (1996), 'Study of the Emerging Trading Environment: The Case of Pakistan', paper presented to the Emerging Trading Environment and Developing Asia Conference on Country Studies, 29-30 August, Manila: Asian Development Bank.

Levinson, Arik (1996), 'Environmental Regulation and Industry Location: International and Domestic Evidence', in Jagdish N. Bhagwati and Robert E., Hudec (eds), *Fair Trade and Harmonization: Prerequisites for Free Trade?*, Cambridge, MA, US: MIT Press, pp. 429-57.

Mohan, Rakesh (1996), 'Comment on "Observations on International Labor Standards and Trade" by Alan Krueger', mimeo.

Panagariya, Arvind (1999a), 'WTO: US Demands Threaten Seattle Meeting', *Financial Times*, 10 November 1999.

Panagariya, Arvind (1999b), 'The Millennium Round and Developing Countries: Negotiating Strategies and Areas of Benefits', chapter presented at the Conference on Developing Countries and the New Millennium Round of Trade Negotiations, 5-6 November 1999, Cambridge, MA, US: Harvard University.

Panagariya, Arvind, M.G. Quibria and Narhari Rao (eds) (1997), *The Global Trading System and Developing Asia: Challenges and Opportunities*, Hong Kong: Oxford University Press

Raychaudhuri, B. (1996), 'The International Trading System and Social Clauses' in *Asian and Pacific Developing Economies and the First WTO Ministerial*

Conference: Issues and Concerns, Studies in International Trade and Investment 22, Economic and Social Commission for Asia and the Pacific, New York: United Nations.

Reza, Sadrel, M. Ali Rashid and Mustafizur Rahman (1996), 'The Emerging Global Trading Environment and Developing Asia: Bangladesh Country Chapter', chapter presented to the Emerging Trading Environment and Developing Asia Conference on Country Studies, 29-30 August 2000, Manila: Asian Development Bank.

Rodrik, Dani (1997), *Has Globalization Gone Too Far?*, Washington, DC, US: Institute for International Economics.

4. Paved with Good Intentions: Social Dumping and Raising Labour Standards in Developing Countries[*]

W. Max Corden and Neil Vousden

1. INTRODUCTION

The term 'social dumping' is popular in Europe. It refers to the export by less developed countries (LDCs) of products that are produced by unduly cheap labour and in poor, often shocking, working conditions. The campaign against social dumping usually includes proposals for governments to enforce certain minimum working conditions, prohibit or limit the use of child labour, often establish a minimum wage above starvation levels, and allow or even encourage the operation of independent trade unions. Sometimes it is proposed that multinationals which operate in LDCs should bring about voluntarily, or under pressure, the necessary improvements.

The advocates of anti-social dumping measures can be found in the developed countries, notably the United States and Western Europe. They have one (or both) of two motives, namely, *humanitarian* and *protectionist*. The latter motive has the objective of reducing the international competition faced by import-competing producers of labour-intensive products in the developed countries. This objective would be achieved if reduction of exports by LDCs, resulting from higher labour costs, significantly raised world prices of these exports. But we shall begin here with a small country model where

---

[*] This chapter uses a two-sector wage differential model to analyse the effects of an increase in labour costs in the export sector of a developing country. The increase is assumed to be a response to humanitarian or protectionist-motivated pressure from developed countries to reduce 'social dumping'. Some labour would shift into the residual sector of the economy, hence lower wages there, and increase wage inequality. The average wage may rise or fall, depending on elasticity conditions. Monopsony in the labour market, mobility of multinationals in response to lower profits and terms of trade effects are allowed for.

the developing country cannot affect world prices. Hence, we start with the humanitarian motive. The protectionist motive – which depends on the terms-of-trade effects of anti-social dumping measures – will be discussed later, in section 5.[1]

Developed countries, or their individual citizens, have several ways of reducing social dumping by LDCs.

The first way is for developed countries' governments to attach conditions about labour standards, minimum wages, trade union rights, and so on, to international trade agreements, so that, in effect, governments of LDCs will face the threat of protectionist barriers against their exports if they do not comply. The threat would probably be directed specifically against exports of particular products or categories where social dumping is believed to be practised, though it might be directed against LDCs' exports in general if labour conditions and wages are believed to be shocking even in non-export sectors of the economy. The threat of protectionist barriers might also be informal, without the intermediation of an actual or potential trade agreement.

A second way is for citizens and non-governmental organisations (NGOs) to practise or encourage boycotts of the LDCs' offending exports, and of firms that import or distribute these products.

A third way is for governments, individuals or NGOs to put pressure on multinationals – again, through threats of boycotts and strikes affecting possibly the world-wide operations of the multinationals – to change their operations in LDCs so as to raise wages, improve working conditions, and encourage trade unions.

This chapter will now assume that the LDC or the relevant multinationals give way to the pressures. The net result is that conditions of employment in the industries concerned improve, and labour costs rise. What are the broader effects in the LDC?

---

1. There is a growing literature on labour standards and trade. Many references are given in Swinnerton (1997). In that paper a distinction is made between 'core' labour standards (the right to collective bargaining, prohibition of forced labour, of discrimination in employment, and of exploitation of children) and other labour standards such as minimum wage and working conditions. The issues are also reviewed by Bhagwati (1997), who argues that universally condemned labour practices, such as slavery, are rare, and in general labour standards cannot be universalised on moral grounds. See also Brown *et al.* (1996) and Organisation for Economic Cooperation and Development(1996).

2.   A SIMPLE MODEL

Figure 4.1 refers to a particular LDC which faces given world prices. There
are two sectors, sector X which produces exports of manufactured goods, and
sector Z which can be thought of as representing the rest of the economy, and
also faces given world prices, whether import or export prices. For the time
being it is assumed that all products and services are tradeable. Capital
(including land) is fixed and specific to each sector, the only variable factor
being labour, which is uniform in characteristics. The horizontal axis shows
the total supply of labour in the economy, divided up between the two
sectors. Curves M_xM_x and M_zM_z trace out the values of the marginal products
of labour in the two industries, with origins, respectively, at X and Z. Labour
is paid its marginal product. Initial equilibrium is at A, with a uniform wage
rate XW in the economy, and a labour allocation of XN in sector X and NZ in
sector Z. We now make two crucial assumptions. First, the measures designed
to improve labour standards and real wages apply only to industry X. This is the
industry which exports manufactures to developed countries where the pressures
to improve labour conditions come from, and is also the industry where the
measures can, to some extent, be enforced. It may also be the industry where the
multinationals under attack primarily operate. Second, the net result of raising
minimum wages, improving labour conditions and allowing the operation of
trade unions, can be represented by a rise in the real wage. There is, of course,
some difference, both for firms and for workers, between an increase in labour
costs brought about by a rise in the paid-out wage, and an improvement in
working conditions. The main point here is that both raise labour costs.

The wage in sector X is raised from XW to XW_1. Hence employment in
sector X is reduced from XN to XN^1. The redundant labour force N^1N then
crowds the market for employment in sector Z, forcing the wage in that sector
down to ZW_2. There are no unemployment benefits and sector Z must absorb all
the potentially unemployed, so that employment in sector Z rises from NZ to
N^1Z.

Sector Z can be given a broad interpretation. It is the residual sector of the
economy. It can include both the self-employed and family employment. The
main point is simply that raising the wage in sector X reduces per capita
incomes in sector Z by increasing labour in that sector even while capital
(including land) is fixed there. It is not actually necessary to assume that all
employment in that sector is wage labour, nor that labour is paid its marginal
product. But, for the time being, we adhere to the assumption that all labour is
paid wages, and that the wage is always equal to labour's marginal product.

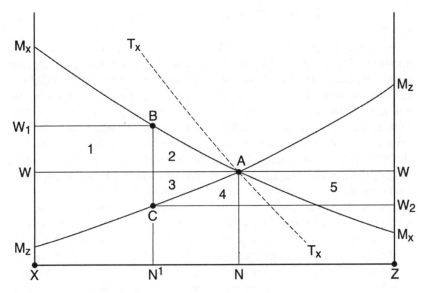

Figure 4.1 Distributional Effects in the 'Wage-Differential' Model

In Figure 4.1, area 1 represents the increased wage bill in sector X for all those privileged workers who remain employed in that sector. It can be interpreted more broadly as representing the net benefit resulting from higher paid wages, as well as improved working conditions resulting from the measures either brought about by the LDC's government under pressure from developed countries, or by the multinational employers in sector X. Area 1 + 2 is the reduction in profits in sector X. Area 3 + 4 is the loss in wages to the workers that have had to transfer from sector X to sector Z, while area 5 is the loss in wages to the workers previously, and still, employed in sector Z. Area 4 + 5 is the gain in profits and rents in sector Z. Netting out gains and losses, the country's efficiency loss from creation of the wage differential is area 2 + 3.

It is clear that inequality within the wage earning sector has increased – or, to be precise in this formal model, has been created for the first time. If we define the poverty level not in terms of the average wage throughout the economy, but by how many workers fall below a defined minimum wage (or income), then the probability is that the poverty level has increased. This would be so in the diagram if the minimum were somewhere below, but close to XW.[2]

What has happened to the total wage bill? It may have increased or decreased. Hence, given the fixed total labour force, the average wage may have increased or decreased. The outcome will depend on the elasticities of the two marginal product curves. For example, if the elasticities over the relevant ranges (from A to B and from A to C) are unity in both cases, then in each sector, and hence the economy as a whole, the wage bill must stay constant. For any given wage increase in sector X, the steeper is AB and the flatter is AC, the more likely is a rise in the total wage bill. The Appendix derives the precise formula. Two extreme elasticity cases are noted in the next section.

The basic model used here comes from the literature of development economics and international trade. The two-sector 'wage differential' model has a long history and plays a key role in the evolution of the theory of protection.[3] In the trade theory literature, the wage differential is usually given, and the implications for the theory of protection are then explored. It is usually assumed that the differential is in favour of import-competing industries in the urban sector, and a third or fourth-best argument for protection of that sector can then be derived. Here we are concerned, rather, with the economic and distributional effects of introducing such a differential in the first place, with unchanged trade and subsidy policies.[4]

3.   HAVE THE HUMANITARIANS A CASE?

It might seem odd for humanitarians in developed countries to press LDCs or multinationals to implement measures that would increase wage (and possibly income) inequality, and probably increase poverty. Furthermore, it would reduce the efficiency of the economy – and hence the tax base – through inducing a shift of labour from more productive to less productive

2. We might assume that in sector Z there are many wage rates distributed randomly around the average wage, W2 being the average after the transfer of labour. A decline in this wage would be likely to increase the number of persons that fall below a specified poverty level wage.
3. See Hagen (1958), Bhagwati and Ramaswami (1963), and Corden (1974) chapter 6.
4. The literature has also introduced 'Harris-Todaro' unemployment or low-income employment resulting from a wage differential. This involves adding a third sector to the model. See Harris and Todaro (1970). If one added this effect here, the efficiency and distributional effects would become more adverse. As shown in Corden and Findlay (1975), the Harris-Todaro model can be expounded in terms of a diagram like Figure 4.1, and Harris-Todaro effects could easily be added to the analysis here. See also Corden (1974) chapter 6.

uses. One might dismiss the views of the humanitarians as reflecting the common tendency of non-economists to thinking in partial equilibrium terms. Alternatively, the simple model just presented might have flaws. Here various modifications to the model, and possible rationales for the humanitarian case, will be briefly explored. The first modification discussed below is clearly the important one.

3.1   Monopsony in the X-Sector Labour Market

It may be that a rise in the real wage in sector X would not lead to any decline in employment there. Possibly the elasticity of the labour demand (M_xM_x) curve is simply zero over the relevant range. This could be so for small changes and in the short run.[5] More plausibly, there may be a monopsony situation in the labour market, so that in that sector, though not in the Z-sector, the wage is below the marginal product of labour.

This is represented in Figure 4.2. Curve M_zM_z is not only the marginal product curve in sector Z, but is also the supply curve of labour facing sector X. It traces out the average cost of labour to employers in that sector. The marginal cost curve derived from it is RR. The demand for labour curve M_xM_x is the same as before, tracing out the marginal value product of labour. Given monopsony in the labour market, the employment equilibrium is then at Q where the marginal product is equal to marginal cost. The wage is at W. Any increase in the wage up to, *but not beyond*, Q would not lead to any reduction in employment and output. In fact, provided the wage were not raised as far as Q, a rise would lead to an increase in employment, with maximum employment at A. Hence there is initially scope for raising the wage (or labour costs more generally) without reducing employment in sector X as a result.[6]

It is likely that humanitarians implicitly have this kind of model in mind. It is a classic model of 'labour exploitation'. It may well apply in the short run in many situations and especially in locations where there is a single big employer, or if employers are cartelised. It will not apply in the long run

---

5.   One can hardly make a general statement applicable to all LDCs, but evidence for the United States and the United Kingdom cited in footnote 6, that *possibly* minimum wage increases have not had significant employment effects, is relevant here.
6.   In Card and Krueger (1995) it is argued – primarily on the basis of a survey – that an increase in the minimum wage in the United States may actually have increased employment, or possibly had no significant effect. Such a conclusion could be rationalised with the monopsony model. The evidence for the United States is thoroughly and sceptically reviewed in Kennan (1995). On the United Kingdom, see Machin and Manning (1996) who also conclude that employment effects have probably not been significant.

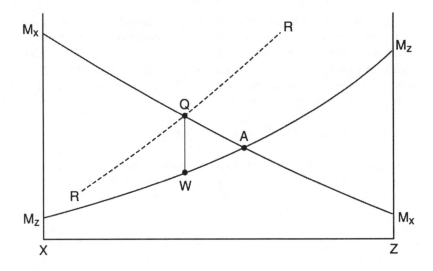

Figure 4.2 Distributional Effects in a Modified 'Wage-Differential' Model

where there is reasonably free entry. Excess profits of employers resulting from monopsony will tend to be competed away so that the monopsony will come to an end.

3.2   Absence of a Sector Z, or Different Specification

It might be argued that minimum wages and improved labour conditions should be imposed throughout the economy and thus a two-sector model is not appropriate. But there has to be a residual sector of some kind if employment in sector X falls. In developed countries with unemployment benefits, there can simply be a pool of unemployment which expands when real wages rise, though even then some of the potentially unemployed are likely to move into a self-employment sector. But in an LDC there has to be a residual sector. In any case, complete enforceability of labour market regulations applied through pressure on governments from international sources, or on multinationals, is quite implausible. Creation of a wage differential is inevitable.

It is true that labour need not get its marginal product in sector Z. Because of income sharing within families and small communities, labour transferring into this sector may be paid more, namely, its average product.[7] But this will not alter the fact that when extra labour has to be absorbed in sector Z the average income in the sector – which will be equated to the wage in sector X – will have to fall, provided there is some tendency to diminishing returns. Furthermore, it will remain true that the transfer of labour from X to Z will generate an efficiency cost. In Figure 4.1 the M_zM_z curve could be reinterpreted as the average product of labour in sector Z, and the efficiency cost of the transfer will be greater than shown there because the marginal product will be below the average product.

If the elasticity of demand for labour in sector Z were infinite (so that the curve would be horizontal through A) extra labour could be absorbed in sector Z without a decline in the real wage there. A rise in the real wage in sector X would still bring about a wage differential and an efficiency loss, but the wage rate in sector Z would not fall, and thus the transferred workers would not actually lose. These conclusions can be readily derived from Figure 4.1. There would be a net rise in the wages bill for the economy as a whole. We have here an extreme version of the well known surplus labour model. The more common version assumed income sharing combined with diminishing returns.[8] As a general assumption for LDCs, absence of diminishing returns in a residual sector seems quite implausible.

So far it has been assumed that the products of sector Z are all traded, with given world prices. But sector Z may also embrace the non-traded goods and services part of the economy. Indeed, since it is the residual sector, it must do so. It can be shown that if sector Z is partly or wholly a producer of non-traded products, the M_zM_z curve will become steeper so that the distributional and efficiency effects of the rise in the real wage in sector X will become greater. The essential point is that a movement of labour out of X into Z (hence leading to a rise in output of Z) will require a fall in the relative price of Z to ensure that extra demand for Z is generated. This is, in effect, a real depreciation. This is verified in the Appendix, which fully expounds the model where Z is non-tradeable.

An interesting result ensues when one combines the monopsony assumption with the assumption that Z consists of, or includes, non-traded goods. Suppose that the monopsonist is a foreign firm repatriating profits. A rise in the sector X wage would then increase total domestic income. With good Z non-traded, this rise in income would increase demand for Z, thus driving up its market-clearing price and the wage paid to sector Z workers.

---

7.   This is the assumption of a standard model originating in Nurkse (1953) and Lewis (1954). See also Ranis and Fei (1964) and Corden (1974) chapter 6.
8.   See again Lewis (1954) and Corden (1974) chapter 6.

In such a case the humanitarian labour standards policy actually benefits *all* workers at the expense of a foreign-owned firm.

3.3 Other qualifications

There are various good reasons why all developed countries regulate working conditions to some extent, and these reasons can also apply to LDCs. Often they have to do with information, or the absence of it, or possibly with externalities. For example, employees may not be aware of unsafe features of particular employment, and even if they were provided with information they may not successfully absorb it. Hence regulations to ensure minimum safety conditions have to be introduced. This is the subject of a large literature and cannot be pursued here.

For the social-dumping issue, which is the subject of this chapter, two points have to be added. First, if labour regulations, however justified, can only be applied in one sector, a wage (or labour cost) differential will still emerge with all the consequences discussed in this chapter. Sector X will become safer and contract, and more workers will crowd into unsafe sector Z. Second, the appropriate nature and extent of such regulations will vary between countries – among other things involving a trade-off between wages and working conditions on the one hand, and employment in the privileged sector on the other. Should this not normally be determined by national governments rather than imposed in response to foreign pressure?

4.   MOBILE MULTINATIONALS

So far we have assumed that capital in sector X is not only specific to that sector but also fixed in supply. But the supply of capital will depend on the rate of return, at least if there is international capital mobility. Reduced rates of return would lead to a reduced supply of capital (and associated techniques and entrepreneurship in the case of multinationals). Thus the long-term scope for squeezing profits in sector X must be limited. In Figure 4.1 this effect increases the elasticity of the M_xM_x curve. Hence employment in sector X will fall more for a given real wage increase in that sector than if capital were not mobile, and the total wage bill (and hence average wage) for the economy as a whole is more likely to fall. Humanitarians need to bear in mind that multinational operations are internationally mobile, at least given time.

5. TERMS-OF-TRADE EFFECTS AND THE PROTECTIONIST CASE

Finally, let us introduce terms-of-trade effects. Import prices are the numeraire and are held constant. Reduction in export supply now raises export prices and so improves the LDC's terms of trade. The M_xM_x curve in Figure 4.1 is drawn for given export prices, and a rise in export prices shifts it upwards. Thus we get the T_xT_x curve which traces out the marginal value product of X, as employment in X is reduced. This curve is steeper than the M_xM_x curve because it allows for the endogenous upward shifts of the M_xM_x curve as export prices rise. Starting at A, a given rise in the real wage to W_1 (the real wage being measured in terms of prices of Z) will lead to a lesser reduction in employment in X than when there was no terms-of-trade effect.

It is important to bear in mind that the terms of trade have improved only because employment in X, and hence the export quantity, has fallen. If there were no reduction in employment in sector X, and hence in the quantity of exports – as assumed in the monopsony case noted above – there would be no such favourable terms-of-trade effect.

The terms-of-trade effect is crucial to the protectionists' case for policies which regulate social dumping. They want the world relative prices of X to be raised. This would reduce the competition they face from 'cheap labour' exports from LDCs supposedly 'dumped' in their markets. Of course, it would at the same time worsen the terms of trade of their own countries. Hence the protectionists' proposals are only useful to them if labour costs are raised in those LDCs which can affect their terms of trade or, alternatively, if they are raised in a large enough group of countries the members of which may be individually small economies unable to affect their own terms of trade but which collectively can influence world prices through reduction in employment in the relevant export industries.

6. A PARADOX: WHAT IS GOOD FOR THE HUMANITARIANS IS BAD FOR THE PROTECTIONISTS

There is a very significant paradox. It has to do with the degree of monopsony in sector X. The humanitarian case really depends on a minimal or zero decline in employment in sector X as a result of the rise in labour costs imposed on that sector. Hence the greater the degree of monopsony in sector X labour market, the stronger the humanitarian case. On the other hand, the protectionist case depends on a reduction in output, and hence employment, in sector X. Such an output reduction is required to raise world prices of X, given that there is a terms of trade effect. The lower the degree of monopsony, the better the outcome from the protectionist point of view. If the rise in labour costs would just lead to a profits squeeze and no decline in output and employment in the sector, the protectionists would have nothing to gain. The paradox is that the monopsony model – which provides the strongest basis for the humanitarian case – is one that yields no benefits to the protectionists from measures directed against social dumping.

7.   CONCLUSION

The campaign against 'social dumping' – that is, the export by developing countries (LDCs) of products produced by cheap labour and in poor working conditions – has both a humanitarian and a protectionist motive. The question addressed in this chapter has been: what would be the effects if LDC governments, or multinationals operating in LDCs, gave way and thus raised labour costs in LDC export industries? This chapter has used the two-sector wage differential model to explore the effects.

Employment in the export industries would fall, labour would transfer into the residual sector, where wages and average incomes would then fall. Hence inequality among wage earners would increase and the average wage for the economy as a whole might rise or fall, depending on relative elasticities as set out in the Appendix. The main qualification concerns the possibility of labour market monopsony in the export sector. In that case, a rise in the wage rate may not lead to reduced employment, but just to lower profits. The humanitarians may have this possibility in mind. It is likely, however, that excess profits of employers resulting from monopsony would in time be competed away so that the scope for raising labour costs without reducing employment in export industries is limited, especially because in the longer run multinationals are mobile.

In most of the chapter it is assumed that the LDC concerned cannot affect its terms of trade, being small in the world economy. Finally, allowance is made for terms of trade effects, so that the reduction in LDC exports would raise their relative world prices, this being the objective of the protectionists in the developed countries. A given rise in the wage in export industries would then lead to a lesser transfer of employment out of export industries compared with absence of terms of trade effects. But an interesting paradox emerges once labour market monopsony is allowed for. If raising labour costs in LDCs' export industries did *not* reduce employment there because of labour market monopsony, it would also not reduce exports and thus would not raise world relative prices of these goods. Hence it would not achieve the objective of the protectionists. On the other hand, it might achieve the objective of the humanitarians, which is to raise wages and working conditions in LDC export industries while not reducing wages in the rest of the economy. What is welcome for the humanitarians is not good for the protectionists.

APPENDIX

This Appendix analyses the two main competitive market models considered in the chapter. In both models, the country in question is small in world markets. The first model has two goods, an exportable (X) and an importable (Z), both produced domestically. In the second model, there are three goods, an exportable (X), an importable (Y) and a non-tradeable (Z). In this model, only goods X and Z are produced domestically; there is no domestic production of the importable. Here, both models are captured in a single framework by treating good Z as a non-tradeable. This reduces to the case where Z is a small-country importable when its domestic demand curve is infinitely elastic (i.e., goods Y and Z are perfect substitutes). Each of goods X and Z is produced using a sector-specific factor (capital) and an intersectorally mobile factor (labour). The resource constraint for labour is

$$N_x + N_z = N \tag{1}$$

where N_i is the labour input into sector i ($i = X, Z$) and N is the economy's total labour endowment (given).

Let the production function for sectors X and Z be given by
$X = F(N_x)$ ($F' > 0$, $F'' < 0$) and $Z = G(N_z)$
$G' > 0$, $G'' < 0$) respectively. Then the labour demands in the two sectors satisfy

$$\left. \begin{aligned} F'(N_x) &= w_x \\ p_z G'(N_z) &= w_z \end{aligned} \right\} \tag{2}$$

where p_z is the relative price of good Z (good X is numeraire so that $p_x \equiv 1$) and w_i is the wage paid to sector i labour ($i = X,Z$). The market-clearing condition for good Z is

$$G(N_z) = D(p_z, I) \tag{3}$$

where $D(p_z, I)$, $(D_p < 0, \ D_I > 0)$, is the domestic ordinary demand for good Z and I is national income given by

$$I = F(N_x) + p_z G(N_z).$$

(4)

Now consider the effect of an exogenous increase in the sector X wage (w_x) on the economy's total wage bill (WB) given by

$$WB = w_x N_x + w_z N_z,$$

(5)

Define η_x and η_z as the sectoral elasticities of labour demand with respect to the sectoral real wage. i.e.

$$\eta_i \equiv - \frac{\partial N_i / N_i}{\partial (w_i / p_i) / (w_i / p_i)}, \quad i = X, Z.$$

(6)

Taking total differentials of (5) and using (6) yields the following expression for the proportional change in WB[9]:

$$\widehat{WB} = \theta_x \hat{w}_x \left[1 - \eta_x + \eta_x \frac{w_z}{w_x} \right] + (1 - \theta_x) \hat{w}_z,$$

(7)

where $\theta_x \equiv \dfrac{w_x N_x}{WB}$ is the share of total wages paid to workers in sector X. Note that $\hat{w}_x$ is exogenously given. It remains to determine $\hat{w}_z$.

---

9. A ^ over a variable denotes proportional rate of change.

We begin by noting that from (1) and the definitions of η_x and η_z

$$\eta_z\left(\hat{P}_z - \hat{w}_z\right) = \hat{N}_z = \frac{N_x}{N_z}\,\eta_x\hat{w}_x.$$

This enables us to solve for $\hat{w}_z$ as

$$\hat{w}_z = \hat{P}_z - \frac{N_x}{N_z}\frac{\eta_x}{\eta_z}\hat{w}_x. \tag{8}$$

To determine $\hat{P}_z$, take total differentials of (3) and use (2) to obtain

$$\lambda_{Nz}\hat{N}_z = -\varepsilon_z^P\hat{P}_z + \varepsilon_z^I\hat{I} \tag{9}$$

where ε_z^P and ε_z^I are respectively the price and income elasticities of the ordinary demand curve for Z and $\lambda_{Nz} \equiv \dfrac{N_z w_z}{P_z Z}$ is labour's income share in sector Z.

Using (2), differentiation of (4) yields

$$\hat{I} = (w_x - w_z)\frac{N_x}{I}\,\hat{N}_x + \frac{P_z Z}{I}\,\hat{P}_z. \tag{10}$$

Substituting in (9) and using (6), we obtain

$$\frac{\lambda_{Nz}\eta_x N_x \hat{w}_x}{N_z} = \left[\alpha_z \varepsilon_z^I - \varepsilon_z^p\right]\hat{p}_z - \varepsilon_z^I (w_x - w_z)\frac{N_x}{I}\eta_x \hat{w}_x,$$ (11)

where $\alpha_z \equiv \dfrac{p_z Z}{I}$ is the share of income spent on good Z. Note that the Slutsky equation implies that

$$\alpha_z \varepsilon_z^I - \varepsilon_z^p = -\varepsilon_z^h$$

where ε_z^h is the price elasticity of the Hicksian compensated demand for good Z. Thus, (11) yields the following solution for $\hat{p}_z$:

$$\hat{p}_z = -\frac{\eta_x N_x \hat{w}_x}{\varepsilon_z^h}\left[\frac{w_z}{p_z Z} + \frac{\varepsilon_z^I (w_x - w_z)}{I}\right].$$ (12)

Substituting into (8) yields

$$\hat{w}_z = -\frac{\eta_x N_x \hat{w}_x}{N_z}\left[\frac{\lambda_{Nz}}{\varepsilon_z^h} + \frac{\varepsilon_z^I (w_x - w_z)N_z}{\varepsilon_z^h I} + \frac{1}{\eta_z}\right].$$ (13)

Finally, this may be substituted into (7) to obtain

$$
\hat{WB} = \hat{w}_x \theta_x \left[1 - \eta_x + \eta_x \frac{w_z}{w_x} \right]
$$
$$
- \hat{w}_x (1 - \theta_x) \frac{\eta_x N_x}{N_z} \left[\frac{\lambda_{Nz}}{\varepsilon_z^h} + \frac{\varepsilon_z^I (w_x - w_z) N_z}{\varepsilon_z^h I} + \frac{1}{\eta_z} \right] \tag{14}
$$

This may be written in a more convenient form as

$$
\hat{WB} = \hat{w}_x \theta_x \left\{ 1 - \eta_x + \frac{w_z \eta_x}{w_x} \left(1 - \frac{1}{\eta_z} \right) \right\}
$$
$$
- \hat{w}_x \frac{\theta_x w_z \eta_x}{w_x \varepsilon_z^h} \left\{ \lambda_{Nz} + \frac{\varepsilon_z^I (w_x - w_z) N_z}{I} \right\} \tag{15}
$$

(a) Two traded goods:

Consider the special case in which the country in question is small in world markets, producing only two goods, an exportable X and an importable Z. In this case, the price of good Z is unaffected by an increase in the sector-X wage. This is the special case of the above model in which the demand curve for Z is infinitely elastic, i.e., $\varepsilon_z^h = \infty$. (12) then implies $\hat{p}_z = 0$ so that the change in the wage bill in (15) reduces to the first group of terms on the right hand side, i.e.,

$$
\hat{WB} = \hat{w}_x \theta_x \left\{ 1 - \eta_x + \frac{w_z \eta_x}{w_x} \left(1 - \frac{1}{\eta_z} \right) \right\}. \tag{16}
$$

It is now straightforward to derive the three special elasticity cases discussed in the text. First, if there is a unitary elasticity of labour demand in both sectors so that $\eta_x = \eta_z = 1$, then $\hat{WB} = 0$ - i.e., there is no change in the average wage. Second, if the elasticity of demand for labour in sector Z is infinite ($\eta_z = \infty$), then (16) can be written as

$$\hat{WB} = \hat{w}_x \theta_x \left\{ 1 - \eta_x \left(\frac{w_x - w_z}{w_x} \right) \right\} \qquad (17)$$

$$= \hat{w}_x \theta_x > 0$$

in the neighbourhood of the initial equilibrium ($w_x = w_z$). Finally note that if the elasticity of labour demand in the X sector is zero ($\eta_x = 0$), then again

$$\hat{WB} = \hat{w}_x \theta_x > 0. \qquad (18)$$

(b) Good Z Non-traded:

When the two sectors of production in the economy are an exportable (X) and a non-traded good (Z), equation (15) gives the full expression for the proportional change in the wage bill. The second group of terms in parentheses captures the additional effect of making Z non-traded. The term is negative and represents the additional fall in the sector-Z wage due to the induced fall in the market-clearing price of good Z. This confirms the statement in the text that introducing a non-traded good in sector Z leads to a larger fall in the sector-Z wage, increased inequality and a smaller increase/larger fall in the average wage for the economy.

REFERENCES

Bhagwati, Jagdish N. (1997), 'The Global Age: From a Sceptical South to a Fearful North', *The World Economy*, **20**(3), 259- 83.

Bhagwati, Jagdish N. and V.K. Ramaswami (1963), 'Domestic Distortions, Tariffs, and the Theory of Optimum Subsidy', *Journal of Political Economy*, **71**, 44-50.

Brown, Drusilla K., Alan V. Deardorff and Robert M. Stern (1996), 'International Labour Standards and Trade: A Theoretical Analysis' in Jagdish N. Bhagwati and Robert E. Hudec (eds), *Fair Trade and Harmonization: Prerequisites for Free Trade?*, vol. 1, Cambridge, MA, US: MIT Press, pp. 227-80.

Card, David E. and Alan B. Krueger (1995), *Myth and Measurement: The New Economics of the Minimum Wage*, Princeton, US: Princeton University Press.

Corden, Warner M. (1974), *Trade Policy and Economic Welfare*, 1st edn, Oxford, UK: Clarendon Press.

Corden, Warner M. and Ronald Findlay (1975), 'Urban Unemployment, Intersectoral Capital Mobility and Development Policy', *Economica*, **43**, 59-78.

Hagen, Everett E. (1958), 'An Economic Justification of Protectionism', *Quarterly Journal of Economics*, **72**, 496-514.

Harris, John R. and Michael P. Todaro (1970), 'Migration, Unemployment and Development: A Two-Sector Analysis', *American Economic Review*, **60**, 126-42.

Kennan, John (1995), 'The Elusive Effects of Minimum Wages', *Journal of Economic Literature*, **33**(4), 1950-65.

Lewis, William A. (1954), 'Economic Development with Unlimited Supplies of Labour', *Manchester School of Economic and Social Studies*, **22**, 139-91.

Machin, Stephen and Alan Manning (1996), 'Employment and the Introduction of a Minimum Wage in Britain', *Economic Journal*, **106**, 667-76.

Nurkse, Ragnar (1953), *Problems of Capital Formation in Underdeveloped Countries*, New York, US: Oxford University Press.

Organisation for Economic Cooperation and Development (1996), *Trade, Employment and Labour Standards: A Study of Workers' Rights and International Trade*, Paris, France: Organisation for Economic Cooperation and Development.

Ranis, Gustav and John C.H. Fei (1964), *Development of the Labour Surplus Economy: Theory and Policy*, Homewood, IL, US: Irwin.

Swinnerton, Kenneth A. (1997), 'An Essay on Economic Efficiency and Core Labour Standards', *The World Economy*, **20**, 73-86.

PART THREE

TRADE, ENVIRONMENT AND
COMPETITION

5. Reforming Environmental Policy: Harmonisation and the Limitation of Diverging Environmental Policies: The Role of Trade Policy

Scott Vaughan[*]

Reflecting upon Wallace Stevens' observation that 'change of style is a change of subject',[1] one insight into changes underway in the trade and environment debate in the past decade can be gained from comparing the two defining slogans of that debate.[2]

The first, contained in Agenda 21 of the 1992 Rio Summit, calls upon trade and environmental policies to be 'mutually supportive'.[3] Although

---

[*]   This chapter is dedicated to the late Ambassador Arthur Campeau, for his unwavering commitment to the environment.

1.   Stevens *et al.* (1999), in Milton (ed.) p. 184.

2.   There have actually been a myriad of slogans since the trade and environment agenda first caught the attention of policy makers in the early 1970s. For example, under the 1972 Stockholm Plan of Action that established the United Nations Environment Programme, the following was noted: 'GATT, among other international organizations, could be used for the examination of the problems [of trade and the environment], specifically through the recently established [GATT] Group on Environmental Measures and International Trade'. However, the GATT Group did not formally convene until almost twenty years later.

3.   United Nations Conference for Environment and Development (UNCED), Chapter 2, Paragraph 2.19, 'Environment and trade policies should be mutually supportive. An open, multilateral trading system makes possible a more efficient allocation of resources and thereby contributes to an increase in production and incomes and to lessening demands on the environment ... An open, multilateral trading system, supported by the adoption of sound

vaguely suggestive of policy co-dependence, cooperation and balance, mutual supportive policies, as set out in Rio, were really about constraining the use of trade restrictions for environmental purposes and asserting the positive economic and environmental effects of a rule-based, multilateral trading system. Mutually supportive references became the polemic backdrop to a dizzying schedule of workshops, symposia and seminars that continue to crowd the trade-environment agenda.

The second slogan, blunter and impervious to malleable interpretations of a mutually supportive vision, was heard not in the muted exchanges of trade and environmental official meetings, but urgently in the streets of Seattle in late 1999. That slogan – 'The WTO: Fix it or Nix It' – summed up the public's judgement that the World Trade Organization (WTO) was a 'broken' institution, in need of either sweeping reforms or a complete dismantling.[4]

While the WTO continues to attract the passionate scrutiny of civil society, far less attention has been paid to reforms underway in environmental policy itself. Granted that environmental policy is by definition inherently dynamic and subject to constant change and reforms, reflecting in part changes in environmental quality and in part changes in the political will of countries to address environmental degradation, this chapter argues that some aspects of environmental policy reform are driven by trade policy considerations. While the post-Seattle debate will in all likelihood revolve around how to reform the WTO, regulatory reforms are underway in the environmental arena which are not primarily influenced by the pursuit of environmental quality, but rather by the principles of trade liberalisation and related open-market principles. It is worth noting that these regulatory reforms continue to proceed largely unnoticed by civil society groups that continue to focus on the WTO.

Two types of policy reforms are described: the harmonisation of domestic environmental policies, and the continued limitation of avenues available in international environmental policy which impede the free movement of goods. These two broad types of reforms are examined in the context of the

---

environmental policies, would have a positive impact on the environment and contribute to sustainable development'.

4. A range of views were expressed at Seattle. Although some called for the dismantling of the WTO, the strongest support centred on halting the launching of a new round of trade negotiations, pending significant changes by the WTO. For example, some 1,500 environmental, development, food security, poverty, human rights and other organisations signed the *'Statement from Members of International Civil Society Opposing a Millennium Round of Trade Negotiations'*, which stated in part: 'in the past five years, the WTO has contributed to the concentration of wealth in the hands of the rich few; increasing poverty for the majority of the world's population; and unsustainable patterns of production and consumption'. See Friends of the Earth UK, November 1999.

European Union (EU), the North American Free Trade Agreement (NAFTA) and Multilateral Environmental Agreements (MEAs).

In looking at these two types of environmental policy reforms, this chapter does not examine the implication of trade rules on domestic environmental policies that contain an extra-territorial application of domestic environmental standards. (This remains the most obvious and keenly discussed area of trade and the environment.) The two WTO trade-environment cases, together with cases involving public health and food safety issues and the two General Agreement on Tariffs and Trade (GATT) tuna/dolphin cases, have been exhaustively examined elsewhere. [5]

1. TRADE AND ENVIRONMENTAL CONCERNS: REHEARSING THE DEBATE

Before looking at these two areas, it is worth rehearsing some of the many concerns that have fallen under the rubric of trade and environment. As Esty (1994) and others have noted, and as the Seattle demonstrations attest, the

---

5. The most visible area in which trade rules can affect environmental policies involves the extra-territorial application of domestic environmental regulations. The topic that has attracted the most attention in this area is the extra-territorial application of regulations covering production process methods (PPM), whereby market access is conditioned by the extent to which a foreign producer complies with the PPM requirements of the importing country. Although there have been only two formal disputes involving environment-related PPMs – the US-Venezuela reformulated gasoline case, and the shrimp/turtle case, involving the US against four developing countries – related cases in the WTO involving the protection of human health underlines the most difficult area of the interface between trade and environment. One commentator from an environmental non-governmental organisation (NGO) has noted: 'The concern of environmental NGOs, in particular in the United States, is that conformity with WTO rules would force changes in various domestic environmental laws which contain provisions which condition market access based on the extent to which foreign producers adopt comparable PPM measures'. The actual effect of WTO panels in forcing domestic environmental laws to conform to Dispute Settlement Body rulings remains unclear, since there have not been enough cases to suggest a clear pattern. In addition, the findings of the Appellate Body of the WTO in the shrimp/turtle case has suggested that the conditioning of market access on imports, based on their environmental or conservation implications, is a legitimate reason to invoke, in principle, GATT Article XX Exceptions. The US response to the findings of the WTO Appellate Body on shrimp/turtle suggests that flexibility does exist in conforming to dispute findings; rather than changing the actual import restriction contained in the US Endangered Species Act, the administration gave notice that it will change the administration of such restrictions, in order to increase transparency and notification procedures, as well as the issuing of new guidelines intended to replace the country-by-country certification requirements regarding the use of Turtle Exclusion Devices by foreign shrimp fishing operations, with a shipment-by-shipment certification procedure.

trade and environment debate encompasses a bundle of related and unrelated issues.

Among the concerns of environmentalists is that free trade will exert direct and indirect negative impacts on environmental quality, and lead to the erosion of domestic or international environmental regulations. Some work has been done in assessing the extent to which trade liberalisation affects environmental quality.[6] However, by far, the focus of analysis has concentrated on the second area, i.e., the extent to which trade policy reform influences environmental policy. This *policy-policy* correlation has revolved around environmental concerns that trade laws and trade dispute bodies will override domestic or international environmental regulations; whether countries with higher environmental regulations will be at a competitive disadvantage *vis-à-vis* countries with lower environmental regulations and/or lax enforcement, leading either to the flight of heavily regulated industries to those countries with lower standards or no enforcement (the 'pollution haven' effect), or else prompt a downwards harmonisation in environmental standards.

Concerns among the trade community have included whether a linking of environmental concerns with market access might lead to an upwards harmonisation in environmental policies, thereby forcing developing or smaller countries either to adopt the higher standards of larger countries, or to be denied market access. Related to these concerns are the extent to which environment-related product requirements act as a non-tariff barrier[7], the extent to which domestic environmental policies condition market access of products based on their production process characteristics opens the floodwaters for unilateral restrictions across a range of areas. Indeed, allowing trade rules to be set aside because of environmental considerations has led to charges of conditionality, as well as concern that the environmental agenda

---

6. Although concern about the negative impacts of trade liberalisation on environmental quality was a key theme of Seattle, the question of how to undertake an environmental assessment of trade agreements remains complex and contentious. For example, among the observations of an Organisation for Economic Cooperation and Development (OECD) workshop organised to examine how to assess the environmental effects of trade, it was noted that 'the art and science of environmental assessment of trade agreements are still in their early stages'. Tarasofsky (2000) in Organisation for Economic Cooperation and Development (ed.) p. 11.

7. Approximately 10-15 percent of all notifications under the Agreement on Technical Barriers to Trade (TBT) over the past six or seven years are related to the environment. Environment-related technical standards represent among the single most important area of notification under that agreement. In addition to the TBT Agreement, WTO Members regularly submit environment-related product notifications under a range of WTO agreements, including the Sanitary and Phytosanitary (SPS), Import Licensing, the Trade-Related Aspects of Intellectual Property Rights (TRIPS) and other agreements. See World Trade Organization (1997).

will lead to a slippery slope in trade policy, whereby allowances for the environment will then lead to allowances for the conditioning of market access based on human rights, labour issues, and a host of other concerns.[8]

Rather than attempting to address most of these, or indeed many of them, the following addresses two policy-policy related issues: the extent to which trade policy reform (and related market integration efforts) influences changes in environmental policy through policy harmonisation, and the limitation on policies that diverge from trade principles.

2. ENVIRONMENTAL POLICY HARMONISATION

The harmonisation of environmental policies is supported by all governments in principle, although increasingly complex to enact in practice. Indeed, the virtues of international cooperation in environmental protection have been recognised for almost a century, and represent one of the oldest areas of international law.[9] To date, roughly 185 MEAs have been adopted by governments, together with approximately 900 regional or bilateral environmental agreements.[10] In addition to work by state actors, there is also evidence of on-going cooperation by the private sector in environmental management at the international level. Examples include the on-going development of the International Standardization Organization (ISO) 14,000 environmental management series, and the adoption by the private sector of well over 50 international voluntary codes of conduct, covering all aspects of environmental policy in such diverse sectors as chemicals and agro-chemicals, transportation and commercial banking and the insurance and pension funds sector.

While such examples reflect the pivotal role of international environmental cooperation, such cooperation is rarely synonymous with the adoption of homogeneous or identical environmental policies. Indeed, MEAs set out objectives and targets that parties are required to meet, but then allow considerable discretion and flexibility as to how signatories will achieve international obligations through domestic policies. For example, under both the Montreal Protocol and the Convention on International Trade in Endangered Species of Flora and Fauna (CITES), considerable scope exists

---

8. For an excellent overview of key environmental and trade concerns, see Zaelke *et al.* (1993).
9. In 1902, the Convention for the Protection of BirdsUseful to Agriculture (Paris) was signed, and entered into force in 1908. This was followed by international conventions to protect fur seals (1911), whaling (1931), flora and fauna (1931). See Birnie and Boyle (1992).
10. See, for example, Tolba *et al.* (1992); Birnie and Boyle (1992); Hunter *et al.* (1998).

that allows members countries to adopt various domestic measures pursuant to international standards contained in the MEAs themselves. The flexibility in MEAs is likely to increase, as countries adopt a mix of domestic and international tools like emissions trading schemes in order to meet national targets for Annex 1 countries under the Kyoto Protocol of the United Nations Framework Convention on Climate Change.

Differences in approaches to similar environmental problems can be explained by obvious distinctions in ecosystems themselves – for example, differences in geographic characteristics, climatic conditions, susceptibility to long range transportation of pollutants through prevailing water or wind currents, etc. Differences in approaches are also reflected by differences in regulatory approaches within and between countries, costs and availability of technologies, access to market information and financing, differences in management cultures, the focus and effectiveness of public environmental lobbying efforts, as well as differences in the effects that non-environmental public policies – such as incentives, fiscal measures or subsidies – exert on environmental policies themselves.

Indeed, the design and implementation of environmental policies is more, rather than less, diverse. This diversity is shaped in large part by fundamental changes in the array of policy options available to address environmental problems. Indeed, most domestic environmental policies in the Organisation for Economic Cooperation and Development (OECD) countries, and increasingly in developing countries, represent a mix of more familiar command-and-control regulations, with market-based instruments and voluntary environmental initiatives.

In light of the broader range of policy options available, the direction of environmental policy is towards greater diversity and change. For example, a recent report by the United States Environmental Protection Agency goes so far as to examine how environmental regulations are subject to regulatory 'reinvention': 'In addition to achieving new efficiencies and better results, reinvention is creating an altogether new mind-set among Agency managers and staff'.[11]

Although the reinvention of environmental policy is often couched in a shift from command and control regulations (that are usually associated with fixed costs that are high, and that inhibit technological or other innovations) to market-based approaches (that are usually associated with least cost options that are inherently dynamic), this dual policy choice is actually a

---

11. United States Environmental Protection Agency, Managing for Better Environmental Results: A Two-Year Anniversary on Reinventing Environmental Protection, Washington, March, 1997. Cited in Markell (2000).

simplification of variables that go into environmental policy. Such variables include:

- Specific statutory requirements, establishing specific regulatory requirements, mandatory technologies, the use of best available technologies;
- Performance-oriented standards, which provide some flexibility in meeting quantitative targets;
- Differential standards, which can be allocated at the sub-form level, based on considerations like past environmental performance;
- Stringency, which can also be flexible within defined parameters;
- Compliance dates, with a preference for identifying long lead times in meeting target dates, to allow polluters to adjust capital and operating costs;
- Compliance assurance, based on monitoring and verification, including systematic and random inspections;
- Informational remedies, including providing information to consumers on environmental characteristics embodied or concealed in products, including through labelling and certification systems;[12]
- Market-based approaches, including subsidies, fees, penalties, permits or offsets, changes in liabilities, bonds, insurance or warranties, tax deferral or differential capital depreciation rates, as well as banking, trading and other instruments.[13]

The one area where environmental policy harmonisation is unambiguously needed from an environmental outcome perspective is in the area of environmental data. Indeed, concerted efforts at the international level involves improving environmental monitoring and improving the comparability of different environmental data sets. This represents the guiding assumption for the creation of the Intergovernmental Panel for Climate Change, the Global Environmental Monitoring System, and many other efforts to ensure comparability of diverse environmental data sets.

---

12. Recent studies suggest a growing link between some government procurement policies and environmental labelling and certification systems. While the performance of consumer-based environmental labels appears to have flattened in the latter part of the 1990s, both public and large institutional procurement policies which give preference to environmental goods and services that can be purchased at a comparable price to like goods and services, appear to be growing. Additionally, procurement policies are turning to labelled and certified goods and services, as opposed to developing stand-alone environmental criteria and verification systems. See Commission for Environmental Cooperation (1999).
13. Morgenstern (1997) p. 34.

Although advances continue in the accuracy of ground and space-based environmental monitoring, statistical surveys, modelling and time-series analysis, a recent report by the United Nations Environmental Programme (UNEP) points to the fact that

> numerous inconsistencies and shortcomings still exist. Even the straightforward mapping of such basic indicators as current GDP, water consumption and fertilizer use is difficult. In particular, little information is yet available on environmental impacts on human health and natural ecosystems, social responses and policy effectiveness. The conversion, integration and moulding of data to information is a complex process.[14]

Given the trend in environmental policies to be designed and implemented in a non-uniform manner, to address specific environmental challenges, an important difference exists between essentially homogeneous trade rules and non-uniform environmental policies. This fundamental difference continues to nurture earnest confusion in both the environmental and trade arenas.[15] That is, while uniform trade rules are applied in the same manner across countries, environmental policies rarely can be, reflecting an obvious point

---

14. United Nations Environment Programme (1999). Among the technical issues related to building comparable data sets include variations in data reporting units, definitions, the coverage of monitoring networks by geographic location, as well as time-series parameters and data measurement methods. In response to these and other technical challenges related to building comparable environmental data sets, considerable attention in international environmental policy remains focused on data comparability and harmonisation-related efforts. Extensive work is underway in strengthening environmental data, and building approaches for the comparability of data. One of the most extensive efforts underway in this area can be found in Working Group I of the Intergovernmental Panel of Climate Change, which helps coordinate national climate monitoring efforts. In the area of chemicals and pesticides, work by the OECD, the United Nations International Programme on Chemical Safety (IPCS) and other organisations focus on harmonising environmental impact assessment procedures, safety assessment procedures (including human health assessment procedures), agreements to support the sharing of assessment information, mutual recognition accords regarding the data testing, procedural harmonisation of testing methods including the development of good laboratory testing practices and certification procedures, the harmonisation of classification terminology, and the harmonisation of national labelling schemes.

15. One example of the extent of this confusion is the transference of perfectly sound principles of trade theory, like the comparative advantage of different countries to produce goods and services, into the environmental policy arena so as to argue for a comparative advantage of countries to receive environmental *bads* (commonly referred to as higher rates of pollution assimilative capacities). The problem with such generalisations is that what is clearly a useful line of reasoning for trade theory is almost entirely without relevance in the environmental arena. Clearly no country has a higher capacity either to accommodate toxic pollutants, nor to accommodate other types of irreversible environmental damages, such as the permanent loss of habitats and the extinction of species. In the latter area, extinction rates today approach the mass extinction era of 65 million years ago. See Wilson (1998).

that economic markets are not synonymous with diverse ecosystems. This difference has been summed up neatly by von Moltke (1999), who noted that trade rules resemble wholesale or uniform rules (national schedules notwithstanding), while environmental policies essentially resemble 'retail' approaches that are designed, adjusted, balanced, implemented and readjusted on an *ad hoc* basis, to address specific environmental problems under differing conditions.

In general, the WTO agreements and NAFTA confer a preference, by way of presumed compatibility, on goods and services that conform to relevant international standards. This builds on objectives set out in the GATT, including Article XXXVIII(2)(e), which calls for feasible methods 'to expand trade for the purpose of economic development, through international harmonization and adjustment of national policies and regulations, through technical and commercial standards affecting production, transportation and marketing, and through export promotion'. The two key WTO agreements that support the adoption of international standards are the Sanitary and Phytosanitary (SPS) Measures – which refer not only to standards, guidelines and recommendations of the World Health Organization (WHO)-Food and Agricultural Organization (FAO) Codex Alimentarius Commission, but also to the International Office of Epizootics and the Plant Protection Convention – and the Agreement on Technical Barriers to Trade, which contains reference to the ISO. Moreover, the WTO contains numerous other references to international standard-setting bodies; although these do not include international environmental agreements, references in the WTO include the Customs Cooperation Council, the World Intellectual Property Rights Organization (WIPO), the International Telecommunications Union as well as international air transport, marine transport and telecommunications agreements.

Although the preference does not preclude the ability of national governments to implement domestic standards that are divergent from international standards, recent WTO panels (and in particular the US-EU Beef Hormones Case) leave open the contentious question of how to allocate the burden of proof in proving that international standards are not applicable in meeting domestic policy objectives.

In light of this general preference towards international standards and organisations, concern has been raised both by the environmental interest, that trade may drive the harmonisation of environmental policies in directions that do not lead to higher environmental quality, and by free traders that the harmonisation of domestic standards may undermine legitimate differences between countries in comparative advantage.

An example of the first type is spelled out in a Report of the Standing Committee on Environment and Sustainable Development of the Canadian House of Commons. Among the key findings of that report is that despite considerable efforts by federal and sub-federal authorities towards environmental policy harmonisation, no clear or compelling environmental justification explained such efforts. Claims that harmonisation was motivated by efforts to clarify jurisdictional overlaps and the duplication of environmental regulations were, according to the Report, 'absent', and that the harmonisation agenda was 'inspired by other considerations. Of particular concern were [the views of many witnesses] that the purpose has not been driven by environmental consideration'.[16]

The following provides examples of environmental policy harmonisation propelled not by environmental considerations alone, but by trade and market-related objectives.

3.   REGIONAL ECONOMIC AND TRADE AGREEMENTS AND REGULATORY HARMONISATION: SINGLE EUROPEAN ACT

The harmonisation of national environmental policies is most pronounced in the EU. This in turn reflects the limitation on national sovereignty accepted by Member countries in pursuit of a common market, including the approximation of national laws within the context of a Community-wide common approach to environmental protection.

Although the Single European Act recognised the priority of ensuring high levels of environmental protection, this commitment is balanced against its core objectives. Although a generalisation, these objectives include support for a common market, including support for the four economic freedoms (free movement of goods, services, persons and capital); avoidance of discriminatory measures; avoidance of trade hindering or competition distorting measures; the adoption of common policies in sectors that include agriculture, transportation and energy; the harmonisation of national regulations and policies; and a constraint on domestic measures that are divergent from common policies.

Within this general approach that balances positive and negative approaches in support of the common market, Member countries have discretion to adopt domestic environmental policies. However, that discretion

---

16. Canada, Parliament, House of Commons, Standing Committee on Environment and Sustainable Development (1997).

resides within more or less clearly defined parameters, parameters which themselves continue to be narrowed.

The clearest examples of positive integration under the Single European Act is the development of Community wide environmental directives. Environmental directives cover key areas of environmental management, from articulating quantitative thresholds on emissions from specific pollutants, to biodiversity protection and other conservation-related areas. It has been noted (Ziegler, 1996) that outside directives identifying quantitative limits on toxic and non-toxic pollutants, considerable flexibility and discretionary powers exist for Members in interpreting community-wide directives, especially relating to risk assessment-related issues.

At the same time, Members are not free to adopt national environmental standards themselves if a Community-wide directive is already in place. As a pre-emptive measure against overlapping domestic policies, this provision in itself increasingly narrows the scope of new national measures, given that there are more than 200 environmental directives which cover all major aspects of environmental management in the EU.

Although the most visible expression of regulatory harmonisation, it has been noted (Ziegler, 1996) that considerable flexibility exists under environmental directives which allow Member States discretionary powers in implementation, particularly for those directives that are not based on quantitative limits on specified pollutants. Even under quantitative restrictions, Member States have some discretion in implementing best available technologies, the interpretation of risk assessment and risk management-based directives.

In addition to Community-wide directives, other measures are in place in the EU which constrain the likelihood of heterogeneous and diverging environmental policies, and support the goal of converging policies. The former Article 100 (and Article 100a) sets out disciplines intended to eliminate domestic regulations, policies and administrative rules that impede, or could impede, the economic freedoms which support the common market.

This balancing of community-wide disciplines with national sovereignty to introduce environmental (or other public policy) objectives has been examined extensively. This balancing includes the environmental objectives contained in the Single European Act (Articles 130r to 130t), coupled with the (former) Article 36 Exceptions Clause,[17] various safeguard provisions,[18]

---

17. Article 36 functions in similar manner to exception clauses under trade agreements, such as GATT Article XX, so as to allow Member States to apply domestic measures which do not conform with other Treaty obligations in exceptional circumstances related to the protection of human health or the control of pests.

and what has been seen as pivotal jurisprudence in the European Court of Justice. Two cases are widely noted: the general findings and implications of the *Cassis de Dijon* Doctrine (rule of reason),[19] and the *Danish Bottles* Case.[20]

In looking at the relationship between homogeneous Community-wide standards, adopted in part in support of underlying economic objectives, and heterogeneous domestic environmental standards, Ziegler (1996) emphasised the complex balancing that must occur. However, this balance can be seen in part against what Ziegler (1996) has characterised as 'a continuous limitation' on Article 36 exceptions, which might be viewed as tipping the balance increasingly towards harmonisation.

4. REGULATORY HARMONISATION AND NAFTA

A second example of a regional economic agreement supporting environmental policy harmonisation can be found in the NAFTA and its so-called 'environmental side agreement', the North American Agreement on Environmental Cooperation. It is worth noting that NAFTA, and its institutions, are significantly less powerful in influencing changes in national environmental regulations outside more familiar trade dispute settlement provisions. Unlike the EU, no supra-national international organisation exists within NAFTA capable of introducing common North America-wide environmental standards to replace domestic ones.

---

18. The Single European Act, Article 130r(2) states in part that 'harmonization measures ... shall include, where appropriate, a safeguard clause allowing Member States to take provisional measures, for non-economic environmental reasons, subject to Community inspection procedures'. Cited in Ziegler (1996) p. 174.

19. In 1979, in response to a previous case involving the ruling on measures that are deemed to have an equivalent effect as quantitative restrictions on imports or exports, the European Court delivered a landmark judgment referred to as the *Cassis de Dijon* Doctrine or rule of reason. The Doctrine found that in spite of potentially broad interpretations related to the difficult task of determining measures having an equivalent effect, 'disparities between national laws relating to the marketing of the products in question must be accepted in so far as those provisions may be recognized as being necessary in order to satisfy mandatory requirements relating in particular to the effectiveness of fiscal supervision, the protection of public health, the fairness of commercial transactions and the defense of the consumer'. Case 120/78, *Cassis de Dijon [1979]*, ECR 649 at 662, cited in Ziegler (1996) p. 49.

20. In decision Case 302/86 *Danish Bottles*, the European Court did not examine the objective of the Danish policy requiring the mandatory re-use of bottles covering 100 percent of the containers used. Instead, the Court noted that the aim of the policy was to reduce waste, which was a legitimate environmental objective, with determining the extent to which the specific provisions were a reasonable means of reducing waste. The Court did not examine the level of protection required under the domestic measure, including a determination of the extent to which the measure restricted trade. See Ziegler (1996) p. 82.

Nevertheless, on at least two fronts, NAFTA remains an innovative trade agreement with regards to environmental issues. First, it contains several references to environmental provisions that appear to go further than suggestions in the WTO and other trade agreements (such as the Free Trade Area of the Americas (FTAA)) to include specific references to the environment. The two most innovative areas in NAFTA in which environmental provisions are included involve trade-related investment provisions, and the clarification of trade rule inconsistencies that could arise from the use of trade measures in identified MEAs.[21]

Second, the NAFTA debate of the early 1990s led to the creation of supporting institutions designed to address a number of environmental and other issues linked to trade expansion. One of the underlying themes of these institutions was the contrast in capacities between the United States (US) and Mexico. These difficulties in the environmental arena included concern about environmental monitoring and enforcement, coupled with a fear that domestic regulations would not be enforced in order to attract foreign investment (the pollution haven theory). Of more immediate concern was the increased manufacturing output, particularly along the US-Mexican border region, as a result of the NAFTA. These institutions comprise the Integrated Environmental Plan for the Mexican-US Border Area, the Border Environment Cooperation Commission, and the North American Development Bank (NADBank), which together focus various types of

---

21. Several references to the environment are contained in the NAFTA. These include a reference in the preamble to trade being 'consistent with environmental protection and conservation', as well as the promotion of 'sustainable development' and the strengthened 'development and enforcement of environmental laws and regulations'. Such language is somewhat similar to the preambular language of the Uruguay Round's reference to 'allowing for the optimal use of the world's resources in accordance with the objective of sustainable development, seeking both to protect and preserve the environment'. References to standards provisions in the NAFTA TBT and SPS are also similar to provisions in the Uruguay Round. However, the NAFTA contains two environmental provisions which differ from the WTO or other trade rules. The first involves reference to the environment in NAFTA trade-related investment rules. Specifically, Article 1114.2 provides that: 'The Parties recognize that it is inappropriate to encourage investment by relaxing domestic health, safety, or environmental measures. Accordingly a Party should not waive or otherwise derogate from or offer to waive or otherwise derogate from such measures as an encouragement for the establishment, acquisition, expansion or retention in its territory of an investment of an investor'.
The second provision, which goes to the heart of the debate between MEAs and trade rules, is contained in NAFTA Article 104. The Article provides that in the event of an inconsistency between NAFTA and the application of trade measures in three MEAs cited in an annex (CITES, the Montreal Protocol and the Basel Convention), the obligations of a party to the MEA 'shall prevail to the extent of the inconsistency, provided that where a Party has a choice among equally effective and reasonably available means of complying with such obligations, the Party chooses the alternative that is least inconsistent with the other provisions of [NAFTA]'.

technical, regulatory, environmental monitoring and financial support (of up to US$2 billion) along the border area.

In addition to these institutions, the North American Agreement on Environmental Cooperation (NAAEC) was created as a kind of side agreement to the NAFTA, with a broad mandate to address various trade-related environmental issues. Several functions are mandated in the Agreement – ranging from the protection of endangered species to the development of ecologically sensitive national accounts. Yet the operational mandate of the NAAEC is found in its Article 10(6):

> The Council shall cooperate with the NAFTA Free Trade Commission to achieve the environmental goals and objectives of the NAFTA by:
> (a) acting as a point of inquiry and receipt for comments from non-governmental organizations and persons concerning those goals and objectives;
> (b) providing assistance in consultations under Article 1114 of the NAFTA where a Party considers that another Party is waiving or derogating from, or offering to waive or otherwise derogate from, an environmental measure as an encouragement to establish, acquire, expand or retain an investment of an investor, with a view to avoiding any such encouragement;
> (c) contributing to the prevention or resolution of environment-related trade disputes by:
> (i) seeking to avoid disputes between the Parties;
> (ii) making recommendations to the Free Trade Commission with respect to the avoidance of such disputes, and
> (iii) identifying experts able to provide information or technical advice to NAFTA committees, working groups and other NAFTA bodies;
> (d) considering on an on-going basis the environmental effects of the NAFTA; and
> (e) otherwise assisting the Free Trade Commission in environment-related matters.

Despite the provisions of Article 10(6) – including the relatively clear instructions that the Council of the NAAEC (comprised of the three environment ministers of Canada, Mexico and the US) 'shall cooperate' with the NAFTA Free Trade Commission (NAFTA FTC) – it is worth noting that not one single meeting has ever been held between the NAFTA FTC and the Environmental Council, despite efforts from at least three prominent Canadian environmental groups to initiate action under Article 10(6) provisions to address environment-related trade disputes underway under the NAFTA Chapter 11 Agreement on Trade-Related Investment.[22]

While institutional cooperation between the FTC and its environmental side agreement remains non-existent, work within various FTC committees and technical working groups continues in addressing various aspects of environmental policy harmonisation. This work has largely centred upon the promotion of mutual recognition and standards equivalence efforts involving environmental, as well as food safety measures. Examples of harmonisation-related activities include:

- In the NAFTA Committee on SPS Measures, among the recommended priority areas of actions are coordinating pesticides regulatory frameworks for the protection of human, animal and plant life;
- The NAFTA SPS Technical Working Groups of NAFTA have worked on 'collaboration on labeling policy [which has] promoted a common NAFTA position in CODEX committees' as well as on issues related to mutual recognition and equivalency;
- In the NAFTA Standards Related Committee, the recommended actions include conformity assessment and the examination of ways to streamline the procedures and reduce costs associated with demonstrating product conformity, including the possibility of negotiating agreements for the mutual recognition of any Party's conformity assessment procedures;
- In the Automotive Standards Council, the work programme includes making national standards-related measures for automotive goods, including emission standards. In addition, the Council is directed to follow work towards the development of global emission standards for automobiles, including under the United Nations ECE.

---

22. Responding to letters from the Sierra Club of Canada, Greenpeace Canada, the Council of Canadians and the Canadian Labor Congress involving at least two investor-state NAFTA Chapter 11 disputes involving S.D. Meyers and Methanex Corporation, the Council suggested that it could not, in most instances serve as a 'point of public inquiry' and referred to work underway under the Council's 10 (6) Environment and Trade Officials meeting. A report of that Group noted that 'the implementation of the NAFTA are the responsibility of the FTC, and the discussions concerning the implementation of the NAAEC are the responsibility of the CEC'. In addition to delineating clearly the NAFTA from the NAAEC, the report noted that with regards to the Council acting as a 'point of inquiry', 'all inquiries would require an acknowledgement, [while] some might fall solely within the mandate and competency of the Council, some might fall solely within the mandate and competency of the NAFTA Free Trade Commission, and some might fall within the mandate and competency of both the Council and the FTC'. To date, the NAAEC has not been involved in any matters relating to the FTC, including environment-based trade disputes. See Council of Canadians (1999).

While efforts relating to environmental policy harmonisation are underway in the NAFTA, work by the NAAEC itself has been more modest, and has concentrated on improving the comparability of environmental monitoring and data collection efforts. Two examples, which together comprise the bulk of the NAAEC's budget and work, underline the efforts of environmental policy itself towards improving environmental data comparability:

1. *Pollutant Release and Transfer Registrar* initiates work towards the comparability of environmental data for individual chemicals from the manufacturing sector, thereby making comparable industrial chemical classifications for specific toxic chemicals. Toxic chemicals included in the harmonised data reporting system of the US and Canada (Mexico has yet to report any emissions and transfers within the harmonised system), include benzene, chloromethane, bichloromethane, ethyl benzene and methenal. Results of data harmonisation are reported in the *Taking Stock*[23] publication of the Commission for Environmental Cooperation.

2. The *Sound Management of Chemicals* which continues to work on improving the management of several toxic chemicals:

- Updating of databases on 12 groups of persistent organic pollutants, including PCBs, dioxins, furons, DDT and endrin;
- Developing common management procedures covering the production, use and trade in toxic chemicals;
- Identifying and evaluating substances for phase out;
- Sampling, analysis and exposure assessments;
- Coordinating research on health and environmental risks;
- Assessing technology to promote technology transfer.

5.   INTERNATIONAL ENVIRONMENTAL AGREEMENTS

The third and final area examined here in which trade policy is initiating reforms in environmental policy can be found in MEAs.

As noted, the WTO and other trade rules confer a preference on countries that adopt relevant international standards by way of presumed comparability. Since 1991, MEAs have been the source of discussion within the GATT and the WTO Committee on Trade and Environment. The major

---

23. Commission for Environmental Cooperation (2000).

emphasis of those discussions has largely revolved around the extent to which different kinds of trade measures contained in MEAs may or may not be compatible with WTO rules. Since no actual case has yet to arise involving the WTO and an MEA, the debate has remained entirely hypothetical. Unfortunately, almost no attention has been paid to the important work that MEAs play in establishing, within their operational frameworks, international standards. Put another way, while the WTO would appear to convey a general preference for international standards developed for instance through the ISO, that same courtesy does not appear to be extended to various international product and performance standards developed under the respective MEA legal regimes. Rather than extending the same kind of presumed compatability of ISO or CODEX Alimentarius standards to MEA-developed standards, much of the WTO debate has centred (at least until 1996 or 1997) on hypothetical incompatibilities.

One example of the international standards developed within MEAs is the on-going technical classification work underway in the Basel Convention on the Transboundary Movement of Hazardous Wastes of different types of hazardous wastes. Since 1995, subsidiary bodies to the Convention have elaborated the hazardous and non-hazardous waste classification list, which in turn clarifies the reach of various operational provisions in the Convention, including the scope of the Basel ban. Another example of international standard-setting work with MEAs, is the on-going work under CITES towards the classification of species within different appendices, reflecting the extent to which those species are partially or fully endangered. Similarly, the Montreal Protocol on the Control of Substances that Deplete the Ozone Layer has, since 1987, classified specific ozone-depleting chemicals that fall under reduction and elimination schedules of the Protocol.

In support of classification activities of these MEAs, arguably their most important *operational* aspect revolves around notification provisions based on the principles of transparency. For example, under CITES, in support of species classification into one of the three appendices, parties are required to issue import and/or export permits, depending on the degree of trade-induced species risk identified in the classification exercise. Similarly, since 1997, the Montreal Protocol requires Parties to issue import and export licences covering trade between parties in the list of ozone-depleting substances. The Basel Convention was originally founded on a system of Prior Informed Notification and Prior Informed Consent for trade between parties in categories of hazardous wastes covered under the original terms of the agreement, as it was negotiated in March, 1989.

Given the emphasis of these MEAs on setting international standards supported by notification provisions, it is surprising that the WTO Committee on Trade and Environment has failed to examine the extent to which international standards contained in MEAs are deemed to be 'relevant' international standards to the trading system. Equally surprising has been the indifference of the Committee to examine ways in which the over 120 WTO notification systems could support the notification provisions that form the operational backbone of MEAs, despite the duplication of several notifications systems. In short, the WTO and MEAs have not examined ways in which their current operations could be supported.

Instead, for seven years, discussions in the WTO have revolved around a series of *hypothetical questions* about the rule inconsistency between MEAs and the WTO, and in what body a legal dispute – should it arise – ought to be heard. Although no single legal dispute has yet arisen between an MEA and the WTO, or for that matter within an MEA itself, this has hardly provided comfort to anyone about the unwelcome consequences of a legal dispute erupting between two international legal regimes.[24]

Concern about the trade hindering nature of MEAs has been the source of long discussions in the WTO, and has focused on two types of trade measures contained in MEAs: trade measures applied between parties to an MEA (including quotas and bans), and trade restrictions that prohibit trade between parties and non-parties to an MEA.

Examples include the use of quotas in CITES to control trade in defined specimens of species between parties; the suspension of trading rights in a clearly defined group of 'products' between parties, if a party fails to conform to the environmental management and administrative requirements contained in the agreements; and the prohibition in all trade between parties and non-parties to an agreement, on the assumption that such trade could

---

24. Although formal dispute settlements have not taken place under the provisions of any international environmental agreement, various procedures have been implemented to address non-compliance by particular parties to meet specific obligations in different agreements. For example, non-compliance procedures have been invoked in the Montreal Protocol in response to repeated infractions from Russia in failing to comply with the reduction of ozone-depleting substances like CFCs and HCFCs, whereby Russia's position as a Party was suspended. However, it has been noted that responses within international environmental agreements to non-compliance significantly differ from formal trade arbitration: in the case of Russia's non-compliance in meeting its obligations under the Montreal Protocol, additional financing was provided through the Global Environmental Facility in order to bolster domestic capacities to meet such obligations. Victor *et al.* (1998) notes that examples like this demonstrate that 'non-compliance is a problem to be solved, and not an action to be punished'.

offset the collective actions of parties to address a common environmental threat (free riders).[25]

Although this question of policy compatibility between the WTO and MEAs remains unresolved, this irresolution has itself acted as a catalyst towards policy reforms within more recent MEA negotiations. Put another way, the unresolved nature of the WTO-MEA debate has limited the options available in new MEAs so as to foreclose measures that could be deemed inconsistent with WTO rules. That is, the trade-environment debate at the international level has led to the same type of continuous limitation on environmental policies that *might* be divergent from trade rules.

The most visible expression of this limitation discipline can be found not only in a discarding of the less blunt trade instruments contained in CITES, the Basel Convention and the Montreal Protocol outside of notification provisions, but in the inclusion of a WTO supremacy or legal savings clause of some form in nearly all new MEA negotiations.

Although difficult to pinpoint exactly when the shift in MEA negotiations occurred, an early indication of action to limit the scope of potentially trade inconsistent measures in MEAs was in the failed negotiations to launch an international forestry convention, under the auspices of the now defunct United Nations Intergovernmental Panel on Forests (IPF). Among the resolutions related to trade in forest products were the following provisions:

> 119.(a) Urged countries to remove all unilateral measures to the extent that they are inconsistent with international agreements.
>
> (b) Requested countries to undertake measures for improving market access for forest goods and services, including the reduction of tariff and non-tariff barriers to trade in accordance with existing international obligations and commitments, and in this context to promote a mutually supportive relationship between environment and trade in forest goods and services, to avoid conflict between measures which affect trade in forest goods and services and existing international obligations.

In addition to general obligations, the IPF negotiations stumbled over the role of forestry labelling and certification measures, and how such mechanisms would relate to WTO obligations in general, and to TBT-obligations in particular.[26]

---

25. An extensive body of literature exists on this unresolved issue of the WTO and MEAs. See for example United Nations Environment Programme (1999) and Organisation for Economic Cooperation and Development (1998).
26. For example, '122.(b) Urged countries to support the application to certification schemes of such concepts as:
   (i) Managers and operators;

The WTO savings clause has found its way, in varying nuances, into both the international negotiations towards a Convention on Prior Informed Consent (PIC) for Certain Hazardous Chemicals and Pesticides in International Trade, as well as the draft Convention on Persistent Organic Pollutants (POPs). In the latter draft, the following language has been inserted in response to concerns about possible inconsistencies between MEA provisions and WTO rules: 'The Provisions of this Convention shall not affect the rights and obligations of any Party deriving from any existing international agreement'.[27]

The final example of the attempted clarification of WTO rules and MEAs is found in the Cartegena Protocol on Biosafety. What is most interesting about the preambular language in the Protocol is that it appears to extend with one hand, by way of the WTO savings clause, and then appears to withdraw with the other. That is, the provision that 'this Protocol shall not be interpreted as implying a change in the rights and obligations of a Party under any existing international agreement', is balanced, or offset as the case might prove to be, by the following: 'the above recital is not intended to subordinate this Protocol to other international agreements'.

Taken together, these two clauses might suggest the limits on environmental policy by trade rules which have been marginally pushed back because of the Seattle debate. (Indeed, as Cosbey *et al.* (2000) has recently noted, one of the reasons the Biosafety Protocol surprised almost everyone during the January 2000 negotiations in Montreal was, in part, because of the sobering message to the trade community from the Seattle demonstrations.)[28]

At the same time, this balance in language provides scant clue as to how a WTO dispute panel – which is the likely forum in which a formal dispute involving trade in genetically modified organisms will be heard – might weigh any further conditioning upon the prescribed trade in genetically modified organisms by reference to the pivoting environmental principle of the Protocol – i.e., the precautionary principle. And indeed, it has been pointed out that asking the WTO to arbitrate a duel of scientific arguments ultimately represents a 'disservice' to the WTO itself.[29]

(ii) Credibility;
(iii) Participation that seeks to involve all interested parties, including local communities;
(iv) Sustainable forest management;
(v) Transparency'.
27. Report of the Intergovernmental Negotiating Committee for an International Legally Binding Instrument for Implementing International Action on Certain Persistent Organic Pollutants on the Work of its Third Session (1999).
28. Cosbey and Burgiel, (2000). Cosbey notes: 'The final text does not settle how the Protocol relates to the WTO and other international agreements. In fact it looks like a conflict postponed, rather than a conflict avoided'.
29. Ward (2000).

6.   CONCLUSION

Although examples of harmonisation and the narrowing of diverging policy choices based on trade policy preferences are noted, this chapter does not provide evidence as to whether trade-related environmental policy reforms lead to better environmental protection policies. Given that they are motivated by trade-related concerns, one assumes that harmonisation and policy limitation lead to better trade policy, either by way of reducing technical barriers to trade, or by eliminating costly legal conflicts between the WTO and MEAs.

What harmonisation is doing to environmental policies remains unclear. However, the 1997 Report of the Parliamentary Subcommittee of Canada on the Environment and Sustainable Development suggests that non-environmental priorities have driven regulatory harmonisation in Canada, which have included the promotion of internal and international trade obligations. Among the key observations of that Report is that the harmonisation of environmental policies within Canada raised a 'potential risk of injury to the quality of the environment'.

Given the importance civil society places on trade and environment issues in the Seattle context, it is worth asking why surprisingly few organisations seem to have paid attention to the important policy reforms underway within environmental policy itself.[30]

The NAFTA trade and environment debate is a useful reference point in this regard. A central concern expressed by several environmental organisations, prior to and during the NAFTA negotiations between 1991 and 1993, revolved around the potentially constraining effects of NAFTA rules on domestic environmental, human health and food safety laws.

Indeed, responding to concerns about the potentially negative regulatory impacts of NAFTA became *the* predominant focus of both the Canadian and US governments' environmental reviews of NAFTA. For example, Canada's environmental review of NAFTA refers to 'the concern frequently mentioned by environmental organizations, and by individual Canadians ... that the NAFTA might require "standards harmonization", that is, making Canada/US

---

30. The NGO community around the world appears to be increasingly involved in the WTO debate. Before Seattle, roughly 1,500 environmental, developmental, human rights, anti-poverty, food security, community rights, indigenous peoples and other groups signed on to a Friends of the Earth Statement, calling for a moratorium on the launching of a new round, until a list of concerns were met. This WTO debate conforms to an observed pattern of NGO activism, which concentrates far more on influencing new negotiations while they are underway, and far less on the implementation of environmental policies that already exist. See Victor *et al.* (1998).

standards the same'.[31] Similarly, the US NAFTA review concentrated on countering concerns that NAFTA might undermine key domestic environmental regulations, including the Clean Air Act, Marine Mammal Protection Act and Endangered Species Act.[32]

Six years after governments responded to such concerns – largely by way of reassurances that no trade panels were likely to alter domestic environmental, public health or food safety laws – more than ten NAFTA Working Groups and Committees convened under the FTC have identified numerous environmental, public health and food safety issues potentially ripe for harmonisation-related efforts by the three NAFTA parties. Such harmonisation work includes mutual recognition, standards equivalency work, labelling, risk assessment and other areas of work.

It should come as no surprise that such work is underway by a trade organisation (the NAFTA FTC), given the preference trade policy places on harmonisation. However, what is surprising is that such work has attracted virtually no attention from the environmental groups who had six years earlier concentrated their concerns precisely on NAFTA-propelled regulatory harmonisation.[33]

One explanation for the absence of scrutiny by environmental groups may be found in a study by Victor and Raustiala (1998) which identifies the focus

---

31. Canada, Government (1992) p. 18.
32. United States of America, Government (1993) p. 92 notes that much of the 'concern about NAFTA and the environment has focused on whether NAFTA will undermine the ability of the U.S. government and the states to establish and enforce their environmental, health and safety laws'. Similarly, the US environmental review of the Uruguay Round noted concerns among environmental groups that 'rules of the Uruguay Round on technical barriers to trade (TBT) and sanitary and phytosanitary (S&P) measures could impinge on U.S. sovereignty by restricting U.S. ability to maintain or strengthen U.S. environmental or product safety laws'. Government of the United States of America (1994), p. 98. In addition to concerns about a downwards harmonisation of domestic laws, NAFTA-related environmental concerns raised by NGOs also centred on adverse scale effects along the US-Mexican border region. Audley (1997) has identified three groupings of concerns: 'financial resources to improve enforcement and monitoring of environmental laws, especially within the border region; assessing the potential impact on the Mexico-border region caused by increased trade; direct integration of some environmental provisions into the trade agreement itself'. For an excellent description of different positions of environmental NGOs during the NAFTA negotiations, and how those positions affected the outcome of negotiations, see Audley (1997).
33. There are a few environmental organisations that continue to monitor NAFTA. However, the focus of such work has not been on the FTC in its work on harmonisation, but rather on several environment-related NAFTA Chapter 11 cases, in which compensation has been sought from operators of foreign companies, under arguments that regulatory changes constitute expropriation. Work in this area has been led by Christine Elwell of the Sierra Club of Canada, and by the International Institute of Sustainable Development. More generally, advocacy groups, such as Washington-based Public Citizen, continue to give the NAFTA low marks because of the erosion of US sovereignty.

at the international level of environmental groups. Most environmental groups concentrate efforts on influencing current negotiations leading to new agreements (or amendments to existing agreements), and very little attention given to the implementation of commitments contained in agreements. While environmental groups were 'increasingly vocal during negotiations to form new legal instruments, ... they have been surprisingly inactive during the implementation process',[34] while, by contrast, industry has been much more involved in technical work related to implementation.

Different reasons may (thus) explain the absence of environmental NGOs in NAFTA – harmonisation-related work in the NAFTA is itself surprisingly opaque compared to the WTO, with FTC meetings closed to the public although industry representatives have been invited to sector specific working groups. The NAFTA is a closed trade agreement, and not likely to be reopened to negotiations. Given the scarcity of resources and technical information and expertise, coupled with the stronger bargaining power of concentrating efforts on new negotiations as opposed to technical implementation, the NGO community seems to have shifted its sights on largely process-related issues of the WTO. Foremost among these is the demand for increased transparency and public participation in that organisation.

Whether the demands of civil society to reform the WTO will lead to a shift in the pace or direction of harmonisation reforms and the WTO savings clause, remains to be seen. However, given the deterioration of environmental quality, the focus of so many NGOs on WTO reforms as a means to secure higher environmental protection seems, at best, to be a circuitous route.

---

34. By contrast, Victor *et al.* (1998) suggest that industry is much more engaged in the implementation of actual environmental commitments at the international level: 'Active participation by industry and other targets of regulations often makes the implementation process more effective: the regulated targets typically have the best information on feasibility and costs, and their inclusion might give them a larger stake in the success of the regulation. "Regulatory capture", a frequently cited fear of target participation, has not been widespread ... Contrary to conventional wisdom, we find that it is rare for [environmental advocacy] groups to serve as "watchdogs" to verify that nations have implemented their international commitments [under MEAs]. This inactivity reflects the fact that few groups devote resources needed to build expertise and gather information to enable them to perform such functions during the implementation process'.

REFERENCES

Audley, John J. (1997), *Green Politics and Global Trade: NAFTA and the Future of Environmental Politics,* Washington, DC, US: Georgetown University Press.

Birnie, Patricia W. and Alan E. Boyle (1992), *International Law and the Environment,* 2nd edn, Oxford, UK: Clarendon Press.

Canada, Government (1992), *NAFTA: Canadian Environmental Review,* Ottawa, Canada: Government of Canada.

Canada, Parliament, House of Commons, Standing Committee on Environment and Sustainable Development (1997), 'Harmonization and Environmental Protection: An Analysis of the Harmonization Initiative of the Canadian Council of Ministers of the Environment: Report', Ottawa, Canada: The Committee.

Commission for Environmental Cooperation (2000), *Supporting Green Markets: An Overview of Environmental Labeling, Certification and Procurement Policies in Canada, Mexico and the United States,* Montreal, Canada: Commission for Environmental Cooperation.

Cosbey, Aaron and Stas Burgiel (2000), 'The Cartegena Protocol on Biosafety: An Analysis of Results', draft, Winnipeg, Canada: International Institute for Sustainable Development

Council of Canadians (1999), 'Progress Report to the CEC Council on the Meetings of Environment and Trade Officials to Discuss Article 10(6) of the NAAEC', Ottawa, Canada: Council of Canadians.

Esty, Daniel C. (1994), *Greening the GATT,* Washington, US: Institute for International Economics.

Hunter, David, James Salzman and Durwood Zaelke (1998), *International Environmental Law and Policy,* University Casebook Series, New York: Foundation Press.

Markell, David L. (2000), 'The Role of Deterrence-Based Enforcement in a "Reinvented" State/Federal Relationship: The Divide Between Theory and Reality', *The Harvard Environmental Law Review,* **24**(1), 1-114.

Morgenstern, Richard D. (1997), 'Conducting an Economic Analysis', in Richard D. Morgenstern (ed.), *Economic Analyses at EPA: Assessing Regulatory Impact,* Washington, DC, US: Resources for the Future.

Organisation for Economic Cooperation and Development (1998), *The Use of Trade Measures in Multilateral Environmental Agreements,* Paris, France: Organisation for Economic Cooperation and Development.

Report of the Intergovernmental Negotiating Committee for an International Legally Binding Instrument for Implementing International Action on Certain Persistent Organic Pollutants on the Work of its Third Session, Annex II, art. N *bis,* Geneva, 6-11 September, 1999, UNEP/POPS/INC.3.4

Stevens Wallace, Adagia and Milton J. Bates (eds) (1999), *Opus Posthumous,* New York: Alfred A. Knopf.

Tarasofsky, Richard (2000) 'Report of the Workshop Methodologies for Environmental Assessments of Trade Liberalization Agreements', in Organisation for Economic Cooperation and Development (ed.), *Assessing the Environmental Effects of Trade Liberalization Agreements,* Paris, France: Organisation for Economic Cooperation and Development, pp. 11-20.

Tolba, Mostafa K. and Osama A. El-Kholy in association with E. El-Hinnawi (eds) (1992), *The World Environment 1972-1992: Two Decades of Challenge,* London,

UK; New York, US: Chapman and Hall on behalf of the United Nations Environment Programme.

United Nations Environment Programme (1999), *Global Environmental Outlook 2*, London, UK: UNEP Earthscan Publications Ltd.

United States of America, Government (1993), *The NAFTA: Report of Environmental Issues,* Washington, DC, US: Executive Office of the President.

United States Trade Representative (1994), *The GATT Uruguay Round Agreements: Report on Environmental Issues*, Washington, DC, US: Office of the United States Trade Representative.

Vaughan, Scott and Ali Dehlavi (1998), *Policy Effectiveness and Multilateral Environment Agreements*, Geneva, Switzerland: United Nations Environment Programme.

Victor, David G., Kal Raustiala and Eugene B. Skolnikoff (eds) (1998), *The Implementation and Effectiveness of International Environmental Commitments: Theory and Practice*, Laxenburg, Austria: International Institute for Applied Systems Analysis, Cambridge, MA, US: MIT Press.

von Moltke, Konrad (1999), 'Presentation to the WTO High Level Symposium on Trade and Sustainable Development', Geneva, March.

Ward, Halina (2000), 'WTO Rules and the Application of the Precautionary Principle', in *Bridges,* Year 4, No.1, 15-16.

Wilson, Edward, O. (1998), *Consilience: The Unity of Knowledge*, New York: Alfred A. Knopf.

World Trade Organization (1997), *Environment-Related Notifications, W/32*, Geneva, Switzerland: World Trade Organization.

Zaelke, Durwood, Paul Orbuch and Robert F. Housman (eds) (1993), *Trade and the Environment: Law, Economics and Policy*, Washington, DC, US: Island Press.

Ziegler, Andreas R. (1996), *Trade and Environmental Law in the European Community,* Oxford, UK: Clarendon Press; New York, US: Oxford University Press.

6. The Relationship Between International Trade Policy and Competition Policy

Edward M. Graham

1. INTRODUCTION

At the ministerial meeting held in Singapore in December of 1998, authorisation was given for the creation of a Working Group on Trade and Competition Policy within the World Trade Organization (WTO). This Working Group served to formalise calls for investigation of how competition policy might interact with international trade policy, calls that had originated within the European Union (EU)[1] but had largely been rejected by certain other key WTO Members, notably the United States (US). The mandate of the Working Group was quite constrained. Reflecting the European interest, the public Declaration issued at the conclusion of the meeting indicated that the goal of the Working Group was 'to study issues raised by Members (of the WTO) relating to the interaction between trade and competition policy, including anti-competitive practices, in order to identify any areas that may merit further consideration in the WTO framework'.

However, reflecting US reservations about the exercise, a press release issued by the WTO at the conclusion of this meeting indicated: 'the issue is not whether the WTO should negotiate rules in this area but whether it should initiate an exploratory or analytical work programme to identify areas requiring further attention in the WTO framework'.

In other words, the Working Group was meant to be engaged in an exercise that might (or might not) lead to the launching of a formal 'work programme', where such a work programme, if launched, would then not

---

1. Formerly the European Economic Community. In this chapter EU refers to either the current European Union or to the predecessor, the European Economic Community.

necessarily lead to an action agenda. The work of the Working Group was thus meant to be limited to a preliminary investigation to determine whether a full-blown investigation was warranted and thus was a preliminary exercise to a preliminary exercise. The reader could be forgiven for concluding that the Group's mandate therefore was, in effect, to do very little. And, indeed, this was a mandate that over the next three years indeed would be fulfilled. The Group's mandate (and existence) was set to end with the WTO ministerial meeting to be held in Seattle in November 1999, at which time the Group was to report to trade ministers with recommendations as to what, if anything, might be done next.

The Seattle meeting however failed to resolve whether there would be any further work in the area of Trade and Competition Policy. Indeed, as is well known, demonstrators opposed to the WTO succeeded in disrupting the meeting to the point where the official participants failed to resolve anything whatsoever. Prior to the meeting, there had been widespread anticipation that the outcome would be the launching of a new round of multilateral trade negotiations. The mission of such a round would have been largely to complete tasks that had been left unfinished at the conclusion of the Uruguay Round that had established the WTO some five years earlier but had left a number of issues unresolved. However, a new round might also have addressed a number of so-called 'new issues' – ones that had not been addressed at all during the Uruguay Round –including trade and competition policy.

Indeed, during the months prior to the Seattle meeting, senior officials of the EU once again cautiously endorsed further work in this area, joined by some other key countries such as Japan. The EU did not, however, suggest that the negotiation of new rules be undertaken; thus any further work probably would have remained in the domain of exploration. Once again, however, the US made known its opposition to further work in this area. Indeed, the preference of the US was, according to some persons contacted by this author who were involved in preparatory work for the Seattle meeting (but who have asked not to be identified), was that the issue be dropped altogether, i.e., that the working group be disbanded and that there be not even further investigative work. In the late spring of 2000, however, there were indications that the US would not stick to this position but rather would be somewhat more flexible on the issue of the future of competition policy within the WTO.

In the meantime, one of the main agreements concluded during the Uruguay Round was the General Agreement on Trade and Services (GATS) and certain of the provisions of this agreement have the effect (or potential effect) of putting elements of competition policy into the WTO, or at least with respect to those activities covered by GATS. This issue is discussed further in the final section of this chapter.

As of the time of this writing (July, 2000), there has been no resolution of the impasse that emerged in Seattle. Whether competition policy would be on the future trade agenda, and in what form, thus remains an unsettled issue.

In light of this development, this chapter endeavours to examine what is the relationship between trade policy and competition policy. It is concluded (section 2) that the substantive goals of these two policies – or at least when trade policy acts further to open markets to imports (and duly noting that some aspects of trade policy accomplish the opposite!) – are largely the same. However, the procedural aspects of the two sets of policies are greatly different (section 3), and one consequence of the differences is that whereas nations' trade policies must conform in large measure to internationally-agreed upon standards, the same cannot be said for competition policies. Thus, competition policies as actually implemented by nations vary substantially from jurisdiction to jurisdiction and, indeed, differences in these policies can lead to inconsistent outcomes. In the light of trends towards globalisation – i.e., interdependencies among the national economies of the world and multi-nationalisation of business activities – these inconsistencies are likely to grow in number and importance. Furthermore, the costs and conflicts associated with these inconsistencies are likely to grow. Whether this calls for some formal linkage of trade and competition policies or for some other form of action on the multilateral front, for example, development of international standards for competition policy, is explored in the final section (section 5) of this chapter.[2]

2.   ARE THE GOALS OF LIBERAL TRADE AND COMPETITION POLICIES THE SAME?

To answer the question posed above, it is of course necessary to ask what the goals of the two sets of policies are. Doing so, it becomes clear that, from an economic perspective, the goals of both sets of policies are in fact one and the same, notably to increase consumer welfare via enhancement of efficiency. But, as little as twenty years ago, most economists would have argued that

---

2.   The focus of this chapter thus is largely on what could be termed the 'cross-border aspects of competition policy' rather than 'competition aspects of international trade policy'. This latter is not a null set, for example, it can be (and is) argued that some elements of trade policy can be highly anti-competitive in terms of the impact of their application. Antidumping, for example, is often mentioned in this regard. These elements warrant mention in their own right. See for example, Lipstein (1997). However, they are not the subject of this chapter.

the routes to achieving this enhancement via competition or trade policies were substantially different. Efficiency gains via trade liberalisation were seen largely to be achieved via realisation of comparative advantage as determined by relative factor endowments. These would result even if the market both before and after trade liberalisation were competitive; indeed, most models of the gains from trade assumed competitive markets for both inputs and outputs. By contrast, efficiency gains through application of competition policy were seen to be realised via elimination of dead-weight losses created by monopolisation of markets by a single seller, or a group of sellers acting collusively.[3] In both cases the outcome entailed better use of resources in the short run. Also, the gains were of a 'one shot' variety, i.e., the gains would occur in a single burst resulting from resource reallocation enabled by the policy change. However, the precise means by which the outcome was created were quite different, one resulting from a different mix of output given competitive markets as a precondition, the other resulting from a different mix of output given changes in the structure of markets and the conduct of sellers in those markets.

Current thinking has evolved away from seeing gains from either trade liberalisation or from moving from less to more effective competition within markets as 'one shot' (i.e., static) in nature. The changed thinking is based on recognition that the main driver of efficiency gains in the medium to long run is not the reallocation of resources in a static sense but rather the enhancement of total factor productivity (generally thought itself to be driven by technological progress). Correspondingly, most of the potential gains from either trade liberalisation or the creation of more competition within markets are now seen as deriving from increased rates of total factor productivity increase, rather than from better static allocation of resources.

The changed thinking in turn leads to a convergence of the goals of liberal trade policy and competition policy. To put it rather simply, it is now accepted by most economists that more competition in markets, under many circumstances at least, fulfils a necessary condition for more rapid total factor productivity increases. This is because firms, when competing with one another, will use gains in efficiency (in practical terms, cost reductions or creation of improved products) as a competitive weapon. Faced with effective competition, firms that successfully implement efficiency gains faster than their rivals will prosper; those that fall behind their rivals will not.

---

3. Or, if the sellers were small in number but did not behave collusively, via entry of new sellers who would drive a Cournot equilibrium price and output closer to a competitive outcome.

This thinking is to some extent in conflict with the notion, commonly associated with Joseph Schumpeter, that appropriability of returns to research and development require that in order to be innovative, a firm must have market power. To be sure, if competition is highly fragmented and diffusion of new technologies from innovating firms to rival firms is very rapid, firms might indeed be deterred from investing in research and development at rates necessary to maintain socially desirable rates of total factor productivity increases. And indeed, in sectors where the second of these considerations (rapid diffusion of technology to rivals) figures importantly, for example, in pharmaceuticals, strong intellectual property protection, giving an innovating firm a limited monopoly right over the commercial exploitation of a new technology, might be necessary to ensure that returns to innovation indeed are appropriated by innovator firms. However, in many other technologically advanced sectors, diffusion of technology is generally not so rapid that the Schumpeterian 'appropriability dilemma' poses a significant practical barrier to innovation. For example, in the semiconductor industry, where there is much capability among firms to imitate rival firms' technology, the rate of technological progress is nonetheless rapid. This seems to be due in large part to lags – between first application of a new technology and imitation of that technology – being sufficiently great that adequate returns on innovation can be realised by 'first mover' firms.[4]

In this light, trade liberalisation (and its 'close twin' foreign direct investment liberalisation) and measures to increase domestic competition in markets can be seen to accomplish almost the same end. The former serves to introduce into markets new sellers that originate from outside a nation, whereas the latter serves to enlarge the number of competing sellers that originate from within the nation. Arguably, what is important in either case is the contestability of the market, i.e., whether or not new entrants, irrespective of national origin, can enter a market if incumbent sellers become complacent and do not match the efficiency of the new entrants. Incumbents who do not wish to compete with new entrants might seek to create entry barriers, including measures at the border to discourage entry by 'foreign' firms and regulatory measures that are biased in favour of incumbent firms. But entry barriers can be created as well by strictly 'private' measures such as restriction of access to distribution and retailing facilities without which potential new entrants cannot succeed.[5] Competition policy, then, is all about

---

4. See, for example, Scherer (1999).
5. Control of such facilities can deter block entry if creation of new facilities entails a large sunk cost that creates a significant 'wedge' between marginal cost of delivering the product to market and the average cost of doing so.

removing such entry barriers to as great an extent as possible. Trade policy, in this context, becomes little more than an adjunct of competition policy, i.e., trade policy is largely concerned specifically about those border measures that might impede market contestability.

This 'new thinking' does not entirely replace 'old thinking' about the efficiency gains from elimination of monopolistic dead-weight loss or realisation of neo-classical comparative advantage, of course. Indeed, there is doubtlessly much static gain yet to be realised, for example, from further liberalisation of textile and apparel trade so that countries that have latent comparative advantage in sewn goods deriving from low prices of semiskilled labour relative to other factor prices can realise this advantage and consumers can benefit therefrom. But for many products and services, and most especially for those associated with the so-called 'new economy' (i.e., most goods and services embodying information technology or biotechnology), most of the potential unrealised gains are dynamic in nature, i.e., associated with increased rates of total factor productivity enhancement. Thus, for example, new initiatives announced in Europe in late March 2000, among other things, were aimed at increased rates of creation and use of information technologies to be achieved in large measure via further deregulation and demonopolization of the telecommunications sector.[6] The main objective was not so much elimination of static dead-weight losses associated with telecommunications monopolies, but rather realisation of faster rates of technological improvement, i.e., faster rates of increase of total factor productivity. Given this, liberalisation of 'trade policy' (including, as a subset of trade policy, policy towards direct investment) could be seen as an integral part of the main objective.

3. THE PROCESSES BY WHICH TRADE POLICY AND COMPETITION POLICY ARE IMPLEMENTED ARE GREATLY DIFFERENT

If competition and trade policy serve the same long-run economic goal, the processes by which they do so could not be more different. Let us start with trade policy. In this domain, economic logic suggests that, except perhaps under very special circumstances, it is in the interests of any nation to maintain open economies, i.e., to allow imports to enter the nation unfettered

---

6. 'EU leaders agree sweeping reforms to create jobs', *Financial Times*, 25/26 March 2000, p. 1 and accompanying story on p. 2.

by tariff or other restrictive border measures, including discriminatory internal taxes or regulatory measures. However, over the long sweep of history, nations have been reluctant to do so, largely because of pressures exerted by domestic producers (often in league with labour interests) that must compete with imports and seek protection against this competition. At the same time, however, governments are also pressured by domestic producers whose exports are internationally competitive and who thus seek access to foreign markets that might be closed because domestic producers in these markets seek protection from imports. Thus, a successful formula for liberal trade policies has been developed whereby governments negotiate with one another to gain market access for domestic exporters and, increasingly, domestic firms wishing to establish local operations in foreign markets via foreign direct investment. As is now well understood, in these negotiations, a government treats measures to further open its own domestic markets as 'concessions' to other governments seeking access for its own firms to these markets, to be traded away for access to foreign markets.

From an economics perspective, the whole process resembles nothing so much as placing the cart before the horse. In principle, it is in their own unilateral interests that nations should open their domestic markets to foreign competition. Hence, multilateral negotiations to achieve this end simply should not be necessary. But, because of the political power of incumbent domestic producers, unilateral opening has often not proven possible for governments to achieve. Thus, unlike the mythical cart before the horse, multilateral trade negotiations as conducted over the past half century or so have largely proven able to deliver the goods in the form of much more open economies than would have been likely in the absence of these negotiations.

Arguably, the origin of the multilateral trading system of today can be traced to the US Trade Agreements Act of 1934, under which the US Congress authorised the US President to seek reciprocal tariff reductions with major trading partner nations. This authorisation was in some ways the forerunner of today's 'fast-track' negotiating authority granted to the President by the Congress to enter into trade negotiations on behalf of the Congress.[7] Under this authority, US Secretary of State Cordell Hull proposed

---

7. The idiosyncratic nature of the US Constitution requires this because, under the Constitution, the Congress holds authority over international commerce of the US whereas foreign policy is in the domain of the US President. Under 'fast-track', the President (via the US Trade Representative) actually negotiates for the US, but if the resulting agreements require changes in US law, these must be enacted by Congress. Also, under 'fast-track', Congress votes for such changes as a package, such that Congress must either pass or reject the whole package, thus preventing Congress from forcing re-negotiation of specific aspects of a trade agreement. At the time of this writing, the 'fast-track' authority had lapsed.

in the closing years of World War II the creation of the International Trade Organization (ITO), which would have been an international organisation that would have acted to implement a set of trade rules that would have bound all of the world's trading nations to common standards agreed to by those nations. Much of the motivation for creation of the ITO was political rather than economic. Although Hull recognised that there were economic benefits that accrue to free trade, Hull was much more concerned with prevention of future wars on the scale of World War II and saw stronger trade ties among nations as one means to reduce the chances that nations would go to war with one another.

The ITO was never launched, however, and in its place was a provisional agreement, the General Agreement on Tariffs and Trade (GATT) which remains as the core agreement of the modern multilateral system. For more than 40 years, the GATT in fact was the only multilateral trade agreement in existence. But it was modified in a series of multilateral trading rounds that took place over the years and that acted in most instances to liberalise international trade, mostly via the reduction of bound tariff levels as embodied in the GATT Article II bound tariff schedules of participating nations.[8]

One matter that largely was settled by the failure of the ITO was that there would be no role for the GATT to remedy the effects of private business practices, even if these practices were to act as barriers to trade. This was because the rejected Treaty of Havana to establish the ITO contained explicit provisions pertaining to restrictive business practices whereas the GATT did not. The GATT nations thus formally interpreted rejection of the Treaty of Havana as rejection of any extension of GATT into the realm of private business practices. Thus, for example, GATT Article XXIII, pertaining to 'nullification or impairment' of 'any benefit accruing to (a GATT Member nation) directly or indirectly (by virtue of another nation's GATT obligations)' cannot be used to raise a dispute concerning nullification or impairment, for example, of an export opportunity created by the GATT but foreclosed because of a private business practice. This is true even in spite of Article XXIII language indicating that the article can be invoked whenever 'attainment of any objective of (the GATT) is being impeded as the result of ... the existence of any other situation'.[9] However, as noted in the

---

8. Following the conclusion in 1979 of the 'Tokyo Round' of multilateral tariffs, the GATT was supplemented with several so-called 'plurilateral' agreements. These were ones to which only a subset of GATT nations were participants.

9. The non-applicability of GATT Article XXIII to private business practices was formalised by the GATT in 1960, and this formalisation carries over to the WTO.

introduction (and developed further in the conclusion) of this chapter, the
GATS concluded in 1995 does reintroduce some new but limited scope for
the WTO to deal with private practices that restrict or foreclose trade,
specifically those that might impede trade in services.

The most recent round of negotiations, the Uruguay Round, resulted in the
creation in 1995 of the present World Trade Organization (WTO) and its
associated agreements, of which the GATT remains the core agreement.
These agreements provide common standards to which the laws of the WTO
Member nations, by common agreement, are supposed to conform.
Importantly, alleged violations by a government to its WTO obligations are
addressed via a state-to-state dispute settlement procedure under which
impartial arbitral 'panels' hear the facts pertaining to a dispute and then rule
whether or not an obligation in fact has been breached. If so, the panel
proposes a remedy to the problem to which the errant nation must either
conform or face the possibility of international sanctions. Anti-globalist
activists claims to the contrary notwithstanding, no nation is stripped of its
sovereignty by this procedure and, indeed, governments are free to ignore the
ruling of a WTO panel and any remedy the panel might recommend.[10]
However, as just noted, if a nation does not remedy the contravention of an
obligation as per the recommendations of a panel ruling, nations that are (in
WTO terms) adversely affected by that nation's practice can impose limited
sanctions on the offending nation. The WTO system is not a supranational
government, but it does provide a framework in which governments can
agree to a common set of standards that work largely in the direction of
opening domestic markets to competition from firms from other nations and
resolve disputes pertaining to these standards.

To a free trade purist, the WTO system is not necessary and, furthermore,
highly imperfect (for example, many exceptions to the principle of
maintenance of open markets are allowed). But even a purist would agree that
the system as constituted is preferred to one where government policies are
dominated by protectionist interests such that their markets are largely closed
to foreign competition.

Whereas the WTO creates a common set of principles and standards to
which the trade law and policies of all WTO Member nations are meant to
conform, there are no such common international principles and standards for
competition policy. This lack of standards reflects both the history and the
intellectual underpinnings of competition policy. With respect to the history
of competition policy, this history varies substantially from nation to nation

---

10. See Jackson (2001) for a study of the WTO dispute settlement process. Jackson concludes
that this process has rendered fair and impartial decisions that tend to be quite narrow.

among the forty or so nations that have adopted competition laws. (More than one hundred nations have no competition laws at all.) In the US, for example, the first such laws were passed during the 19th century largely in response to populist sentiment against very large business enterprises. Such firms appeared in the US economy during the second half of that century and, in some cases, these firms grew to hold monopolies in certain key sectors.[11] In some instances, the monopolies were regional in nature, in others they were national in scope.[12]

Over the years since that time, the specific focus and objectives of US competition policy have evolved, but the populist roots of this policy have never quite disappeared. First actual application of the law, during the early 20th century, reflected populist sentiment when US authorities proceeded to break up two large 'trusts' (i.e., large, monopolistic groups of firms, specifically Standard Oil and American Tobacco).[13] The US enthusiasm for 'trust busting' ended at about the time of the conclusion of World War I, and a long period followed when, under Republican administrations, there was little actual enforcement of the various statutes. When antitrust was revived under the Roosevelt administration during the 1930s and early 1940s, the focus shifted from breakup of monopoly to vigilance, first against cartels (especially international cartels), and later against 'incipient monopoly', to be accomplished largely via merger review.

But also, especially during the 1930s, there emerged an issue in US policy that has its roots in populist sentiments and has not been completely resolved to this day. This is, is it the role of competition policy to protect individual firms from larger rivals, even where the larger rival succeeds by virtue of its greater efficiency? Most scholars, even during the 1930s, likely would have answered with a resounding 'no'. But, this notwithstanding, the US Congress during the 1930s passed the Robinson Patman Act, which in fact was motivated by the desire of the Congress to protect certain types of firms (especially small retailers) against competition from large rival firms (specifically, at the time, regional and national chain stores). This Act prohibited most price discrimination, but allowed it under a number of

---

11. Canada is the only country with a competition law older than the earliest US law, the Sherman Act. Unlike US law, Canada's law has been substantively changed since its initial passage.
12. Populist sentiment first grew against the railroads, which were regional monopolies. Sentiment later shifted to national monopolies, such as that held over oil products by the Standard Oil Trust or the tobacco industry held by the American Tobacco Trust.
13 Even though abusive monopolistic practices by US railroads fomented the populist sentiment that led to the passage of the Sherman Act, the railroads were never actually touched by US competition law; rather they were subjected to price regulation under the authority of the Interstate Commerce Commission.

specific circumstances. Most economists would argue that the overall effect of enforcement of this Act would be to slow or halt the pace of enhancement of efficiency but that the exceptions did serve to negate the worst of these effects. This law is still extant in the US but little enforced.

US policy was characterised by activist merger review during the decades stretching from the 1950s through the 1970s. During this period, the only real criterion against which mergers were evaluated was whether or not a merger would lead to significantly greater market concentrations. Most scholars now believe that this was the wrong criterion on which mergers should be evaluated and the issue to be addressed was not whether market structure would be altered by a merger but rather whether firm conduct would thus be altered. One result was that merger review of that period, by almost all accounts, was overzealous. There was a shift in policy during the 1980s when, under the Reagan administration, mergers were evaluated under dual criteria of whether these would lead to creation of market power and whether they would enable the realisation of efficiencies. With respect to the former, the authorities determined whether or not the merger would likely lead to monopolistic conduct by the merged parties. With respect to the latter, it was up to the parties to the merger to demonstrate to the authorities that efficiencies could be achieved as a result of the merger –i.e. if the likely existence of efficiencies could be demonstrated as a defence offsetting the creation of market power. Even so (and, some might argue, especially so during the Clinton years), US policy has reflected some element of populism, for example, much of the recent case of the US government against Microsoft has been based on alleged misconduct of Microsoft towards rival firms.

European competition law is of quite different origin to US law. Such a law did not exist in Europe (with the exception of Germany, where an anti-cartels law was forced upon West Germany by the occupying powers following World War II, and was retained after the occupation ended and the modern Bundesrepublik was created) until the creation of the European Economic Community. The Treaty of Rome, creating the EU, that came into force during the closing years of the 1950s contained specific provisions pertaining to competition and, furthermore, gave special powers to the European Commission (created by the Treaty) to enforce these provisions. Thus, European competition law, unlike that of the US, was supranational in character. Also, unlike that of the US, European competition law was seen from the outset as being linked to trade liberalisation or, more generally, to economic integration among the Member nations of the EU. Part – or, indeed, most – of the motivation behind the creation of the EU was to end (or at least to channel) political strife among European states, strife that twice during the 20th century erupted in devastating wars. The reasoning of the

EU's founders was that if the economies of these states could be made sufficiently interdependent, another European war would be unthinkable. Thus, although economic objectives were not irrelevant to the goal of European integration (and, arguably, economic objectives have become relatively more important with the passage of time), the major objective underlying this integration was political, not economic, in nature.[14]

Central to achieving European integration was the ending of most border measures restricting the flow of goods and services (and, ultimately, factors of production, including capital and human beings) among the European nations. Competition policy was seen as a necessary adjunct to this mission. The original intent was that neither cartels nor other private business practices (specifically, the exercise of misuse of a 'dominant firm position') should act to offset the effects of ending border restrictions.

De facto, over time, this quite different initial motivation for European competition law has led European enforcement agencies to deal with most of the same issues as the US enforcement agencies, for example, control of incipient monopoly via mergers review (the European Commission has had explicit authority to review mergers only since 1989), control of cartels, regulation of vertical restraints (for example, such issues as resale price maintenance, exclusive dealership arrangements, exclusive supplier arrangements, price discrimination, and the like), and regulation of monopolistic practices (in Europe, 'abuse of a dominant firm position') such as allegedly predatory pricing. However, European law and policy nonetheless differs from that of the US markedly in terms of procedures. For example, certain infractions in the US can be treated as criminal offences, but not so in Europe. The scope for private antitrust action in the US is much larger than in Europe. And, most importantly, major cases in the US are heard in courts of law – the major power held by the US enforcement agencies is the ability to bring such a case to court – whereas in Europe the European Commission, through its Directorate General (DG) IV, decides on most cases.[15]

Furthermore, even if the basic issues treated under the two sets of law are similar in the US and the EU, specific substantive aspects of law and its application can be quite different. For example, current European policy tends to be much stricter towards vertical restraints than does US law, which

---

14 Thus, the history of European competition policy has been, in terms of its underlying original rationale, much more akin to that of the multilateral trading system, which also was originally motivated by the political objective of reducing the likelihood of armed conflict, than to the US antitrust laws. Perhaps for this reason the EU is much more open to issues of competition policy being explicitly included in the WTO agenda than is the US at this time.

15. An appeal procedure does exist in Europe whereby firms can contest DGIV decisions.

allows for a larger scope of efficiency-based defences for such restraints as exclusive dealing. However, Europe grants block exemptions whereby whole sectors are, in effect, allowed to pursue certain practices that would otherwise be illegal. In contrast, the US has no equivalent to block exemptions, save for the one rather odd case of a complete exemption from antitrust granted to major league baseball.[16]

Importantly, whereas US competition law concerns itself almost exclusively with private practices that might reduce competition in markets and does not concern itself with government practices of policies that might have the same effects, European law does grant competition authorities some competence in the latter. In particular, the European authorities have powers to regulate the use of state aids to industries or regions and even to order such aids to be paid back if the effect of these is to distort competition.

One procedural element that US and European competition policy does seem to have in common, in spite of the many differences between the two, is that in practice those cases of alleged infringement of competition law that are examined by enforcement agencies are often triggered by complaints received from firms that compete with the alleged offender.[17] Importantly, it is not official policy in either location that such complaints automatically lead to investigation by the enforcement agencies, nor are those cases that are investigated necessarily ones that are raised by competitors. However, as a practical matter, the agencies do receive much of their information regarding instances of possible misconduct from firms that believe themselves to be victim of the misconduct, and hence rival firms' complaints do act as the major trigger of investigations.[18]

In a sense then, the enforcement agencies act similarly to the WTO dispute settlement procedures in the narrow sense that both sets of bodies act to mediate (or adjudicate) disputes among parties. Even in the US, where

---

16. However, European policy has been changing in directions that act to bring it and US policy into greater mutual conformity. This is in some large part a consequence of new thinking (new since the 1970s!) among economists about the economic consequences of vertical practices. This thinking recognises that some such practices, even if these might discourage new entry at some level into a market, can nonetheless serve to enhance efficiency. This is especially so of vertical measures that discourage 'free rider' entry, i.e., entry that piggy-backs off large sunk costs incurred by incumbent firms. If 'free riding' is allowed, or so goes current thinking, the result will be disincentives for firms to make necessary (and socially desirable) investments because 'free rider' competitors will bid down returns on such investments to levels unacceptable to investors.

17 On this see Fox (1997b). A comprehensive treatment of the US versus EU competition law is contained in a series of essays in the volume edited by Evenett, Lehmann and Steil (2000).

18. This statement does not apply to merger review; merger review is generally self-initiated by the enforcement agencies on the basis of information that must be supplied by the merging parties to these agencies.

antitrust cases are often settled in courts of law, the enforcement agencies often, in effect, act as mediators or adjudicators by acting to bring settlement to cases out of court. In such instances, cases can nonetheless wind up in court if parties to the case do not accept the remedies as proposed by the agencies. However, as noted earlier, private parties can bring antitrust cases in the US directly to court, by passing the enforcement agencies altogether, something that generally is not possible in Europe.

This is not to claim that there is any convergence between procedures for settling disputes in the domain of competition policy and those for settling trade disputes. Rather, there are huge differences between these two sets of processes. The biggest difference, of course, is that the WTO procedures are meant to settle disputes among governments of sovereign nations and not private parties, whereas competition enforcement agencies often, in effect, settle (or attempt to settle) disputes among private parties.

Indeed, perhaps the biggest difference in general between competition policy and trade policy is that the former deals mostly (even in Europe) with private practices that impede market contestability whereas the latter deals with government measures, mostly those taken at the border, that have the same effect. A large lacuna is thus created: neither set of policies is equipped to deal with competition distortions that result from some combination of private practice and government law or policy that enables (or even fosters) that practice. Thus, for example, if incumbent sellers in a market conspire among themselves to fix prices and to limit output, this practice can be subject to remedial action by competition authorities. If the same prices and output are fixed and limited by government regulators, this practice generally cannot be touched by competition officials. Ironically, if the effect of a private cartel agreement to fix prices and limit output is to foreclose a national market to imports from other nations, the practice generally cannot be touched by trade policy (i.e., through WTO dispute resolution) unless perhaps it can be shown that the agreement directly stems from government measures. It is often argued that foreclosure of one nation's market to imports from another market results not from a specific governmental measure to create and enforce a cartel agreement, however, but rather from government toleration of private arrangements (i.e., failure to act under domestic competition law). Whether such governmental forbearance of cartels with import foreclosure effects generally can be the basis for WTO dispute settlement procedures is untried but dubious.

Apart from the US and the EU, other countries have their own unique histories with respect to competition law and policy. Thus, for example, Mexico implemented a competition law in order to further an on-going process of reform of domestic economic policy in an effort to make this policy more market-driven, less *dirigiste*, and less nationalistic than historically had been the case. Although in some specific regards Mexico's motivations were similar to those of Europe, the underlying reasons for these motivations differed in Mexico from those in Europe. Thus, Mexico, like Europe, sought to open its domestic markets to greater foreign competition and to use competition policy to help prevent private practices conducted 'behind the border' from offsetting market opening measures taken at the border. But the underlying objectives for Mexico to do so were much more economic and less political than for Europe. Unlike Europe, Mexico's recent history has not been dominated by highly destructive wars. But Mexico during the century just past has experienced economic setbacks, including a depression following the debt crisis of the early 1980s and a financial crisis in 1995. Mexico thus saw domestic reform and the role of competition policy in this reform as a means to foster better economic growth as a goal in its own right. In contrast, while Europe has also viewed competition policy as a means to achieve an economic goal, this goal has been one of integration, which itself has not been viewed as the final goal but rather as a means to achieve a still bigger end.

To summarise, the key differences between competition policy and trade policy are as follows. First, the trade policies of most of the world's nations, those that are WTO Members, are subject to a common set of standards establishing obligations to which these policies must conform (or face sanction through the dispute settlement process). Failure of a nation to implement laws and policies that do conform to WTO obligations opens that nation to disputes being lodged in the WTO. Competition policies, by contrast, are not subject to international standards and, in fact, competition law in differing countries varies substantially in terms both of substantive content and procedures for enforcement. These differences among countries in turn reflect differences in the underlying objectives that competition policy is meant to achieve. Indeed, to say that 'competition law in differing countries varies substantially' is a considerable understatement. In many countries, of course, there is no compeition law at all.

Furthermore, unlike with trade policy, there is no formal means available by which nations can resolve disputes that might arise as a result of differing approaches to competition policy. A prerequisite for such dispute resolution would be that there be a common international competition standard against which the issues in a dispute could be judged. But there has not been to date any willingness of nations to attempt to harmonise their competition law or policy so as to reduce the large differences that exist among them, let alone to create common standards. Further, where there might be an overlap between multilateral trade rules and private competition issues, by common agreement, these rules cannot be brought to bear on the private practice at issue. This is because failure of the Treaty of Havana established a precedent whereby private business practices that might foreclose exports are not subject to multilateral trade rules (and, hence, by default, are subject only to national competition laws). There has been great reluctance to reverse this precedent. Competition authorities in most nations have shown a reluctance either to see WTO rules extend into the domain of competition policy, or to create any sort of international agency to administer an international competition law.

Does the resulting lack of uniform competition policies result in international problems? Will these problems grow? The next section suggests that the answer to both questions is 'yes'.

4.   INTERNATIONAL TRADE DISPUTES OFTEN HAVE A COMPETITION DIMENSION

If there were, in spite of the commonality of trade and competition policies in terms of their ultimate objective, a clean separation of their actual application, then neither the procedural differences between the two sets of policies nor the substantive and procedural differences among differing nations' competition policies would really matter a great deal. Trade policy would, in these circumstances, concern itself with border measures enacted by governments. Competition policy would largely concern itself with the complementary issues of behind-the-border regulation and private business practices that affect conditions of market entry.[19] The two sets of policy could largely coexist peacefully.

Even so, a concern might exist that competition policy in each nation be applied on a 'national treatment' basis, for example, that complaints about private business practices that might foreclose (or limit) market opportunities to potential new entrants have as much standing when raised by foreign parties as when raised by domestic parties. Such concerns have been raised. For example, part of the motivation of the WTO dispute over photographic film raised by the US against Japan was concern that Japanese authorities had not dealt with alleged infringements of the Japanese antimonopolies law by

---

19. As noted previously, however, competition policy does not generally in fact concern itself with governmental behind-the-border measures, even if these act to reduce contestability of markets. Again, the main exception is competence granted to the European Commission to regulate state aids to industry.

the dominant producer of film in Japan in a way that led to a fair outcome from the point of view of a US-controlled rival firm (this case is discussed further below). Concerns have also been raised that, in certain developing nations, competition law has been enforced so as to protect incumbent domestically-owned firms from competition by more efficient multinational firms. Such enforcement resounds with populist and nationalistic overtones. As suggested earlier in this chapter, populist overtones can also be found in the US law.

But such concerns could be addressed via reform of domestic competition law enforcement in those nations where the law was not applied on a national treatment basis. This issue is often tied to the bigger issue of whether the courts of a country are fair and impartial. It is a well taken point that in many countries courts are not fair and impartial, that judges are corrupt, and that outcomes of judicial proceedings do not reflect due process of law. It further goes almost without saying that multinational firms are not necessarily always the victims of corrupt legal proceedings; sometimes, in fact, these firms themselves are the corrupting agents. What does go without saying is that competition law and policy cannot serve well to protect the process of competition, including ensuring that this law and policy is enforced on a non-discriminatory basis, if the courts that must ultimately interpret and enforce the law are corrupt. In many countries, the most significant unfulfilled prerequisite for an effective competition policy is that an impartial judiciary that upholds rule of law does not exist.

However, even if competition law and policy existed in every country in the world and was administered on an impartial basis in courts that were not corrupted, problems might arise between this law and policy and liberal trade policy. This is because, in the modern world economy, hundreds of firms operate on a transnational basis (giving rise to the so-called 'globalisation' of economic activity). Thus, many of the concerns addressed by competition policy arise on a cross-border basis. One clear example of this is mergers. During the late 1990s, almost half of all mergers reviewed by US authorities were cross-border transactions, usually ones involving one European and one American party.[20] Ten years earlier, only a small fraction of mergers reviewed by these authorities were cross-border ones. Those transactions involving both American and European parties can be subject to review by European authorities as well, leading to a potential for jurisdictional conflict if the two authorities reach opposite conclusions as to whether to clear the

---

20. US Department of Justice (2000).

merger.[21] Obviously, this possibility becomes greater if those authorities judge the merger against dissimilar criteria than if the two sets of criteria are 'harmonised'. And, also obviously, even if the authorities arrive at compatible conclusions, the transactions costs to parties to a merger of complying with merger review requirements of multiple jurisdictions are greater than if only one such review is required. If nothing else, multiple jurisdictions claiming authority over review of the same merger add substantially to the frictional costs of completing such transactions.

Some but not all of the problems suggested above might be solved (or at least reduced) by greater formalised cooperation among competition authorities. Most promising of various schemes for cooperation is what is termed 'positive comity'. Under positive comity, there would be agreement among such authorities that any particular situation involving competition law (whether it be a merger or a possible violation of law, for example, a cartel, an illegal vertical restraint, an abuse of a monopolistic position by a firm, etc) would be handled by only one authority, presumably the one with the greatest interest in the case. However, this authority would take into account the interests of other authorities, especially if the 'effects' of the case (or remedies) were to spill into the territory of jurisdiction of the other party. In turn, these other authorities would agree, within limitations prescribed by their own law (or, better, under waivers to these limitations), to provide the lead authority with relevant information pertaining to the case.

To this end, a number of formal bilateral international cooperation agreements (ICAs) have already been struck among competition authorities, and more are in the offing.[22] Furthermore, a recent high-level committee assembled by the US Department of Justice has recommended that the way to deal with the growing interface between international trade policy and competition policy issues is to extend and deepen such cooperation.[23] Current

---

21. Indeed, mergers between parties that are both legally 'American' nationals can be subject to review in Europe and mergers between parties that are both legally 'European' can be subject to review in the US – for example, where the parties are multinational firms holding operations on both sides of the Atlantic. One of the most contentious cases of recent times was the merger of the American firm McDonnell-Douglas into the Boeing Corporation, also an American firm. The merger was reviewed by authorities on both sides of the Atlantic, who initially reached opposite conclusions. The resulting conflict was resolved only at diplomatic levels.

22. Some of these have been enabled by the US International Antitrust Enforcement Assistance Act of 1994. To date, only one full-blown agreement has been concluded under this Act, with Australia. Another agreement is expected to be completed soon with Canada and what amount to exploratory agreements have been struck with the EU and Japan. Other bilateral agreements not involving the US exist, for example, between the EU and Japan, but these mostly are also essentially exploratory in nature.

23. US Department of Justice (2000).

agreements vary in terms of the amount and level of cooperation that is enabled and, clearly, much more could be done than has been done in these existing agreements. But, equally clearly, no such agreement can hope to resolve fully the conflicts that are intrinsically created by fundamental incompatibilities in substantive standards among differing nations' laws and policies. Current ICAs call for cooperation and, in some cases, procedural harmonisation but not harmonisation of substantive law.

Greater cooperation thus might solve some of the problems associated with conflicting jurisdictions as these affect merger review and other aspects of competition policy, but it is not likely to solve all of them. The main question for this chapter is whether there are likely to be conflicts that remain unresolved regarding market access for foreign sellers in nations' domestic markets.

Issues of market access can, in fact, be raised by mergers. For example, the US express delivery firm UPS has alleged that European postal monopolies (specifically, the Deutsche Bundespost and the Royal Mail) have been acquiring independent local express delivery firms (for example, acquisition by Deutsche Bundespost of DHL) in order to expand their legal monopolies in regular postal services to the express delivery market. The further allegation is that traditional postal monopolies are being used to cross-subsidise the operations of the postal agencies in the express delivery market, an allegation that, if correct, is tantamount to price predation designed to foreclose the market from competition.

It is not the purpose here to comment on whether the allegations in this specific case are correct. The issues, rather, are whether merger review procedures undertaken by European authorities will fully consider the market access issue and, were it to be determined that the postal mergers have indeed created a situation of abuse of dominant firm position, whether effective remedies will be found to render this market more contestable.

More generally, the issue is whether or not it is satisfactory for cases of alleged foreclosure of a non-national firm from a nation's market to be judged and resolved solely by authorities of that nation. In the WTO, of course, disputes arising from failure of a government to abide by obligations so that a foreign firm faces market foreclosure are raised by other governments (generally, the home government of the foreclosed firm) and decided by impartial panels. But when the reasons for foreclosure fall into the domain of competition policy, however, all that the aggrieved firm can do is to seek relief from the government of the affected country. This is not necessarily a problem if the relevant authorities are fair, neutral, and objective. The question is, what if they are not?

Mergers are, of course, not the only domain of competition policy where issues of market access for foreign firms arise. The photographic film case against Japan pursued by the US Government arose because a US-based firm, Kodak, believed that expansion of its market share was foreclosed by virtue of exclusive dealing relationships between domestic rival Fuji Film and several distributors. (The Kodak case arguably was weakened somewhat because, in fact, Kodak did have its own exclusive dealing relationship with another distributor; thus, Kodak's case was not that it was foreclosed from Japan altogether but, rather, constrained in efforts to enlarge market share.) Kodak did not believe that its concerns were addressed fairly by the Japanese Fair Trade Commission (JFTC), which had looked at the relevant markets and determined that there was no violation of the domestic antimonopolies law. Thus, the US Government brought a case against Japan in the WTO, but could not base this case on the vertical restraints that unquestionably existed in Japan for reasons already discussed. Instead, the US case was based on evidence that these restraints were enabled by measures taken by the Government of Japan. The dispute settlement panel did not accept the US arguments and ruled in favour of Japan.

Although the photographic film case has been the only dispute brought to the WTO that explicitly involved competition issues, such issues have figured in a number of bilateral trade disputes that have not been formally brought to the WTO. These have included US complaints regarding Japanese business practices having alleged export foreclosure effects in automobile, flat glass, and paper markets. The automobile complaints centred around exclusive dealing relationships between Japanese automakers and their distributors which allegedly foreclosed sales both of finished US automobiles and US-made auto parts in the so-called 'aftermarket'. Japanese authorities denied the existence of foreclosure in these instances. In flat glass, by contrast, the JFTC has concurred with at least some US allegations that a producers' cartel in Japan exists and has coerced (by threat of boycott) independent distributors from handling imported flat glass, even though the imports were priced significantly below substitutable domestically-produced goods. However, the JFTC has not formally investigated this sector, nor has it required remedial measures to be applied. Allegations similar to those for the flat glass sector have been directed towards the Japanese paper market. A 1992 agreement was signed between the Japanese and US governments to increase market access for foreign sellers of paper products in Japan but, at least according to one source, the agreement has 'not had its intended effect'.[24]

Other complaints have been made concerning anticompetitive business practices in Japan that have foreclosure effects on Japanese imports. These involve the electronic equipment market and the soda ash market. While again the US Government, responding to US producers, has been the main complainant, the Americans have been joined by European sellers. In all of these cases, a common thread has been the perception that the JFTC has been lax in enforcing Japan's own Antimonopolies law.

Other trade disputes invoking competition issues have occurred involving nations other than Japan. Thus, for example, there have been quarrels between the US and Europe over access to airline reservations systems. The US has complained that US aerospace firms have not been able to win contracts to supply parts to the Airbus consortium because of exclusive dealing relationships between the consortium and European suppliers. Similar complaints have been raised by the US Government over market access in Europe of telecommunications equipment manufacturers, with the added twist of concern that European technical standards in this sector are designed to serve as market access barriers. Similar complaints have been raised by the USTR concerning the markets for telecommunications equipment in a number of non-EU nations. The EU has investigated a number of cases of alleged international cartels that have acted to raise prices of relevant products internally in Europe.

The WTO Working Group on Trade and Competition policy received submissions from a number of countries that identified business practices within their own borders that had possible import foreclosure effects or acted to retard entry of foreign firms via foreign direct investment. The EU, France, Canada and the US all presented examples of such practices.

A common element in many of these case examples is that private business practices are often enabled or abetted, intentionally or unintentionally, by government policies or practices, usually in the form of regulatory measures. One question that naturally arises in such instances (and indeed figured in the WTO photographic film case noted above) is whether or not foreclosure caused directly or indirectly by such measures might be subject to the WTO dispute resolution. As already discussed, private practices are not subject to WTO but, under GATT Article XXIII, government measures that cause 'nullification and impairment' certainly are (and, hence, in the photographic film case, the US Government based its case

---

24. US Department of Justice (2000).

on alleged existence of such measures, albeit unsuccessfully). This, of course, opens the door for certain types of foreclosure potentially being subject both to competition policy and trade policy, for example, it is not out of the question that competition authorities might investigate a case to determine whether private restraints impeded market entry and, simultaneously, a WTO panel might investigate the same case to determine whether government measures that enabled those private practices constituted nullification and impairment. And, just as differing competition authorities having jurisdiction over the same merger raises the potential for conflicting outcomes, so the possibility of WTO panels and competition authorities investigating the same case (albeit from different perspectives) also creates potential for conflicting outcomes.

As suggested in the opening sections, such potential conflicts are likely to proliferate over time. The reasons are several. First, as noted, mergers and acquisitions once took place largely within national boundaries of particular countries, but these are becoming more and more international. Second, markets for many products are becoming increasingly global, even in sectors where cross-border mergers do not figure. And, third, those sectors where government regulation figures importantly, for example, telecommunications, financial services, pharmaceuticals, are among those sectors that are most rapidly becoming globalised. Furthermore, as suggested in section 3, many of these cases suggest a major lacuna created by the combination of trade and competition policy. Namely, while trade policy is concerned with government border measures that might reduce market contestability and, through the GATT national treatment and nullification and impairment clauses, at least some behind-the-border measures that might have the same effect, and while competition policy is concerned with private practices that might have the same effect, neither set of policies addresses combinations of governmental regulation and private practices that create pro-incumbency biases and hence reduce market contestability. Cooperative arrangements among competition enforcement agencies do not offer much potential for filling this lacuna, and to date no work programme has emerged in the WTO to address the issue. Nonetheless, many of the specific examples of trade disputes discussed in this section would seem to fall into this particular category. There appears to be a real problem for which no remedy is available or proposed.

5.   IS THERE A WAY FORWARD?

What emerges from the previous two sections is as follows. On the one hand, the conflicts and costs associated with non-uniform principles and procedures of competition policy, as it has been implemented across the globe, are likely to grow (section 4). But, on the other hand, there is little effort or will among nations to take those steps necessary to reduce the inconsistencies that give rise to these costs and conflicts (section 3). Especially anathematical, at least as perceived by the US Government, would seem to be any effort to embody competition standards in the WTO.

One of the main reasons for the reluctance of nations to 'internationalise' competition policy is that nations have exhibited in recent years a growing unease with the extent to which they have already yielded sovereignty to international institutions such as the WTO, the International Monetary Fund (IMF) and, in Europe, even the Commission of the European Union itself. Such unease is reflected, *inter alia*, in moves in Europe towards greater 'subsidiarity' (code language for shifting the responsibility for decision-making away from the European Commission in Brussels and back to national capitals) and provisions in US trade law allowing the US Congress to end US Membership in the WTO. At least some of the antiglobalist demonstrators in Seattle in November 1999 were protesting alleged loss of national sovereignty to the WTO. In those countries requiring financial 'bailouts' from the IMF during the Asian financial crisis in 1997, there have developed elements of backlash against the IMF itself, motivated in part because decisions over matters normally considered to be within the sovereign prerogative of national governments were seen to be taken by the IMF and not by governments themselves.[25]

Compounding the issue of whether there should be international competition standards is the problematic issue of what the standards should normatively be, even if there were to be consensus that some such standards indeed should exist. Competition policy, when it works well, often involves a delicate balance between how much market power should be allowed on the part of one firm and the efficiencies that this market power might enable the firm to realise. Hard and fast *per se* rules to guide determination of what is the correct balance are infeasible. One consequence is that competition law in the US (where procedures used by competition authorities to determine what is the correct balance are arguably the most advanced) has, for most issues,

---

25. Ironically, in some countries, reforms demanded by the IMF were in fact ones that senior officials of the affected governments themselves knew were necessary but were blocked from doing so because of internal deadlocks.

moved away from application of *per se* rules and towards 'rule of reason' (i.e., each case is decided on its own merit). In light of the complexities of most competition cases, a rule of reason approach is to be desired. However, a rule-driven procedure such as the Dispute Settlement Mechanism of the WTO is not especially well-suited to this approach. Most WTO dispute settlement involves a relatively simple interpretation of whether or not an action taken by a member government is or is not consistent with obligations under relatively unambiguous WTO rules, not a balancing of one goal against another.

There might appear some conflict between these statements and earlier ones to the effect that the economic goals of competition policy and liberal trade policy are largely the same. In fact, core WTO obligations are largely consistent, as noted earlier, with the basic goal of competition policy to foster consumer welfare via ensuring that competition among economic agents does take place. Most WTO dispute cases as decided by dispute resolution panels involve determination of whether or not a practice by a government that violates a core obligation falls within the scope of an allowed exception. While it could be argued that most competition policy cases that are adjudicated involve a similar decision – i.e., whether or not a private action that potentially reduces competition falls within an allowed exception, including one based on efficiency – the difference comes down to there existing much more ambiguity in many competition cases as to what should be an allowed exception, than in most WTO cases. One consequence is that the amount of discretion that must be allowed the deciding authority is necessarily greater for most competition cases than for most WTO disputes. Given this, one factor that mitigates inclusion of competition issues in the WTO is reluctance of nations to have cases involving national interests to be decided by tribunals which must exercise discretionary authority. In this matter, as just suggested, WTO panels do not enjoy much discretionary authority. Rather, their authority again is quite limited to deciding a case on the basis of relatively non-ambiguous rules. But almost all experts in the area of competition policy believe that to try and establish non-ambiguous *per se* rules to govern competition policy on a global basis would be folly.[26]

All of this militates against anything like 'global competition policy', or at least against such a policy being administered on a supranational basis

---

26. This is true even on the part of authors who have generally been in favour of some role within the domain of competition policy for the WTO, such as Scherer (1994) and Graham and Richardson (1997). Those who have favoured such rules, for example, Fox (1997a), have tended to see these rules covering a limited subset of the specific issues covered by competition policy, for example, rules on hard cartels with boycott.

through the WTO or any other international organisation. Yet, as noted above, there are aspects of the globalised economy that do seem to call for a competition policy that is not confined within the borders of one nation. Further, a case can be made for standards that are uniform across boundaries, and for competition policy that is consistently applied across the globe. More importantly, perhaps, pressures for such consistency are likely to grow.

What will be the response of governments to such pressures? One response doubtlessly will be expansion of the nascent network of cooperation agreements among competition enforcement agencies, with more agencies participating in cooperative arrangements. Out of such cooperation there might in fact develop some harmonisation, if not of substantive standards then at least of certain procedural aspects of enforcement. For example, for merger review, one outcome could eventually be uniform information reporting requirements, such that all relevant agencies at least worked with the same information. Uniform, or at least similar, requirements for information reporting would reduce costs to business firms of complying with merger review requirements and, moreover, would render current restrictions against the sharing of information among enforcement agencies debatable. Such restrictions, which are often embodied in national competition law, in fact are one major obstacle to international cooperation among enforcement agencies. Further down the line, it is not to be ruled out entirely that cooperation and consultation among enforcement agencies might lead to some harmonisation of substantive standards. On this last matter, there are some competition-related issues where harmonisation might in fact prove relatively easy to accomplish, the remarks of previous paragraphs notwithstanding. For example, at least among the Organisation for Cooperation and Economic Development (OECD) nations, substantive law with respect to cartels is already quite similar from jurisdiction to jurisdiction, and further convergence might not be difficult.[27] However, on other issues, such as vertical restraints, substantive differences in current law and practice among nations are quite great and convergence on such issues would likely be a long way off, if ever.

Intensified efforts at cooperation thus is the likely response of competition policy itself, as carried out by competition enforcement agencies, to global pressures for consistency. Is there a role for trade policy in achieving this consistency? As of the time of this writing, there is in fact some indication that the US might be willing to be somewhat more flexible than in the immediate past with respect to the EU call for competition policy to be

---

27. See, for example Organisation for Economic Cooperation and Development (1998).

included on the multilateral trade agenda. However, for all of the reasons already indicated, this is not likely to lead in the near future to actual negotiation of competition-related rules in the WTO. Rather, what might be anticipated is a renewed mandate of the Working Group on Trade and Competition, where the mandate might include the group making recommendations as to whether there is a case for such rules at some time in the future. Such rules might be envisaged, for example, to counteract government regulations that have the intended or unintended effect of protecting incumbent interests in a particular market and thus exclude foreign suppliers from that market. Such rules would be in the spirit of existing WTO obligations pertaining to national treatment, whereby imported goods are meant to receive treatment no less favourable under tax, regulation, or other government laws and policies than equivalent domestically-made goods.

In fact, however, skeletal competition-based rules already exist in the WTO within the existing General Agreement on Trade in Services (GATS). This agreement, of course, covers only service sectors, and many of the obligations created under GATS apply only to those sectors whereby (WTO) Member nations undertake market access commitments as listed on Members' Schedules. (In other words, the obligations only apply to those specific sectors that an individual nation elects to open to international competition.) Activities within such sectors are subject to national treatment along the lines suggested in the previous paragraph although nations can, for these listed sectors, also list sector-specific exceptions to national treatment.

Even so, and irrespective of whether a sector is one in which a Member undertakes a market access commitment, GATS Article IX states that 'Members recognize that certain business practices of service suppliers, other than those falling under Article VIII (designated monopolies), may restrain competition and thereby restrict trade in services'. Accordingly, the article indicates that 'Each Member shall, at the request of any other Member, enter into consultations with a view to eliminating practices (that restrain competition)'. It is not, however, indicated what form these consultations might take or what agencies will represent governments in these consultations, (i.e., would the consultations take place among trade officials, or might these be competition officials?). Thus, one possibility might be for the WTO to try to link GATS Article IX with the growing network of competition cooperation agreements, for example, to encourage competition agencies to include within these agreements arrangements for consultations on GATS-related issues pertaining to private practices that impede market access.

Furthermore, the GATS calls for the WTO Council for Trade in Services, through 'appropriate bodies it may establish', to develop disciplines regarding regulation of services suppliers (specifically, qualification requirements and procedures, technical standards and licensing requirements) to ensure that these 'do not constitute unnecessary barriers to trade in services'. In the interim, prior to introduction of such disciplines, for sectors where specific commitments have been undertaken, a Member is bound not to apply licensing and qualification requirements in a manner in which they 'nullify or impair' its specific commitments. Again, there might be some formal role for competition policy in this domain. For example, the competition experts who constitute the trade and competition working group might be invited to work with the Council on Trade in Services (or be constituted as one of the 'appropriate bodies') of this group to work on developing the called-for measures to insure that regulatory practices do not unduly impede market contestability.

It is widely noted that the GATS has put the WTO into the competition policy business. What seems to be called for, along the lines of the suggestions above, is that this is recognised by the world of competition policy. That is not to say that the WTO should embark upon a course whereby its role is expanded towards becoming a world-wide competition agency. Rather, what needs to be done in the near-term is to ensure that the competition role that has already been defined for the WTO is meshed effectively with the nascent network of competition agency cooperation arrangements, so that the latter works with, and not apart from, the WTO. To this end, competition agencies might be better advised to work on building upon that which already exists in the WTO, rather than (as seems to have been the case in recent years) to work on trying to keep the worlds of trade and competition policy separate and distinct.

REFERENCES

Evenett, Simon, Alexander Lehmann and Benn Steil (eds) (2000), *Antitrust Goes Global: What Future for Trans-Atlantic Cooperation?*, Washington, DC, US: The Brookings Institution and The Royal Institute for International Affairs, London, October.

Fox, Eleanor M. (1997a), 'Towards World Antitrust and Market Access', The American Journal of International Law, 91(1).

Fox, Eleanor M. (1997b), 'US and EU Competition Law: A Comparison', in Edward M. Graham and J. David Richardson (eds) (1997), pp. 1-25.

Graham, Edward M. and J. David Richardson (eds) (1997), *Global Competition Policy*, Washington, DC, US: Institute for International Economics.

Jackson, John H. (2001) (forthcoming), *The Role and Effectiveness of the WTO Dispute Settlement Mechanism*, Washington, DC: The Brookings Institution.

Lipstein, Robert A. (1997), 'Using Antitrust Principles to Reform Antidumping Law', in Edward M. Graham and J. David Richardson (eds) (1997), pp. 405-38.

Organisation for Economic Cooperation and Development (1998), *Recommendation of the Council Concerning Effective Action Towards Hard Core Cartels*, Document No. C98(35) final, Paris: Organisation for Economic Cooperation and Development.

Scherer, Frederic M. (1994), *Competition Policies for an Integrated World Economy*, Washington, DC, US: The Brookings Institution.

Scherer, Frederic M. (1999), *New Perspectives on Economic Growth and Technological Innovation*, Washington, DC: The Brookings Institution.

United States Department of Justice (2000), International Competition Policy Advisory Committee to the Attorney General and Assistant Attorney General for Antitrust Final Report, Washington, DC, US: United States Government Printing Office.

PART FOUR

MULTILATERAL AGREEMENTS

7. European Lessons for Multilateral Economic Integration: A Cautionary Tale[*]

Peter Holmes and Alasdair R. Young

---

1. INTRODUCTION

The basic theme of this chapter is that the European Union (EU)[1] occupies a very peculiar role in the global system: it is simultaneously an international actor and an international institution. It is both a protagonist in the global system and a potential model for that system. This potential is due to the fact that it was designed to liberalise economic exchange between states. We argue, however, that the challenges to the world trading system that have arisen during the past few years, especially since the 1999 World Trade Organization (WTO) Ministerial in Seattle, have counterparts within the EU. Thus, while the EU experience has much to offer, it would be wrong to conclude that the way to address the new challenges to liberalisation is simply to copy the approach the EU has pursued internally.

The EU's potential as a model is arguably becoming increasingly relevant as the global trading system moves beyond tackling 'at-the-border-issues' – particularly tariffs and quotas – and into addressing seriously 'beyond-the-border issues' – technical barriers to trade (TBTs) and domestic regulations governing services and investment, as well as competition. Essentially,

---

[*] Earlier versions of this chapter were presented to the ECSA Sixth Biennial International Conference, Pittsburgh, 2-5 June, 1999; the Workshop on 'Challenges for EU External Economic Policy in the Next Decade', 13-14 April 2000; and 'The Political Economy of Change and Adjustment in Europe' Conference, 6-7 July, 2000. We thank the participants, particularly Seamus O'Cleireacain and Sam Laird, for their comments.
1. Although the term European Union is legally inaccurate, as all of the issues we discuss fall within the first pillar of the EU and as it is the European *Community* that is a Member of the World Trade Organization, we adopt common usage.

differences in product regulations can present barriers to trade. National regulations governing competition, services or establishment and their pattern of enforcement can hinder investment and entry.

We, not terribly controversially, assume that the vast majority of regulations are intended to address legitimate public policy objectives. Nonetheless, they may do so in ways that impede free economic exchange. In addition, some regulations are adopted as disguised protectionism. Consequently, as 'at-the-border' measures become less important, a tension emerges between further liberalisation and preserving legitimate regulatory sovereignty. This tension is evident in the current transatlantic dispute over hormone-treated beef, and was a factor in the collapse last year of the negotiations on a multilateral agreement on investment (MAI). One particularly difficult aspect of this tension concerns how to deal with different national attitudes and approaches to risk.

We argue that this is something that the EU has tackled before. Although it does not frame the issue in the way in which we have, the EU, particularly the European Commission, is explicitly or implicitly arguing that its own experience should inform multilateral rule-making (see, for example, Commission 1998). The most striking example in the current context is competition policy where the Commission has invested heavily in persuading the rest of the world, and above all its immediate neighbours, to adopt a philosophical approach based on the EU's experience. The EU would claim to have pioneered mutual recognition as a way out of the dilemmas posed by attempts at strict harmonisation. In telecommunications services, in particular, there has been a fairly successful adaptation of the EU model, with its emphasis on competition policy instead of regulation, to the global stage. The EU's state aids rules, arguably, inspired the WTO's subsidy code (Woolcock, 1993).

There are, however, substantial limits to the suitability of the EU as a model for the global system. Only where the EU has pursued trade liberalisation on a scale that essentially anticipates multilateral action might it be seen as a pioneer. Where the EU is truly *sui generis* and is to some extent creating some of the attributes of a state or at least a confederation, it is unlikely to be appropriate. There is thus a risk that the WTO might seek to pursue the kind of beyond-border 'deep integration' discussed by Lawrence (1996) in a context where there is not the kind of 'club' of countries, which, he suggests, is needed for it to work. Moreover, we also argue that attempts to transpose EU-like approaches to the wider stage can and do have feedback effects, some unanticipated, on the EU itself.

This chapter is more about defining a research agenda than providing definitive answers. Nonetheless, in addition to characterising the EU system of regulation and contrasting it with the multilateral developments to date, we aim to identify which aspects of the EU model might be appropriate for application at the global level and in which areas. Our central finding, which is perhaps not surprising, is that the EU's less highly developed internal regimes, whether now or at some previous stage in the integration process, are more likely to serve as models for the multilateral system. Whether the EU is an appropriate model or not, its experience with these issues may provide valuable insights into how (or how not) to advance multilateral liberalisation.

We consider the appropriateness of EU models in four areas that are now rising to the top of the international trade agenda. These are:

- technical barriers to trade, focusing on issues of risk;
- services;
- investment; and
- competition policy.

We begin, however, by addressing what we see as one of the fundamental challenges to further liberalisation – respecting regulatory sovereignty, particularly as it reflects different attitudes to risk.

2. LIBERALISATION VERSUS REGULATORY SOVEREIGNTY?

Divergent national regulations can, and do, pose barriers to trade. While regulations adopted as disguised protectionism might be eliminated much as quantitative restrictions (QRs) have been, most regulations serve legitimate and necessary purposes. Consequently, they cannot simply be swept aside. Squaring the circle by replacing divergent national rules with common rules, as even the EU has discovered, is fiendishly complicated and time-consuming, at best; and at the multilateral level probably impossible. In the absence of common multilateral regulations, how can the tension between liberalising trade and addressing market failures be satisfactorily addressed?

The problem exists because there are a number of legitimate reasons for national regulations to diverge (Hancher and Moran, 1989; Previdi, 1997). First, and most straightforward, different countries face different problems. This naturally results in different policy responses. Second, there are cultural differences in attitudes towards risk. When devising rules for assessing the safety of substances no formula will be perfect. There is the double-edged risk of mistakenly banning something that is quite safe or of mistakenly permitting something dangerous. No test is perfect. Statisticians distinguish 'Type I' and 'Type II' errors, i.e., falsely rejecting a true hypothesis versus falsely accepting an untrue one. They tell us that for any given amount of evidence you cannot reduce the risk of one type of error without increasing the risk of the other. The choice on the trade off depends on subjective preferences regarding the consequences of error – the 'loss function' (see Bernstein, 1996). Where these differences are cultural, as we contend they are at least in part, national regulatory frameworks will be set such as to opt for more of one or other risk. The United States (US), and to a lesser extent the United Kingdom (UK), tend to err on the side of putting the burden of proof on those who want to act, and thus require high levels of scientific proof before introducing regulations. Denmark and Germany, however, are more concerned about the potential risk of the new and tend to place much greater emphasis on the 'precautionary principle' (Héritier, 1994).[2]

Last, but not least, even if two countries face the same problem and have the same attitude to risk, politics would produce different outcomes. As different countries (including the EU) have different constellations of societal interests and different political institutions, the political interplay between them would be expected to produce different regulatory outcomes.

Given the legitimate bases for differences in national regulatory approaches, the question arises as to how the multilateral system should cope with the tension between trade liberalisation and regulatory sovereignty. The international system faces a trade off between the risks of allowing national bans that are ostensibly for consumer protection, but actually are sheer protectionism (letting the guilty person go free), versus the danger of preventing countries banning products merely because their collective preferences are different (convicting an innocent).

Moreover one country's choice of system is likely to provoke responses by others. So if country A acts in an ultra-cautious manner and gets permission from the world system to do so, that would give authorisation to others to do the same. This would have the additional costs of hurting country A's exports, and it might deny consumers in the other countries freedom of choice and competition, as they would be in country A. This spillover effect may be in the same or different sector. There is in fact no economic welfare reason for the US to deny its non-risk averse consumers EU-made products that the EU itself does not permit, if, in fact, the US consumers do prefer choice. Thus if the EU presses the WTO to allow it to opt out of internationally agreed standards, it is asking for others to have this right too.

---

2. There is no risk-minimising free lunch here, as attention paid to any one risk may distract from another (Jaynes p. xiv).

Once, this would have been accepted readily, but with the increased political weight of *export* interests at the expense of importers (Milner, 1988) this is no longer so easily agreed.

Moreover, there is a dynamic interaction between EU and multilateral rules. If the EU as a whole has accepted a norm at WTO level, then degree of differentiation *within* the EU and the processes for managing it become subject to WTO disciplines.

3.　ECONOMIC INTEGRATION THE EU WAY

A crucial feature of the EU's regulatory approach is that, despite having engaged in a greater degree of regulatory approximation than any other group of countries, a significant degree of variation between national rules is still permitted. It is this acceptance of variation, albeit within limits, which we argue holds the key to the EU's potential as a model for the multilateral system.

An important aside here is that the EU has shown much greater tolerance for differences in regulations of production processes (such as social legislation and some environmental measures) than it has for those that affect market access (such as product characteristics). Apart from worker safety legislation, which often actually concerns equipment safety, the EU has made very little attempt to harmonise working conditions – the work-time directive[3] being the prime exception. Most environmental legislation that addresses pollution from production processes has taken the form of minimum directives, which set only the regulatory floor. This approach is reinforced by the treaty provisions on worker safety and the environment (Articles 118a and 130t, respectively, of the Single European Act) which explicitly permit the Member governments to maintain or introduce national measures more stringent than those agreed at the European level. Further, environmental, process directives, the large combustion plant directive[4] being a marked example, often formally accept significant degrees of national variation in the form of derogations. Lastly, there has recently been a move to make greater use of environmental quality targets, as opposed to the

---

3. Council Directive 98/104/EEC, *Official Journal of the European Communities*, L 307, 13 December 1993.
4. Council Directive 88/609/EEC on the limitation of emissions of certain pollutants into the air from large combustion plants, *Official Journal of the European Communities*, L 336, 7 December 1988.

approximation of limits on particular emissions from specific sources. This permits much greater flexibility at the national, and even regional, level.

Although there is a strong economic argument (see, for example, Holmes *et al.*, 1998) for not worrying about production processes when seeking to liberalise international economic exchange, the shape and nature of the EU's approach has been dictated by regulatory politics (Young and Wallace, 2000b). The Member governments have different preferences, which cannot always be readily reconciled within common rules. Given the problems the EU – compared to the world, a relatively small and homogeneous club of countries – has had tackling these issues, it is highly unlikely that the global system will make much progress towards common standards, despite concerns in parts of the developed world about social and environmental 'dumping'.

Although the EU is less tolerant of variation with respect to regulations that affect market access, it is not *in*tolerant. Again, politics matter. Progress on trade liberalisation within the EU has been possible only because the approach acknowledges and respects the Member governments' prerogative to pursue legitimate public policy objectives, even at the expense of interfering with the four freedoms (Young and Wallace, 2000b). The result is that although the EU system is predicated on liberalising inter-state economic exchange, it accepts legitimate national restrictions. To understand how this works and how it might be applicable to the multilateral system, it is necessary to summarise briefly the key aspects of the EU's regulatory regime, the *Acquis Communautaire*.

The starting point is, of course, the Treaties, particularly, for our purposes, the 1957 Treaty of Rome. The Treaty of Rome established the core principles of non-discrimination and the free circulation of goods, services, capital and people, albeit crucially within certain bounds (see Table 7.1). Significantly, however, national rules, at least in part because they addressed valid public policy objectives, could not simply be swept away by the application of treaty principles. Consequently, secondary legislation, which introduced a degree of regulatory approximation, had to be adopted in a number of areas. Thus John Pinder's (1968) distinction between 'negative' and 'positive' integration, while analytically useful, is rather too stark.

Crucial to both the functioning of the EU regime and to its suitability and transferability to the multilateral level, is the central role played by the European Court of Justice (ECJ) in interpreting the provisions of the treaties and the Member States' compliance with them and subsequent secondary legislation. In particular, the ECJ is charged (at least implicitly) with assessing whether national rules that impede the four freedoms do so within the acceptable limits set by the treaties. Acceptance by governments of

Table 7.1 The EU Framework of Regulation

	Treaty principle	Treaty qualification	Secondary legislation
Goods	Quantitative restrictions on imports and all measures having equivalent effect shall, without prejudice to the following provisions, be prohibited between Member States. (Art. 30 (28))	... Articles 30 to 34 shall not preclude prohibitions or restrictions on imports, exports or goods in transit justified on grounds of public morality, public policy or public security; protection of health and life of humans, animals or plants; the protection of national treasures possessing artistic, historic or archaeological value; or the protection of industrial and commercial property. Such prohibitions or restrictions shall not, however, constitute a means of arbitrary discrimination or a disguised restriction on trade between member States. (Art. 36 (30))	mutual recognition new approach directives detailed harmonisation centralised authorisation
Services	... restrictions on freedom to provide services within the Community shall be progressively abolished during the transitional period in respect of nationals of Member States who are established in a state of the Community other than that of the person for whom the services are intended (Art. 59 (49))		*transport::* abolition of quantitative controls + common qualitative measures (incl. safety). *financial services:* approximation of prudential supervision + home country control *telecommunications:* rules to ensure market access
Investment	... restrictions on the freedom of establishment of nationals of a Member State in the territory of another Member State shall be abolished by progressive stages in the course of the transition period (Art. 52 (43))	The provisions of this chapter and measures taken in pursuance thereof shall not prejudice the applicability of provisions ... providing for special treatment for foreign nationals on grounds of public policy, public security or public health (Art. 56 (46))	liberalisation of capital movements and abolition of exchange controls. service-sector-specific rules works-council directive merger control regulation

negative judgements, particularly in the light until recently of no coercive powers, hinges upon the legitimacy of the ECJ.

3.1 Goods

The inability of the Treaty alone to deliver economic integration was, in many respects, most evident with respect to goods, although there were also particular problems with transport services (see below). Following the creation of the customs union in 1968, it became evident that TBTs were the most significant remaining obstacles to free trade. Most of these rules, however, safeguarded legitimate public policy objectives and so could not simply be swept aside. The Commission's initial response was to seek to agree detailed common rules to eliminate the awkward national differences that impeded trade. This proved extremely cumbersome, slow and unsatisfactory (Dashwood, 1983).

In the early 1980s, the EU changed tack. The Commission, building upon the ECJ's *Dassonville* and *Cassis de Dijon* judgments, advanced two core innovations – the mutual recognition principle and the new approach to harmonisation – which paved the way for the single European market programme (SEM) (Young and Wallace, 2000a). The mutual recognition principle assumes that although the Member States' rules might differ in substance, unless proved otherwise, they should be considered to be equivalent in effect. Consequently, the default scenario is for the Member governments to accept products legally on sale in other Member States.

The mutual recognition principle, particularly the assumption of equivalence, has been tested numerous times. Significantly, the ECJ has not required governments to provide conclusive proof that a product would harm human health before it can exercise its prerogative under Article 36 (Weatherill and Beaumont, 1993). This was illustrated in the *Eyssen* case, in which the Dutch government's ban on the preservative nisin in processed cheese was challenged as an unfair trade barrier. Although existing scientific evidence on the health risk of nisin was equivocal, the ECJ took the view that a government is entitled to protect its public from substances the safety of which is subject to scientific doubt. In other words, application of the precautionary principle is sufficient to justify action under Article 36.

The mutual recognition principle applies to products accounting for approximately 25 percent of industrial production (Commission, 1996b). This indicates that, even within a relatively homogeneous club of countries that is the EU, only a relatively small proportion of regulations can be assumed to be equivalent in effect.

Even when European regulation is required, it does not necessarily have to be detailed. This is where the new-approach directives come into play. In some areas, the European institutions confine themselves to agreeing common 'essential minimum requirements', which tend to establish only ends, not the means of achieving them. Developing detailed specifications to meet these requirements is delegated to the European standards bodies – the European Committee for Standardisation (CEN), the European Committee for Electrotechnical Standardisation (CENELEC) and the European Telecommunications Standards Institute (ETSI). Even those European standards, although bringing advantages, are not mandatory; any standard that is certified to meet essential minimum requirements can circulate freely within the EU. Products falling under the new approach directives – such as toys, construction products, pressure vessels and recreational craft – account for about 17 percent, and growing, of EU industrial production (Commission, 1996b).

As a consequence, detailed harmonisation is restricted to relatively few products – most notably cars and chemicals – that are regarded as particularly dangerous. There are also centralised authorisation procedures for pharmaceuticals and genetically modified crops and foods. Although restricted to relatively few product groups, because of their economic importance, detailed harmonisation affects products accounting for about 30 percent of industrial production.

Finally, even when common EU product standards have been adopted, it is possible, under certain circumstances and with the prior approval of the Commission, for Member governments to impose more stringent national standards under Article 100a(4). This provision was included in order to address the Danish and German governments' concern that single market rules adopted under qualified majority voting, with them in the minority, might force them to accept products that they consider unsafe or environmentally harmful (Ehlerman, 1987). This was underlined by Denmark's (not legally binding) Declaration in the Single European Act to the effect that

> in cases where a Member State is of the opinion that measures adopted under Article 100a [single market measures] do not safeguard higher requirements concerning the working environment, the protection of the environment or the needs referred to in Article 36, the provisions of Article 100a(4) guarantee that the Member State in question can apply national provisions.

According to the Commission (1996a), governments have invoked Article 100a(4) most often in the chemical sector. As far as we know, the only legal challenge to have been concluded was the French government's challenge of the Commission's approval of Germany's ban on PCPs. The ECJ, in 1994, overturned the Commission's approval of the ban on procedural grounds.

The Treaty of Amsterdam substantially modified Article 100a(4). These changes require the Member government to notify the Commission of the reasons for maintaining the provision, but also permit Member States, with the permission of the Commission, to *introduce* national provisions based on new scientific evidence after the adoption of common measures.

3.2 Services

There are two particular aspects to services that make transnational liberalisation particularly challenging: they are often subject to high levels of domestic regulation and often the provision of services requires the physical proximity of supplier and consumer and, thus, often involves establishment. The EU, as did the General Agreement on Trade in Services (GATS) (see below), makes a distinction between the cross-border supply of services and those involving establishment. We shall follow their lead and focus here on the cross-border provision of services, including establishment in our discussion of investment, below.

Despite the general difficulties of liberalising cross-border trade in services, European action was required in only a relatively few service sectors: financial services, transport, telecommunications, broadcasting and advertising (Commission, 1996b). Significantly, the Treaty of Rome explicitly allocated special treatment to financial services and transport, and the liberalisation of telecommunications services was not even considered at the time. In fact, that trade in services could be liberalised was not widely appreciated until the 1980s (Drake and Nicolaïdis, 1992).

The transport sector was given special treatment in the Treaty, as it was in the Member States, because of its importance to national economic development. Its special role was protected through economic regulations that set quantitative restrictions, explicitly or implicitly through monopolies, and often price controls. Cross-border transport services were governed by bilateral arrangements between the Member States, which also limited numbers of service providers and set prices. European regulation liberalised cross-border provision of transport services, in all but rail, by eliminating quantitative restrictions and price controls, replacing them with common qualitative criteria and safety measures. This is roughly analogous to the mutual recognition principle on the basis of equivalent national rules (or minimum essential requirements).

An essentially similar approach was adopted towards financial services. Here, the comparison with essential minimum requirements and mutual recognition is even more striking. The centre-piece of the approach was approximation of national prudential regulations (minimum essential requirements) combined with 'home-country control' (mutual recognition). Under this system, with the exception of some aspects of personal life insurance, the EU-wide operations of a financial institution – whether provided across borders or through establishment – are regulated by the government of the state in which it has its headquarters.

The move to liberalise telecommunications services in the EU came only in the late 1980s, and thus, more than in any other sector paralleled multilateral developments. As a result, the EU's internal liberalisation efforts explicitly referred to the establishment of a 'fair international trade environment' (see, for example, Council Resolution of 22 July 1993). The key to liberalising cross-border telecommunications services was abolishing discriminatory conditions for access to the existing network. The most important elements, however, concerned establishment, to which we now turn.

3.3 Investment

Unlike with goods and services, there has been relatively little secondary legislation implementing the EU's internal investment regime, which is based almost entirely on the Treaty of Rome. Nonetheless, some common rules have been necessary to ensure the free flow of investment between Member States. The most important of these concern the liberalisation of capital movements and the abolition of exchange controls and the establishment of basic conditions with respect to financial, transport and telecommunications services, mentioned above.

Prior to the SEM programme, transport was the only sector to which the right of establishment did not apply. The SEM, however, created common definitions of European firms and established frameworks that enabled them to operate freely throughout the EU. Establishment in financial services was less of a problem, although it did require a national licence for each Member State in which operations were conducted and sometimes licensing conditions were discriminatory. The establishment of 'home-country control', described above, addressed both of these problems.

In telecommunications, common rules were adopted to eliminate exclusive rights on mobile, data and satellite services and, more recently, basic telecommunications. The 1998 package of liberalisation measures requires: objective, transparent and non-discriminatory licensing of network operators and service providers. Although various conditions, including for universal service, may be attached to licences, the number of licences available cannot be limited except where necessary for technical reasons. Particularly relevant for our purposes, is the regulatory framework to ensure that competitors have access to and interconnection with the network on reasonable terms. This regime, enshrined in the EU's 1995 open-network provision directive[5], provided the model for the GATS 'Reference Paper' on anti-competitive behaviour (Holmes *et al.*, 1996.)

A wide range of non-investment-specific European rules also affect cross-border investments within the EU. The works council directive[6] and the merger control regulation[7], for example, apply only to firms with operations in more than one Member State. Other rules, such as controls on state aids (subsidies), rules on regional aids, the work-time directive, and environmental measures affect foreign investment as well as domestic firms.[8] Arguably, the interlocking web of general European rules obviates the need for an extensive regime specific to extra-EU inward investment.

3.4   Competition Policy

The Commission is extremely active in promoting something resembling the European idea of competition policy as a model for the global system, (see Commission 1995, 1996c). The trade-related dimension of EU rules makes this a very interesting idea, but we argue that there is need for considerable caution here.

EU competition policy (Treaty of Rome, Articles 85-94) appears on the face of it to be a straightforward form of anti-trust for the European market. It is, however, worth noting that the Treaty is targeting not inefficiency or harm to consumers *per se*, but measures and actions that 'distort trade between Member States'. The objective is to ensure that as tariff barriers and other state-controlled border measures disappear they are not replaced by subsidies or by various forms of market entry barriers put in place by private or state-owned firms. Thus, the Treaty targets cartels that enable the fragmentation of the European market and abuses of dominant position that allow a firm in one market to rip-off consumers while preventing rivals from elsewhere entering its home market. Rapacious abuses that do not affect trade are acceptable.

---

5. Council Directive 90/387/EEC, Official Journal of the European Communities, L 192, 24 July 1990.
6. Council Directive 94/45/EC, Official Journal of the European Communities, L 254 30 September 1994.
7. Council Regulation 4064/89/EEC, Official Journal of the European Communities, L 395, 30 December 1989.
8. See Brewer and Young (1995) for a full description of EU policies with implications for FDI.

This explains the emphasis in the initial years of EU competition policy on the removal of vertical restraints – such as restrictive selective and exclusive distribution agreements – which allowed producers to segment (national) markets. Thus the Commission's 1996 Green Paper on Vertical Restraints notes that EU competition policy is unusual in having 'market integration' *per se* as a goal (Commission, 1996c). One reason for this appears to have been to prevent firms with a dominant position in one market using that as a springboard to sell at lower prices into other parts of the common market, while using control of the distribution system to prevent 'sell-back' into the higher priced market, thus allowing 'predation'. This helps to explain the emphasis placed on competition policy in the Europe Agreements with central and east European countries. It must, however, be remembered that competition policy is not the only tool for promoting market integration and, whatever one may read into the Treaty, integration is not the sole goal of competition policy.

As the single market became a reality, EU competition policy came to a turning point. It could be argued that, if the single market worked properly, each national market could be considered 'contestable' as it would be so open to entry that European competition policy would be made redundant. Alternatively, firms might respond to the completion of the single market in ways – such as pan-European mergers, cartels, and market sharing arrangements – that would frustrate the intensification of competition. Thus, competition policy needed to be applied more vigorously if the single market was to be meaningful. The EU took the latter view, most clearly in the adoption of the 1989 merger regulation,[9] which gave the Commission authority to vet mergers that might affect the common market. Many Member States had no merger rules at all before this and welcomed the new regulation. The size threshold for Community competence was much disputed, though logically the criterion should have been whether or not mergers were capable of affecting intra-EU trade.

EU competition policy has been especially successful in the telecommunications sector, in which the EU has moved from domination by state monopolies to an essentially competitive market in barely ten years. It did this in part through the deployment of the Commission's powers in competition policy in a context where the establishment of Community *regulatory* authority would have been unthinkable.

---

9. Council Regulation 4064/89/EEC, Official Journal of the European Communities, L 395/1, 30 December 1989

We should note that within the EU, state aids are treated as part of the competition policy process as another element in 'levelling the playing field'. The EU has had some influence in persuading its WTO partners of the value of its approach to distinguishing trade distorting subsidies from others (for example, those for pre-competitive R&D).

4.   MULTILATERAL EFFORTS TO DATE

The multilateral system has begun to tackle the types of issues discussed above only relatively recently. The Uruguay Round (1985-1993), in particular, saw significant advances with respect to TBTs and trade in services, including establishment, in particular. Investment rules, to date, have been discussed essentially among only the developed countries in the Organisation for Economic Cooperation and Development (OECD). With the latest effort, the Multilateral Agreement on Investment (MAI) collapsing in 1998, renewed attention has turned to the WTO as the possible forum for a multilateral framework for investment (MFI). The links between both trade and investment and trade and competition policy have been the discussion of WTO working groups set up following the Singapore Ministerial. There have not been any truly multilateral efforts at international competition policy, most international efforts have been essentially bilateral co-operation agreements.

4.1   Goods

Historically, the General Agreement on Tariffs and Trade (GATT) sought to freeze ('bind') and periodically reduce tariff barriers and to replace quantitative restrictions (QRs) with tariffs, which were then subject to reduction. The notion of a QR under the GATT was much less sweeping than the Treaty of Rome's inclusion of 'measures having equivalent effect'. In addition, the 1947 GATT had no provisions for harmonising laws in order to ensure free trade.

Starting with the 1979 Tokyo Round agreement, however, the multilateral system began to impose disciplines on national regulations that impeded trade – TBTs. This was challenging as the GATT – with several Members from the then socialist bloc – even more than the EU, had to recognise diversity of policy and market structures. Nonetheless, its Members sought above all to ensure that whatever systemic diversity existed did not have discriminatory effects on trade. Thus it is not surprising that prior to the

WTO, free traders (for example, Low, 1993[10]) argued that not only were GATT disciplines too weakly defined, they were also too laxly enforced.

The Uruguay Round made major changes to the rules on trade in goods sweeping the main additional agreements (but not that on government procurement) along with the GATT itself under the umbrella of the WTO and its tougher dispute settlement understanding. The combination of new restraints on standards and technical barriers and binding dispute settlement makes the parallels (and intersections) between multilateral and EU approaches to trade in goods particularly intriguing.

In a nutshell, the Uruguay Round agreement on technical standards is based on the Tokyo Round code. Both stress the procedural elements of standard setting, emphasise non-discrimination, and insist that *unnecessary* obstacles to trade must not be created. The 1994 code (Article 2) goes a bit further in saying that international standards shall be used where they exist, unless they are ineffective to pursue legitimate ends. It adds that in any departure from international norms, scientific evidence must be 'among the relevant considerations'. The 1994 code (Article 2.7) also says that Member States shall 'give positive consideration' to mutual recognition of others' norms that achieve the same effect.

Jackson (1997) notes that there is ambiguity about the burden of proof regarding the scientific basis of contested measures. However, he notes, there is far less ambiguity in the separate code governing sanitary and phytosanitary (SPS) measures. This is the subclass of technical regulations governing food and animal health.[11] Hoekman and Kostecki (1995) note that the US was particularly dissatisfied with the weakness of the TBT code as a means of addressing EU bans on certain US agricultural products and hence pressed for tighter SPS measures.

The SPS agreement is remarkable in that it goes well beyond the TBT agreement in many respects. It lays down a tighter regime of scientific testing (Articles 3 and 5), and states that members 'shall accept' others' standards even if different so long as the exporter can 'objectively' demonstrate that they are equivalent in effect (Article 4). It also goes much further than the TBT agreement in requiring member States to base their rules on international standards, specifically the Codex Alimentarius. Jackson (1997) reports US satisfaction at the much more specific rules in the SPS agreement

---

10. Low (1993) p. 5 is not untypical in writing, 'Seriously buffeted by multiple challenges to its authority and integrity the [GATT] system has proven less and less capable of mediating trade relations among countries'.
11. For reference, about 70 of the 300 proposals contained in the Commission's 1985 white paper on completing the single market proposals concerned sanitary and phytosanitary measures.

than the TBT agreement regarding the way scientific evidence could be used to justify measures stricter than those agreed in the Codex.

The wording appears to deny the Member governments much discretion to set higher standards. Lang and Hines (1993), writing before the conclusion of the Round, expressed concern that the combination of new WTO rules and a modification of the Codex rules on beef hormones sought by the US would make illegal the EU ban, which it seems was previously GATT-compatible. Indeed, this proved to be the case. Invoking these new rights under the SPS agreement, the US, supported by Canada, challenged the EU's ban on hormone injected beef, arguing that there was little or no scientific evidence that the specific substances in question posed an actual risk and that the onus of proof lay with the EU. The EU relied on the fact that there was some indirect evidence that this class of hormone was carcinogenic and above all on the precautionary principle – i.e., that there might be a risk and the public did not want to take it.

The WTO's Dispute Settlement Panel (August 1997) and the Appellate Body (January 1998) both found against the EU, although the Appellate Body rejected two of the Panel's three findings. As a result, the issue turned on whether the prohibition was based on a satisfactory risk assessment. Neither WTO group carried out tests of their own, but gave more credence to the experts called by the US who said that evidence used by the EU could not justify the measures applied. A detailed procedural requirement was thus turned into a substantive finding by the WTO.

Further research is needed for a detailed comparison of this decision with the ECJ jurisprudence. A superficial comparison, however, would suggest that the ECJ gives greater weight to the precautionary principle, and thus may be more sensitive to subjective consumer fears.

Significantly, the Cartagena Protocol to the UN's Biodiversity Convention on trade in genetically modified organisms incorporates a stronger and more specific statement of the 'precautionary principle', largely at the insistence of the EU and developing countries (Cosbey and Burgiel, 2000). The status of the agreement in relation to the WTO was left ambiguous, however, because of strong differences between the US, which wanted it to be subordinate to the WTO, and the EU, which did not.

4.2   Services

The GATS, concluded as part of the Uruguay Round, is the first multilateral and legally enforceable agreement governing trade and investment in services. With the limited exceptions of the agreements in basic telecommunications and financial services, the GATS did not significantly advance liberalisation in services. Nonetheless, it did establish a foundation for future liberalisation.

The GATS establishes a general framework containing general concepts, principles – most importantly the most-favoured-nation principle (non-discrimination between foreigners) (MFN) – and rules that apply to all measures affecting trade in services, which apply to all sectors unless explicitly excluded (a 'negative list' approach). The meat of the agreement, however, is made up of specific national commitments on national treatment and market access. These commitments are made on the basis of a 'positive list' approach – they apply only to those sectors and modes of supply (movement of customer, cross-border, establishment, temporary residence) explicitly identified by each government.

The GATS included several other general principles, including that relevant policies must be published in a timely fashion and that the domestic regulation must be based on objective and transparent criteria and not be more burdensome than necessary.

The agreements on basic telecommunications and financial services were concluded after the end of the Uruguay Round and went further towards liberalisation. The basic telecommunications agreement differs from the general GATS Agreement in that a number of countries (including some EU Member States) took advantage of the negotiations to accelerate their liberalisation plans, and almost all countries signed up to regulatory principles designed to ensure access to infrastructures and to constrain anti-competitive behaviour by market incumbents. In this respect, the telecommunications agreement bore some of the hallmarks of the EU regime, which anticipated it, in leaving the basic regulatory responsibilities with the Member States, but subjecting these to an external regime in which competition principles are central (Holmes *et al.*, 1996). The telecommunications regime goes further into detail in this respect than do other parts of GATS, thus raising the prospect that the EU will be put under pressure to ensure that its own definition of anti-competitive behaviour is aligned with any emerging GATS jurisprudence.

The financial services protocol follows the general framework of the GATS and concentrates only on access for and treatment of service providers. Consequently, it does not impinge upon governments' conduct of macroeconomic policy or on prudential regulations, unless they are used as a means of avoiding commitments or obligations under the agreement. Governments may also retain non-prudential regulations, such as requirements to lend to certain sectors or to offer preferential rates to certain people, so long as they are not discriminatory, are not intended to restrict access to the market, and do not constitute unnecessary barriers to trade.

220 Multilateral Agreements

Members may also introduce temporary restrictions in the event of serious balance-of-payments and external financial difficulties, subject to consultations with WTO Members.

4.3 Investment

The GATS is also the only binding multilateral framework that directly addresses investment, but only with respect to services. The GATS Agreement applies the MFN and National Treatment (NT) principles to the right of establishment. As noted above, however, NT applies only to those sectors that a government explicitly says it does. In addition, the GATS distinguishes between pre- and post-establishment. Meanwhile the WTO Agreement on Trade-Related Investment Measures (TRIMs) actually dealt more with investment-related trade measures (but IRTMs would have been hard to pronounce).

The most ambitious attempt to establish a plurilateral framework for investment were the negotiations on the MAI in the OECD. The negotiations began in May 1995 and broke down in October 1998 after France walked out of the talks. The negotiations adopted a broad definition of investment, which included portfolio investment and intangible assets (particularly intellectual property rights). It would have provided for investor and investment protection and deployed the principle of non-discrimination (the better of either MFN or NT treatment) through a negative-list approach. Several members, notably the US, however, tabled extensive lists of exceptions.

Significantly for our purposes, the autonomy of national regulators, particularly with respect to the environment, was one of the crucial issues that contributed to the collapse of the talks. There was concern, particularly in environment ministries and among non-governmental organisations, that multinational corporations might be able to use the MAI's binding investor-state dispute settlement provisions to challenge national rules that were discriminatory in *effect*, as well as those that were discriminatory in law. This prospect was brought to life by Ethyl Corporation's (of the US) challenge of Canada's ban on the chemical MMT, of which it was the sole producer and importer, under Canadian law and the dispute settlement provisions of the North American Free Trade Area (NAFTA), on which the MAI's provision was based. As with beef hormones, the case hinged on the quality of the scientific risk assessment. In July 1998, while the MAI was in hiatus, the Canadian government lost the case under Canadian law, and settled the NAFTA dispute. The negotiators were already making progress to defuse the potential – the April 1998 negotiating text included a draft 'additional article', that would protect government regulators and their 'normal non-discriminatory work', particularly with respect to environmental and labour standards (OECD, 1998).[12] However, concern about the shift of power from the public to the private was one of the reasons cited by the French prime minister Lionel Jospin (1998) before the Assemblée nationale in October 1998 announcing, in response to a question, France's withdrawal from the talks.

4.4 Competition

Although there are a lot of regional and bilateral agreements which address competition issues, the EU regime is *sui generis*. There are essentially two types of international competition agreement, those based on approximation and those requiring cooperation:

1. approximation: the EU has agreements with its immediate neighbours – notably those in the European Economic Area (EEA), the Central and East European Countries and Turkey – which require that competition policy in each mimic the effects of EU rules addressing possible trade-distorting effects of private arrangements. The EEA agreement goes further and requires a supranational authority to enforce these rules.
2. cooperation: there are a number of bilateral cooperation agreements of which the most notable is the EU-US deal, but also including EU-Canada, Canada-US, Australia-New Zealand, Australia-US and Japan-US. In reality the extent of the legal obligations is very limited.

It is worth recalling that these types of arrangement are quite separate. A requirement to approximate competition rules in order to prevent trade distortions does not necessarily imply *cooperation*. That is to say, the EU's partners must act in certain ways but there is no obligation to exchange information, etc. Nor, curiously, does approximation for the purposes of avoiding trade distortions require detailed harmonisation of laws with respect to internal competition rules. The CEECs, for example, can have an efficiency defence in their merger laws even though the EU does not, so long as any resulting mergers do not then create trade barriers. The same is indeed true of EU Member States.

In practice, these aspects often go together. Private trade barriers *between* separate markets do not require harmonisation. This is the logic of the Europe Agreements and the EEA. Formally they require domestic law to ensure no

---

12. p. 27.

distortions of trade, rather than being a domestic transposition of the essentially transnational rules embedded in the Treaty of Rome. Their experience, however, makes it clear that this is a necessary, but not sufficient, condition for the end of contingent protection (for example, anti-dumping).

The relevance of our discussion of risk, here, is that there is a trade-off among the kind of errors one is prepared to make. Some states will be more willing to tolerate less competition – including less entry by foreign firms in exchange for more stable market conditions. A question arises as to how far trade integration or even the broader notion of efficiency must be adopted if a country has other goals.

5. SUITABILITY OF THE EU AS MODEL(S)?

The EU undoubtedly addresses a far wider range of issues much more thoroughly than can be contemplated at the multilateral level, certainly for the time being. Nonetheless, as our preceding discussion has indicated, the EU's regulatory regime is not as rigid, nor necessarily as advanced, as is commonly perceived. It is in these areas where we would anticipate that the EU is most likely to provide models for aspects of the international system. This potential is explored directly below.

5.1 Goods

Of the areas we have considered, it is probably in goods that the EU holds the greatest potential as a model for a multilateral regime. There is a clear need to strike a balance between liberalising trade and running rough-shod over national regulatory preferences. The EU, for all its appearance of striving for harmonisation, actually is quite respecting of national differences, not least because that has been a condition of the Member governments' willingness to proceed with economic integration. Nonetheless, it has only been possible due to a number of unique features, including the direct effect of European law, the ability to agree on minimum standards to underpin mutual recognition (see Gatsios and Holmes, 1998) and the existence of a number of compensation elements in package deals. Finally, and crucially, the ECJ enjoys a high level of legitimacy and, perhaps relatedly, shows a sensitivity to the different national regulatory traditions.

There are indications that, particularly in the light of the hormone-treated beef judgment, the EU considers the precautionary principle to be underdeveloped in the WTO's provisions. In an informal discussion paper to trade ministers in mid-May, the Commission (1999) indicated that 'non-trade concerns' – such as human health, consumer safety and environmental protection – will have to be adequately addressed in the negotiations on agriculture, and that the SPS and TBT agreements may have to be examined. The US, by contrast, considers the principles incorporated in the SPS agreement 'balanced and sound' and stresses the importance of the 'reliance on science' in avoiding disguised protectionism (USTR, 1998).

5.2 Services

Although in telecommunications one aspect of the EU's internal regime proved a useful element of multilateral liberalisation, this is probably a one-off. As EU experience has demonstrated, in most service sectors entry barriers are not significant. In those sectors where they are significant – financial services and transport, in particular – the transfer of host country control, barring a degree of regulatory approximation, is simply not politically acceptable. As yet, such regulatory approximation seems beyond multilateral agreement. The EU's lesson here is to be realistic and to aim for realistic targets – such as, eliminating discrimination in licensing procedures for financial service providers.

5.3 Investment

The EU's internal regime for FDI is too supranational and dependent on the broader European regulatory framework to be a suitable model for a multilateral framework. In the light of the MAI being a 'step too far' for even the developed countries, even the more intergovernmental NAFTA approach, on which the MAI was modelled, appears too ambitious for the multilateral system. Again, it will be a case of picking and choosing those elements of the EU framework that address specific problems.

It may be that the EU has the most to offer in addressing what we would argue, particularly in the light of the collapse of the MAI, is the fundamental issue for an MFI – squaring liberalisation with regulatory sovereignty. The Commission (1997) actually sought to do just that during the MAI negotiations, proposing general exceptions for public security and public health subject to an anti-abuse clause, along the lines of Article 56 of the Treaty of Rome.

5.4 Competition Policy

The intra-EU regime derives from a real fear that private trade barriers can frustrate liberalisation, but it requires a degree of supra-nationality of law and of enforcement that is unimaginable in the WTO arena. A number of initiatives (such as Scherer, 1994; DIAC, 1993) that drew on this were shot down in the 1980s. The EU's own regime does not face the problem of diverse national rules, but its bilateral agreements do. The EEA, the Europe Agreements and the EU-Turkey agreement go further towards harmonisation – while still not guaranteeing exemption from anti-dumping – than WTO Members are willing to consider. Even the EU-US agreement does not address harmonisation.

6.   CONCLUSION

We are inclined to the view that while the EU has much to offer the world by way of experience in liberalisation, any simple transposition of EU frameworks is likely to be very tricky. In some ways the competition rules might seem to offer the best model, as they were originally developed as a way of dealing with non-border measures that might frustrate agreed trade liberalisation. However, their supra-national character and the fact that they now apply to what is an 'internal' market make them a rather special case, and there is nothing in the EU's experience to suggest that it contains the key to overcoming the emerging resistance to some aspects of trade liberalisation. For some of the problems the EU has its own rather specific solutions; for others the EU is experiencing troubles that it cannot yet resolve. We are therefore sceptical about the argument that in the principle of mutual recognition the EU has discovered the philosophers' stone that will reconcile market opening and national regulatory sovereignty.

Our reading of the regulatory convergence debate is, broadly speaking, that unqualified openness requires a certain degree of commonality in regulatory approaches. This is less of a challenge in the EU than in the wider world since the EU, although by no means homogeneous, is composed of only 15 relatively developed countries.

This issue applies to many areas of public policy. For example, attitudes towards the desired intensity of competition versus market stability differ across countries, and it is only relatively recently that the EU has moved towards the beginnings of a single competition regime for a single market.

Increasingly, we would argue that this divergence is going to be most tested with respect to attitudes towards risk in a narrower sense. Where states have fundamentally different approaches to risk and valid reasons for not accepting mutual recognition (or not just relying on labelling in simple cases), then so long as the national regulations are based on legitimate grounds both harmonisation and mutual recognition have limits. Even within the EU, questions of legitimacy have been posed where the Commission or the ECJ decides (sometimes is left to decide) whether a national rule is legitimate. Enlisting an external constraint, in order to resist lobbies seeking purely protectionist measures, is not the same as agreeing to allow (non-majoritarian, unaccountable) outsiders to decide what measures are and are not protectionist. These legitimacy problems are likely to be particularly profound where the judgement comes down to differences in risk aversion.

Arguably, this implies that the Uruguay Round, both tackling beyond-border issues and applying binding dispute settlement, may have gone too far. Either step by itself would have been far less controversial. The combination may challenge the legitimacy of the multilateral system.

This may hold even for successful exporters of rules to the multilateral level. Where one jurisdiction (whether the EU or the US) succeeds in persuading others of the desirability of adopting their system as a model, the price of this exporting of the system is that it can take on a life of its own in the outside world. If the move from GATT to the WTO is to mean anything at all, then signatories of WTO codes will no longer be able to interpret them as they see fit, but will be subject increasingly to pressures such as that in the beef hormones case where a WTO tribunal defined a correct 'risk assessment'. We are already seeing similar developments in telecommunications services where the EU, having inspired the global regime, is faced with the fact that its ability to invoke special exemptions from the GATS telecommunications annex is defined by what it negotiated at the WTO, and how a panel will interpret this.

The EU's strength, as a potential model for the world system, is its history of seeking to create a regulated balance between open markets for their own sake and the right of governments to safeguard legitimate public policy objectives. The US has not tackled this question. It tends either to have common rules, or to leave matters to the market. Not for a long time has it had to set up mechanisms to cope with interstate differences in taste.

It would appear that the international system will never be able to totally eliminate TBTs and other rules that may inhibit commerce. The relevance of the EU is not so much as a model to be admired, but as a living lesson that even here there are some limits to harmonisation – limits which nonetheless can be regulated. Ensuring that national rules remain within acceptable limits requires policing and adjudication – what might be called 'bounded variation'.

While policing can be diffused to those reporting harm, the judges need to be accepted as legitimate. In the almost certain absence of democratic legitimacy, the legitimacy must be based on transparency and performance, including showing due sensitivity to different regulatory preferences. The

ECJ has been remarkably successful in persuading EU Member States to accept its interpretation of rules they themselves drew up. It remains to be seen what happens if the WTO takes on an analogous role. It is arguable that theq world may not be quite ready for this. Even from a free trade point of view, one may be wary of a possible backlash.

REFERENCES

Bernstein, Peter L. (1996), *Against the Gods: The Remarkable Story of Risk*, New York, US: John Wiley & Sons.

Brewer, Thomas L. and Stephen Young (1995), 'European Union Policies and the Problems of Multinational Enterprise', *Journal of World Trade*, **29**(1), 33-52.

Commission (1995), *Competition Policy in the New Trade Order: Strengthening International Cooperation and Rules*, Report of a Group of Experts, COM (95) 359 final, 12 July, Brussels: European Commission.

Commission (1996a), 'The Single Market in 1995 – Report from the Commission to the Council and the European Parliament', COM (96) 51, 20 February, Brussels: European Commission.

Commission (1996b), 'The Impact and Effectiveness of the Single Market', COM (96) 520 final, 30 October, Brussels: European Commission.

Commission (1996c), 'Green paper on Vertical Restraints in EC Competition Policy', Brussels: European Commission.

Commission (1997), 'Multilateral Agreement on Investment (MAI): State of Play of the Negotiations and Priorities for the Months to Come', internal document, March, Brussels: European Commission.

Commission (1998), *Towards a More Coherent Global Economic Order*, Luxembourg: Office for Official Publications of the European Communities.

Commission (1999), 'The New WTO Round: Informal Discussion Paper for EU Trade Ministers, Berlin 10-11 May 1999', 26 April, Brussels: European Commission.

Cosbey, Aaron and Stas Burgiel (2000), 'The Cartagena Protocol on Biosafety: An Analysis of the Results', An IISD Briefing Note, February, Winnipeg, Canada: International Institute for Sustainable Development.

Dashwood, Alan (1983), 'Hastening Slowly: The Communities' Path Towards Harmonisation', in Helen Wallace, William Wallace and Carole Webb (eds), *Policy-Making in the European Community*, 2nd edn, Chichester, UK: John Wiley & Sons, pp. 177-208.

DIAC (1993), 'Draft International Anti-Trust Code' in *Anti-Trust and Trade Regulation Report*, 19 August 1993.

Drake, William J. and Kalypso Nicolaïdis (1992), 'Ideas, Interests and Institutions: Trade in Services and the Uruguay Round', *International Organization*, **46**(1), 37-100.

Ehlerman, Claus-Dieter (1987), 'The Internal Market Following the Single European Act', *Common Market Law Review*, **24**, 361-409.

Gatsios, Konstantine and Peter Holmes (1998), 'Regulatory Competition', in Peter Newman (ed), *New Palgrave Dictionary of Economics and the Law*, London, UK: Macmillan.

Hancher, Leigh and Mike Moran (1989), *Capitalism, Culture and Economic Regulation*, Oxford, UK: Clarendon Press.

Héritier, Adrianne (1994), '"Leaders" and "Laggards" in European Policy-Making: Clean Air Policy Changes in Britain and Germany', in Frans van Waarden and Brigitte Unger (eds), *Convergence or Diversity? The Pressures of Internationalisation on Economic Governance Institutions and Policy Outcomes*, Aldershot, UK: Avebury, pp. 278-305.

Hoekman, Bernard M. and Michael M. Kostecki (1995), *The Political Economy of the World Trading System*, Oxford, UK: Oxford University Press.

Holmes, Peter, Jeremy Kempton and Francis McGowan (1996), 'International Competition Policy and Telecommunications: Lessons for the EU and Prospects for the WTO', *Telecommunications Policy*, **20**(10), 755-67.

Holmes, Peter, Alasdair Smith and Alasdair R. Young (1998), 'Regulatory Convergence between the EU and CEECs,' in Jens van Scherpenberg and Elke Thiel (eds), *Towards Rival Regionalism*, Baden-Baden, Germany: Nomos, pp. 146-63.

Jackson, John H. (1997), *The World Trading System: Law and Policy of International Economic Relations*, 2nd edn, Cambridge, MA, US: MIT Press.

Jaynes, E.T. (2001), Probability Theory: The Logic of Science, (unpublished work) available at http://bayes.wustl.edu/etj/prob.html.

Jospin, Lionel (1998), 'Réponse à une question de Robert Hue au sujet des négociations sur l'AMI à l'OCDE', Questions d'actualité à l'assemblée nationale, 14 October.

Lang, Tim and Colin Hines (1993), *The New Protectionism: Protecting the Future Against Free Trade*, London, UK: Earthscan Publications Ltd.

Lawrence, Robert Z. (1996), *Regulation, Multilateralism and Deeper Integration*, Washington, DC, US: Brookings Institution.

Low, Patrick (1993), *Trading Free: The GATT and US Trade Policy*, Washington, DC, US: Twentieth Century Fund.

Milner, Helen V. (1988), *Resisting Protectionism: Global Industries and the Politics of International Trade*, Princeton, NJ, US: Princeton University Press.

Organisation for Economic Cooperation and Development (1998), 'Commentary to the MAI Negotiating Text (as of 24 April 1998)', Paris, France: Organisation for Economic Cooperation and Development.

Pinder, John (1968), 'Positive Integration and Negative Integration: Some Problems of Economic Union in the EEC', *The World Today*, **24**(3), 88-110.

Previdi, Ernesto (1997), 'Making and Enforcing Regulatory Policy in the Single Market', in Helen Wallace and Alasdair R. Young (eds), *Participation and Policy-Making in the European Union*, Oxford, UK: Clarendon Press, pp. 69-90.

Scherer, Frederic M. (1994), *Competition Policies for an Integrated World Economy*, Washington, DC, US: Brookings Institution.

United States Trade Representative (1998), 'Preliminary Outline of Issues for Consideration by the Committee as Part of the Triennial Review of the SPS Agreement: Submission by the United States', Washington, DC, US: United States Trade Representative.

Weatherill, Stephen and Paul Beaumont (1993), *EC Law*, London, UK: Penguin.

Woolcock, Stephen (1993), 'The European *Acquis* and Multilateral Trade Rules: Are they Compatible?', *Journal of Common Market Studies*, **31**(4), 539-59.

Young, Alasdair R. and Helen Wallace (2000a), 'The Single Market: A New Approach to Policy?' in Helen Wallace and William Wallace (eds), *Policy-Making in the European Union*, 4th edn, Oxford, UK: Oxford University Press, pp. 85-114.

Young, Alasdair R. and Helen Wallace (2000b), *Regulatory Politics in the European Union: Balancing Civic and Private Interests?*, Manchester, UK: Manchester University Press.

Index

antidumping 49
Aquis Communautaire *see* EU
ASEAN 6
Australia 102, 121, 221

balance of payment 4, 11, 13, 14, 21, 220
  Brazil 7
  Committee *see* WTO
  provisions 5
  and domestic policies 26
    see also policy reversals
banana dispute 9-10
Basel Convention 163, 165
Beef Hormones case 8, 155, 204, 218,
  220, 222, 225
Bergsten, Fred 8-9
Bhagwati, Jagdish N. 103, 104, 113, 118,
  121
Bleaney, Michael 15
Boltho, Andrea 7-8
Brada, Professor 6

Cartagena Protocol on Biosafety 218
cartels 24, 27, 36, 181, 182, 185, 192,
  196, 214
child labour *see* labour
childrens' rights 114
CITES 151, 163
  quotas in 164-65
Clean Air Act 168
Clinton, President 102, 182
Codex Alimentarius 155, 161, 163, 217
Committee on Trade and Environment
  see WTO
comparative advantage 18, 21 69, 77,
  101, 109, 116, 155, 175, 177
competition policies 8, 9, 10, 11, 22-24,
  31, 172-99
  and international standards 194-98

and GATS provisions, 37, 173-74,
  197-98
and GATT 179, 192-93
goals of 23-24, 174-77
history of 180-83
implementation of 177-87
and international cooperation
  agreements 189-90
and Japan 191-92
local 26-27
multilateral agreement on 26-27, 34,
  35
see also Graham; Holmes; Young
Mexico 185-86
procedural aspects of
relationship with trade policy 172-99
and Seattle 173-74
and Singapore Ministerial 172-73
United States and European Union
  24, 183-85
and Working Group of WTO 172-73,
  192
and WTO 37, 172-74, 197-98
and WTO Council for Trade in
  Services 37, 197-98
and WTO dispute settlement 191-93
Convention on International Trade and
  Endangered Species of Flora and
  Fauna *see* CITES
Convention on Persistent Organic
  Pollutants (POP) 166
Convention on Prior Informed Consent
  (PIC) 166
Corden, W. Max v, x, 12, 18-19, 124-43
current account balance
  and Japan and US pressure 12
Customs Cooperation Council 155
custom unions 7, 210

Dispute Settlement Body *see* WTO
Drabek, Zdenek x, xii-xiii, 1-39, 78

efficiency gains 175
employment *see* labour
Endangered Species Act 168
Environment
  Canada 156, 167-68
  data 153-54
  groups 169
  Intergovernmental Panel for Climate
    Change 153
  international agreements (MEAs) 162-
    66
  Montreal Protocol 163
  Mexican-US border area 159
  Victor and Raustiala study 168-69
  and NGOs 169
  and NAFTA 167-69
  and pollution haven effect 150
  and WTO 37, 148, 169
  see also MEAs; Shrimp/Turtle case
Environmental policy 9, 10, 11, 20
  domestic 20, 147-69
  European Union 21, 149, 156-58
  harmonisation of 147-71, 151-56
  international 20, 147-69
  NAFTA 20, 158-62
  NAFTA Free Trade Commission 160-
    61
  North American Agreement on
    Environmental Cooperation 158, 160
  OECD countries 152
  regulatory harmonisation 158-62
  variables of 153
  WTO 20
  Ziegler 157-58
  and multilateral agreements 27-28
  see also Vaughan, Scott
Esty, Daniel 149
Ethyl Corporation case 220
EU
  Acquis Communautaire 32, 208
    vertical restraints 215
    telecommunications 215
  environmental directives 157
  European Court of Justice 158, 208-
    210, 212, 218, 222, 225, 226
  four freedoms 156, 208

framework of regulation table 209
goods 210-12, 222-23
home-country control 213
merger control regulation 214
minimum essential requirements 212,
  213
model at global level 203-28, 222-24
multilateral agreements 203-28
mutual recognition principle 210, 212,
  213
open-network provision directive 214
products standards 211
regulatory approach 207-16
standards bodies 211
telecommunications services 204, 212,
  213
Treaty of Amsterdam 212
Treaty of Rome 208-210, 212, 213,
  214, 222, 223
Turkey agreement 224
US agreement 224
works council directive 214
and *Cassis de Dijon* case 158, 210
and competition policy 204, 214-16,
  223-24
and *Dassonville* case 210
and *Danish Bottles* case 158
and *Essyen* case 210
and investment 213-14, 223
and services 212-13, 223
  transport 212
  financial 212-13
European Economic Area
  and competition policy 221, 223-24
European Union *see* EU
exchange rates 12, 13, 14
  see also overvalued exchanged rates

Feldstein, Martin 12
Fielding, David 15
FDI 20, 22-23, 176, 178, 192
food safety laws 167, 168
free riding 165
Free Trade Area of the Americas
  (FTAA) 159

Gasoline case 121
GATS
  Article IX 37, 197

Article XIV 31
  most-favoured-nation principle 219
  and investment 220
  and services 212-13, 218-20
GATT
  Article II 179
  Article VI 6, 17
  Article XII 4
  Article XVIIIB 4
  Article XIX 6
  Article XXIII 179, 192
  Article XXIV 7
  Article XXXVIII(2)(e) 155
  and goods 216-18
  and quantitative restrictions 216
  see also balance-of-payments; MFN
General Agreement on Tariffs and Trade
  see GATT
General Agreement on Trade in Services
  see GATS
Generalized System of Preferences 103,
  118, 119
genetically modified 8, 9
globalisation 1-37
  criticism of 2-3
  Geneva Social Summit 2
  policies 35
  Seattle attack *see* Seattle
  threats to 9
  Washington demonstration 2
  World Bank treatment of 2
gold standard 11
goods
  EU 210-12
  EU model suitability 222-23
  multilateral efforts 216-18
Graham, Edward M. x, 23-24, 26, 28,
  32, 33, 37, 172-99
  see also competition policies

Holmes, Peter x, 26, 32, 35-36, 203-28
Hull, Cordell 178-79
human rights 9, 16, 23, 151
  see also labour standards

ILO 9
  core labour conventions 36, 112-15
  see also labour
IMF 2, 3, 5, 10, 13, 58, 194-95

India
  and labour standards 105, 110
intellectual property 104, 120, 176, 220
  see also TRIPS agreement
International Monetary Fund *see* IMF
International Labor Organization *see*
  ILO
International Office of Epizootics 155
International Standardization
  Organization (ISO) 151
International Telecommunications Union
  155
International Trade Organization (ITO)
  33, 179

Jospin, Lionel 3, 221

Kazakhstan
  customs union 7
  devaluation in 47-49, 52, 69
  overvaluation in 46

Kodak-Fuji dispute 24, 31, 187, 191-92
  see also competition

labour
  child 2, 9, 16, 105-106, 110-11, 118,
    119, 120, 124
  core conventions 16, 27-28, 36, 107,
    112-15, 119
  exploitation model 129-30
  migrant workers 108, 111
  and multilateral agreements 27-28
  see also labour standards
labour policies 9, 10, 11, 15-19
  and ILO 101, 106, 116
  and Singapore Declaration 101-102,
    106
  and Singapore Ministerial 101
  see also social dumping
labour standards
  comparative advantage 109
  Consumer Utility and Trust Company
    106
  core labour standards 16, 27, 36, 107,
    115
  developing countries 111-12, 124-43
  EU 116, 119

Globalisation Under Threat

fair trade argument 109-10
GSP 119
ILO 121
ILO-UNCTAD Expert Group 121
minimum wage 124
moral values 106-108
OECD 120
pauper-labour argument 109-10
race-to-the-bottom argument 109-10
Trade Act 1974 s502(4) (US) 117
TRIPS 120
TWIN-SAL 106
workers' rights 118
WTO 104-106, 119, 120-21
pressure for 115-19
and humanitarian policy 128-32
and protectionist policy 133
and WTO working party on 102-103,
116-18
see also ILO; social dumping;
universal standards

LDCs
raising labour costs in export industries
124-43
less developed countries *see* LDCs
liberalisation *see* trade liberalisation
linkages 13, 33-34
trade-competition 172-99
trade-environment 19-22, 147-71
concerns 149-51
critics of 20
trade-macroeconomics 11-15, 43-74,
75-97
trade-labour 99-144
compromise or solutions 119-21
EU position 116
pressures for 115-19
see also Corden; Panagariya; Vousden
Low, Patrick 217

macroeconomic policies 9, 10, 75-97
global institutions 10
see IMF; World Bank; WTO
and protection 77-80
literature on 77-78
trade and macroeconomic determinants
of protection 78-79
trade policy and stabilisation 79-80

and trade policy reversals in transition
countries 81
Dornbusch and Frankel 77, 57, 88,
89, 92
macroeconomic developments 83-88
estimation results 88-92
policy issues 92-94
Czech Republic 83-85, 92
Hungary 85-86
Poland 86-87
Slovak Republic 86-88, 92
trade policy developments 81-83
MAI 120, 204, 216, 220, 223
Marine Mammal Protection Act 168
market access 165, 178, 190-92, 197,
207-208, 209, 219
MEAs 27-30, 34, 149, 151,
international standard setting 162-66
trade measures in 164-65
and WTO 29, 165-66
MERCOSUR 6, 7
mergers
and competition 190-91
Mexico
competition policies 185-86
MFN 29, 119, 219-20
Minimum Age Convention 28
minimum wage 112, 119, 124-27, 130
monopsony 129-34
Montreal Protocol 151, 163, 165
Multi- Fibre Agreement 7
multilateral agreements 24-33, 201-28
complementarity of 30-31, 36
market failures 25-26
policy failures 25-26
and competition *see* competition
policies
and EC Expert Report 1995 26-27
and environment 27-28
and labour 27-28
and regulatory sovereignty 205-208
see also Holmes; Young
multilateral agreement on investment *see*
MAI
multilateral agreements on labour 37
multilateral environment agreements *see*
MEAs
multilateral institutions 24-33
multilateral trading

origin of 178-79
legitimacy of 35-36
multilateral institutions 35
see IMF; WTO; World Bank
multilateral efforts 216-22
competition 221-22
EEA 221
financial services protocol 219
goods 216-18
investment 220-21
OECD countries 216
services 218-20
telecommunications agreement 219
multinational firms,
operating in LDCs 18-19, 124-42

NAFTA 6, 149
Canada review of 167-68
Chapter 11 Agreement 161
Automotive Standards Council 161
food safety measures 161
SPS measures 161
SPS Technical Working Groups of 161
Standards Related Committee 161
US review of 168
national treatment principle
and GATS 220
and TRIMs 220
New Trade Agenda 33
non-tradeables 13
North American Agreement on
Environmental Cooperation (NAAEC) 160, 162

OECD
harmonisation of cartels in 36
and competition policies 196
and investment 220
overvalued exchanged rates 14, 43-74
diverse versus uniform tariff structure 69-70
econometric evidence
Argentina 56
Chile 57-58
Malaysia 59, 60-61
Turkey 58-9
Uruguay 44, 47, 56-57
Ghana case study 64-65

problems of 51-61
England (1924), 53
CFA zone 53-55
Chile (1999), 55
Table of great depressions 54
and black market premium 14, 43
and internal balance 50
and Korea 59-60
and Kazakhstan 47-49
and Sub-Saharan Africa 62-68

Panagariya, Arvind ix, 18, 19, 101-23
Pettigrew, Pierre 116
policy reversals 4
evidence of 6
and balance of payment 4
see also Sorsa, Piritta
policy slippages *see* policy reversals
positive comity 189
precautionary principle 206, 210, 222
and Cartagena Protocol 218
production process 17, 34, 150, 207-208
see also Shrimp/Turtle case
protectionism 2, 12
increase trade barriers 8
modern protectionism 8
pressures 15
and labour policies 16
see also labour standards

regionalism 6
east Asia 8
regional groups 6
and threat to liberal trade regimes 6
regulatory convergence 32, 203-26
regulatory sovereignty 205-207, 223
Rio Summit 147

sanitary and phytosanitary measures 30
Agreement on 31, 155, 217, 218, 223
Seattle 2, 3, 19, 25, 33, 148, 149, 203
Shatz, Howard J. x, 14, 15, 43-74
Shrimp/Turtle case 17, 21, 121
Shumpeter, Joseph 176
see also competition policies
Singapore
Declaration 101, 102, 106
Ministerial 172
single European market programme

(SEM) 210, 213
Single European Act 156-58, 207, 211
social dumping 16, 124-43
  monopsony model of 129-30
  terms-of-trade effects 133
  and humanitarian policy 16, 18-19,
    124-28
  and mobile multinationals 132
  and protectionist policy 16, 18-19, 133
Sorsa, Piritta xi, 6, 14, 15, 75-97
sovereignty 33 *see also* multilateral
  agreements
Stevens, Wallace 147
structural policy 11-12
  see also exchange rate policy

Tarr, David G. x, 14, 15, 43- 74
technical barriers to trade 30, 225
  Agreement on 31, 155, 217, 218, 223,
    225
Tinbergen, Jan 106
Tokyo Round
  goods 216, 217
trade
  barriers 216
  and competition policy 172-99
  and macroeconomic policy 41-97
  see also trade liberalisation
trade liberalisation 148
  goals of 176
  versus regulatory sovereignty 205-207
trade-labour link 99-143
  advocates of, 103-12
    Bhagwati , Jagdish N. 104
    Ramaswami 104
    efficiency issue 103-104
trade policies 1-37
  goals of 174-77
  instability of 4-11
trade policy reversals *see* overvalued
  exchange rate policies; Sorsa, Piritta;
  Shatz, Howard and Tarr, David
  and transition countries 75
trade-related investment measures *see*
  TRIMs
Treaty of Havana *see* universal standards
Treaty of Rome *see* EU
TRIMs 220
TRIPS agreement 31, 120, 121

Tuna/Dolphin case 17, 21, 149

UNCTAD 118, 121
UNESCO 9
United Nations 9
United Nations Environmental
  Programme 154
United States Environmental Protection
  Agency 152
United Nations Framework Convention
  on Climate Change 152
United Nations Intergovernmental Panel
  on Forests 165
universal standards 10, 20, 21, 24, 29,
    30-32
  economic consequences of 30, 124-42
  political sensitivity of 32-33
  transplantability of EU 32 *see also*
    Holmes; Young
  and Treaty of Havana 33, 179, 187
United States,
  competition policies 24, 183-85
  'core' labour conventions 115, 118-21
  environment 152, 158-60
  labour standards 101, 103, 106, 107,
    108, 110, 111
Uruguay Round 15, 25, 219, 225
  goods 217
Vaughan, Scott xi, 20-21, 22, 28, 147-71
  see also environmental policies
Volkswagen 22-23
von Moltke 155
Vousden, Neil xi, 18-19, 124-43

wages
  'wage-differential' model 126-28
  modified 'wage-differential' model
    129-30
WIPO 121, 155
World Bank 2, 3, 7, 9, 10, 14, 61, 65, 68,
    70
World Health Organization 155
  World Health Organization-Food and
    Agricultural Organization 155
World Trade Organization *see* WTO
WTO
  agreements 9, 26,
  Balance of Payment Committee 4, 5
  Committee on Trade and Environment

31, 162
Council for Trade in Services 37, 197
dispute settlement procedures 25, 180
environment cases 149 *see*
    Shrimp/Turtle case; Tuna/Dolphin
    case
role of 9, 37
savings clause 165-66, 169
subsidy code 204
Working Group on Trade and
Environment 9
Working party on labour standards
    102, 103, 116
and multilateral environment
    agreements 29
    see also GATT

Young, Alasdair R. xi, 26, 32, 35-6, 203-
    28